FLORENCE

An appreciation

of her beauty

Piero Bargellini

Florence

An appreciation of her beauty

Historical and artistic guide

Florence ARNAUD Publisher

CONTENTS

FIFTH ITINERARY:

SIXTH ITINERARY:

SURROUNDINGS OF FLORENCE:

OUTLINE
OF THE POLITICAL, ARTISTIC AND
LITERARY HISTORY OF THE CITY

Etrusco-Roman period - From the Roman Empire to a little after the year 1000 From the year 1000 to the end of the thirteenth century - The fourteenth century The fifteenth century - The sixteenth century The seventeenth and eighteenth centuries From the nineteenth century to our days.

The ancient Etruscan cities were usually situated high up. On the top of a hill it was easier to defend oneself, and healthier to live in.

Fiesole was a knot in the network of Etruscan roads which ran over Tuscany. It was reached by way of mountain roads which were the safest, even if very tiring.

The hills of Fiesole formed the last promontory of the woody Appennine chain. The Arno river, flowing from east to west, with its stream, and even more with its marshes, barred the way to whoever wanted to go from north to south.

The crossing of the river, by flat-bottomed boat or bridge, was at all times possible at the point where the waters narrow, and that is the spot where the Ponte Vecchio still stands, at the foot of what are today called the *Colli*, a little above the meeting-point of the Mugnone torrent, which used to flow into the Arno where the Ponte Santa Trinita was later built. Downstream the marshes began again.

From Fiesole groups of homes spread towards the river. And one of these, sprung up on the last slopes of the hills of Fiesole, had its cemetery where was later the cemetery of Florence: a cemetery which goes back to a thousand years before Christ, and from which have come a few ash-urns of the type used at Chiusi.

Another nucleus ventured into the marshy ground, forming a station on the river, and left a huge cemetery of terracotta ossuary vases, of the Villanova type.

Etruscan sculpture: the so-called Chimera (Archaeological Museum).

In the meantime the Etruscan civilization spread over Tuscany. In the VIIth. cent. B. C., the whole region had become covered with the network of the **Lucumoniae.**

Fiesole dominated the central valley of the Arno and the Etruscan nucleus fixing itself on the river ought to have become its direct dependant. Perhaps it had a name, but we do not know. It was at the same time a traffic point and a bridge-head. Fiesole was high up, defended by thick walls. And this species of paludal village, beside the river, subject to the floods and to enemy assaults, had, on account of its position, to undergo rather dramatic vicissitudes.

In the 3rd and 2nd centuries B. C., Rome, enlarging its dominions, was bound to meet with the Etruscan cities, and first of all with nuclei like that which was situated at the crossing-point of the Arno. The Romans, spreading out from their cities, and constructing roads, gave great importance to crossing-points. We remember how the roads were called by the names of the Consuls, and that a magistrate had the title of « Pontifex », or bridge-builder.

Before blotting-out Fiesole, the Romans occupied the bridge-head over the Arno. The place had the importance and name of **municipium,** and after the wars of Sulla and Catiline here was founded a colony of veterans from Caesar's army. The agrarian law of 59 B. C. gave the veterans the right to found new cities. Mindful of their past, the veterans became colonists, giving their cities the form of the military « castrum », that is the quadrangular form of the camp of war, divided into four by two cross-intersecting roads.

The name of the new colony was that of **Florentia.** The ancient legends imagine an old king of Fiesole, called Fiorino, killed and buried in a field of lilies by the bank of the Arno. Some have thought that the name of Florentia is derived from the « flowing » (fluenti) waters of the river. Instead, it must be believed that the name of Florentia was one of those augural names which the veterans gave to their colonies. The augury was that the new city should prosper and become « flourishing » (florens).

The augury came true and the colony certainly did flourish. The old Roman « castrum » of rectangular form, or rather trapezoidal, as the part down-river was slightly longer than the part up-river, was all situated on the right bank of the Arno. In the brick walls (the first circle), four principal gates opened, flanked by towers, according to the cardinal points. The southern one gave access to the crossing of the river, opposite the present Ponte Vecchio (in the Middle Ages this gate was called Por Santa Maria).

Of the old Roman city there has remained the topographical impress upon the centre of Florence, where it is possibile to recognize the « cardo maximus » in the present Via Strozzi, Via degli Speziali and Via del Corso; the « decumanus » in the Via Por Santa Maria, Via Calimala and Via Roma. The centre, or Forum, was where now stands the Piazza della Repubblica. Nothing has remained of the old Roman architecture, except a few pieces recovered during casual excavation work and now to be seen in the Archeological Museum. They are fragments and relics of little artistic value. They reveal nothing exceptional in a city which later gave to the world a vision of unparalleled beauty.

So we must imagine Augustan Florence as very similar to all the other cities of Roman origin and civilization. In the centre, the *Forum* (now Piazza della Repubblica) where the citizens met for their affairs. On the Forum stood the *Capitol* (where now are the arcades of the Gambrinus cinema). The adjacent street still bears this name (Via del Campidoglio), from the great Temple which faced to the East, and which was reached by a marble stairway, leading to a portico with six or eight columns of Lunigiana marble, in Corinthian style, surmounted by a triangular pediment, or tympanum. The temple was divided into three parts, with images of the greater gods; Jupiter in the middle, sitting, Juno and Minerva, standing at the sides. The *Theatre* was near the present Piazza della Signoria, between the Palazzo Vecchio and the Palazzo Gondi; the *Baths*, where is the present Via delle Terme, running from Piazza Santa Trinita to Via Por Santa Maria. Outside the walls, near the present Piazza Santa Croce, was the *Amphitheatre*. On its perimeter were later built the houses of the Peruzzi, which have in fact a curved façade. The road which circles it is still called Via Torta (bent).

We think that the city was dedicated to Mars, god of war. In the times of Dante there existed at the foot of the Ponte Vecchio, an old statue of a warrior on horseback, which tradition indicated as Mars. It was carried away by a river flood. For a long time it was believed that the Baptistery was built on an old pagan temple dedicated to that god, and that St. John, patron of the city, had changed places with Mars. But this, however, has not been confirmed by the excavations, and we think that the Baptistery was an original Romanesque construction.

FROM THE ROMAN EMPIRE TO A LITTLE AFTER
THE YEAR 1000

During the Imperial period Florentia saw its prosperity grow with trade. It was chosen as the residence of the **Corrector Italiae**, or Governor of the united regions of Etruria and Umbria (287-366 A. D.).

Christianity appeared in Florence in the time of the persecutions of Emperor Decius, during which Saint Miniatus was martyred, in 250. But only in 313 have we news of a Bishop of Florence, Felice. Eighty years afterwards, in 393, the Church of San Lorenzo was consecrated outside the walls, by St. Ambrose, Bishop of Milan.

During the barbarian invasions, the city, still protected by the circle of the Roman walls, suffered sieges and devastation on the part of the Ostrogoths of Radagasius (405), of the Byzantines (539) and particularly of the Goths of Totila (541), whom legend confuses with Attila.

From the Longobard invasion (570) to the first news of a Duke of the city (c. 784), the city life was gathered about the **Bishops**, custodians and defenders of civilization. To this period goes back the construction of the oldest monasteries, real fortresses of culture and centres of peaceful work, in the middle of the turbulence and arrogance of the barbarian over-lords.

In the monasteries was begun or taken up again with new, let us say industrial, criterions, the working of wool which later became the basis of the artisan life of the city and the greatest source of wealth.

When the Longobards were routed by the Franks, the **Count** was substituted for the **Duke** as governor of the city. On his first journey to Rome,

Charlemagne stopped at Florence where he celebrated Christmas in 786. To him the city's knightly nobility owes its origin.

During the reign of Charlemagne, in peace and relative justice, Florence developed so rapidly, economically and also its buildings grew so numerous, that later people said that the city had been refounded by that Emperor. The legend that Attila had destroyed Florence and Charlemagne rebuilt it, goes to indicate in its summary frankness, that the city life, almost dead under the Goths reflourished under the Franks.

Then, to the Counts, governors only of the city in the name of the Emperor, there succeeded the **Marquesses**, governing all the March of Tuscany. Of these, the MARQUESS UGO who in 1001 fixed the capital of his marquessate in Florence, left a good and unforgettable memory. Pious and just, he is still annualy remembered, with a ceremony of suffrage and remembrance in the Church of Badia which he founded. His good repute was even surpassed by the gentle and fair COUNTESS MATILDA (1046-1115), who supported also with arms, in 1085, Pope Gregory VII in the struggle against the Emperor Henry IV. The Florentines conceived such an admiration for this magnanimous lady, that she remained in the popular imagination the ideal Countess, the symbolic Countess. For at least four centuries, the Florentines continued to baptize their girls with the name of Contessa or Tessa, in honour of her who had defended the Church from the arrogance of the Empire.

Within and without the walls, rebuilt almost on the perimeter of the old ones, with new towers and battlements (second circle), there was in this period, about the year 1000, an extraordinary growth of religious buildings. There were renewed or there sprang up new monuments of capital artistic importance, in keeping with the Romanesque forms spread everywhere as a result of religious fervour.

Therefore the *Baptistery*, which had already sprung up in the centre of the city, was re-decorated. The *church of San Salvatore* (at the back of the Archiepiscopal palace), the *church of San Jacopo Sopr'Arno* (near the Ponte Vecchio) were rebuilt. Outside the walls grew up the monastic churches of *San Miniato al Monte* and the *Badia Fiesolana*.

Lid of an Etruscan sarcophagus (Archaeological Museum).

Other religious buildings, like the *Badia Fiorentina, Santa Reparata, San Pietro Scheraggio*, grew up in Romanesque style, but one does not recognize them because they were later transformed or destroyed. One may conclude that the style of these buildings was the same as that of the basilicas which grew up, at that time or a little earlier, in other parts of Tuscany and Italy, because the unity of style corresponded to that of the Monastic Orders and of the marquess' government in the great orbit of the Holy Roman Empire.

Notwithstanding this, the Florentine Romanesque architecture is distinguished from all the others of the period for its geometrical composition, for its calm equilibrium, for the perfect stillness which dominates in the alternate play of the white and the black. Still one cannot say that it gave rise to a Florentine art, but already it announces what will be the character of Florence: soberness and elegance; composure and measure; equilibrium and perfection.

We look at the Baptistery. No other architectural work, after the Greek ones, joined such an equilibrium of volume to such elegance of design, to the most perfect harmony of colour. And just this Baptistery is the white seed fallen into the centre of the city, from which was to be germinated all Florentine art. This fact came to pass in Florence: art, coming from outside, engrafted itself to the Roman root, giving that marvellous combination of forms typically Florentine, which on a classical basis had manifestations of a realism which was in no way vulgar.

Romanesque architecture, for example, which everywhere else was heavy, yet having at the same time the frivolity of the decorative small arches endlessly repeated, at Florence, blending itself with the two-coloured marble, again found the elegance of the round arch and the strength of line in the cornices.

The Florentine Renaissance, with Brunelleschi, took its origin from the line of this architecture. And from the necessity to revivify, by means of colours, the architectural austerity, the great school of Florentine painting sprang up.

FROM THE YEAR 1000 TO THE END
OF THE THIRTEENTH CENTURY

In order to decorate in mosaic the vault of the Baptistery, in the first years of the thirteenth century, the Florentines called Byzantine artists from Venice, a sign that in Florence there not yet existed artists capable of that enterprise.

The same happened for sculpture, when at the beginning of the fourteenth century they wanted to give the Baptistery a sculptured door which should be more beautiful and richer than those existing in Sicily, in the Campania, in Apulia and in Tuscany. They had to have a Pisan artist, ANDREA DA PONTEDERA (1290-1348). And from Venice came the bronze-founders, who, being foreigners, cast the door of a foreigner. A Sienese, TINO DI CAMAINO (d. about 1337), at the same time showed to the Florentines to what expression one may arrive in funeral monuments.

Florence was rich, but still did not possess an art adequate to its conquered power.

Detail of the Baptistery.

Profiting from the battle between Church and Empire, keeping close to its Bishop, Florence had achieved, at the end of the twelfth century, its effective communal autonomy.

In the thirteenth century, the government of the city, shaking off the power of the Marquess, was exercised by two, three or more **Consuls**, assisted by two **City Councils**.

We can understand how the Consuls as much as the Councillors, came to be chosen from the upper class and among those who had the right to the honorary title of « messere ».

And so was born rivalry between the various families which contended for the predominance of the posts. Some families joined together in alliances of blood or interest, called **consorterie**. This political condition goes also under the name of **Società delle torri** (Society of towers). Every house inside the narrow circle of the walls, grew up very high, and formed the « tower » for two reasons. First of all because the lack of space did not permit the use of a larger area, and so the towers were nothing but medieval skyscrapers; then secondly the towers corresponded to the war technique of the period. Every tower-house became, when required, a fortress and was joined by movable wooden bridges, across the narrow streets, with the towers of allied families forming a system of easily-defended towers.

The singular condition of city life imposed this civil architecture of houses vertically elongated, with thick walls of flat stone blocks, narrow openings, holes and brackets for the fixing of the bridges. The laws of war tactics were more important than those of hygiene or aesthetics without taking account of interior illumination and avoiding ledges which might be used during assaults.

Naturally the city of tower-houses had very narrow streets and was almost without squares. Unhappy clearances have made open spaces in the town inconceivable in the old days. Only in front of the Romanesque churches a short « sagrato » (church-square) widened out, as one can see in front of the church of Santi Apostoli or of that of Santo Stefano.

In vain, to maintain peace and justice, they had recourse to the institution, at first exceptional (1185), later regular, of a citizen **Podestà** (one of the first was Gherardo Caponsacchi, in 1193). In the end they had recourse to a foreign Podestà (1200), who had no ties of local interest.

The quarrels between the various families became increasingly more serious and resulted in the formation of the two great parties, called **Guelphs** (from the German surname Welf) and **Ghibellines** (from the German surname Weiblingen). The Guelphs, faithful to the Pope, were hostile to the power of the Emperor. The Ghibellines, faithful to the Emperor, were hostile to the influence of the Pope. The ancient family jealousies fanned the fire, so that if one family was Guelph its enemies were sure to be Ghibelline.

The same took place in the various Tuscan cities, who were Guelph or Ghibelline, depending whether the enemy cities were Guelph or Ghibelline. For example, if Florence was Guelph, Arezzo and Pistoia had to be Ghibelline and so on.

But the division was not really justified by an effective attachment to the politics of the Pope or the Emperor, and, by complicated subdivisions of party, often the two factions came into conflict, or even into war, with the authority from which they took their name.

The war between the two great parties had its occasioning motive in the murder, for reasons of feminine jealousies, of Boundelmonte dei Boundelmonti, which took place at Easter 1215 close to the Ponte Vecchio, by the Amidei, helped by the Uberti.

The Society of the towers divided itself then into two camps. At the centre of one were the tower houses of the Buondelmonti; at the centre of the other, the tower-houses of the Uberti.

From the beginning, the Ghibellines, favored by the Emperor Frederic II, had the upper hand, and in 1249 threw the Guelphs out of the city. It was the first time that a party had banished the components of the opposing party, and the sad fact constituted a dangerous precedent.

The Ghibelline success was short-lived. The Florentine root, already from the times of the Countess Matilda, was Guelph. A city like Florence, where the artisan work formed the principal source of income, had to break from the Imperial control and to maintain itself free among free cities. Political liberty meant liberty of work and above all liberty of commerce.

So, as soon as Frederic II died, in 1250, the Guelphs again took the upper hand. The Commune had the arrangement called that of the **Primo Popolo,** constituted by the **Signoria,** formed by the **Podestà,** watched over by the **Capitano del Popolo** and by the **Councils** of the twelve **Anziani** (Elders) and the thirty-six **Buonomini** (Good men), all by popular choice.

From 1250 to 1260 Florence had ten years of great prosperity. Only two years after the Guelph victory, in 1252, the well-known « golden florin » was coined, a sign of political and commercial independence, and was soon the money which held the first place on the European market for the purity and constancy of its alloy.

A certain tolerance made living together between Guelph and Ghibelline families possible. The agreement permitted also the expansion of Florence towards the Appennines and the Tyrrenian sea. They began to conquer

Tower-house in the Via Por Santa Maria.

the district, weakening the various feudal lords, secluded in their manors, and building along the roads many « artisan castles », that is places encircled with a wall, like many miniature towns, connected by commercial arrangements and dependant, not to the feudatory, but to the Florentine Signoria.

In this fortunate period fall the gains of Volterra, San Gimignano, Poggibonsi, Marradi, and pacts of alliance were imposed on the proudest neighbouring republics, weakened or intimidated: Lucca, Pistoia, Siena, Pisa, Arezzo.

But the revival of the Imperial fortunes, with the first undertakings of King Manfred, excited the Ghibellines, poor supporters of the « Primo Popolo » regime. They attempted a sudden revolution, which ended in nothing. Chased from Florence they gathered in Siena. The Florentine Guelphs, blinded by hatred, imprudently came up even beneath the walls of the enemy city. And on the 4th of September 1260, attacked on all sides, the Florentines suffered a disastrous rout at Montaperti, in the valley of the Arbia river, which Dante called « coloured red » by their blood. In truth, the day did not cost the Florentines more than 4000 dead and prisoners. But the collapse of illusions was so great, the defeat considered so irreparable that the Guelphs openly gave up the defence of Florence, though it was well equipped and defended. They left the city, even before the conquerors entered it. The latter thought of razing Florence to the ground reducing it to the undefended suburbs, that is, to those popular and artisan quarters which had formed themselves outside the city gates.

And it was even a Ghibelline, FARINATA DEGLI UBERTI, who at the Empoli Congress boldly defended his own city and saved it from destruction.

Florence then had, for six years, a Ghibelline government, headed by an **Imperial Envoy**, who was Guido Novello dei Conti Guidi, from Arezzo. To him was due the opening of the straight Via Ghibellina, in the direction of Arezzo, his country and a Ghibelline city.

But also this period of Ghibelline domination, which weighed heavily upon the people with hard fiscal impositions, lasted but briefly. It ended with the death of Manfred, routed and killed in the battle of Benevento (1266).

The Guelphs again quickly took up the initiative, and the people succeeded, without bloodshed, to enjoin the departure of Count Guido Novello and his German troops.

The Guelph side, supported by the victor, King Charles of Anjou, definitely established themselves, giving a new political and administrative aspect to the city.

Of great importance were then the **Corporations of the Arts**, divided into Major and Minor. All the citizens, whether noble or of the people, had to be inscribed there if they wished to participate in the government. Excelling among the major arts were the *Arte della Lana* and that of *Calimala*. The former organized the activity of the woolworkers, whose products went even to the most distant lands. That of Calimala looked after the finishing and refining of the wool stuffs imported from other countries. These two arts especially brought to Florence her industrial prosperity and her economic wealth.

With this wealth came the desire to embellish the city, and they began, as we have seen, from the Baptistery, described by Dante as the « fine San Giovanni ». The golden florin was so called because on one side of it was

Fourteenth century model of the Cathedral (fresco in the Spanish Chapel).

the Florentine coat-of-arms, the flower of the lily, while on the other side was engraved the figure of St. John, patron of the city.

The saint of rectitude, the precursor of Christ was considered by the Florentines made enthusiastic by success, as the symbol of their mercantile correctness, the precursor of the power of the Republic. His temple, therefore, should be of the greatest splendour, representing in concrete mode the power and fortune of the city.

We have seen how in the first years of the thirteenth century the Florentines had to call in Venetian mosaic-workers for the decoration of the Baptistery cupola. Together with the Venetians, in the lower parts, worked later local artists, like ANDREA TAFI, the so-called GADDO GADDI (1259-1332), and almost certainly CIMABUE (1240-1303). This last is considered the father of Florentine painting, and it was he who gave to the artisan and traditional painting of the Byzantine masters, a power and vivacity until then unknown.

In sculpture, the example of the Pisan Andrea da Pontedera and the Sienese Tino di Camaino was taken up by an artist of genius, ARNOLFO DI CAMBIO, from Colle Val d'Elsa (1232-1301), whom we know also as a very great architect, and who must be considered the founder of that school from which came, later, the great Florentine sculptors.

The triumph of the people brought also the triumph of its language, that is the « vulgar » tongue, which, continuing the Latin « sermo plebeius », became always more established, not only as a spoken language, but also as a written language for domestic and mercantile use. Among all the vulgar dialects the Florentine one was nearest to the Latin, and the most harmonious. And as the artisan people and mercantile class, that is the part of the laymen, showed the desire to educate themselves, already the Chancellor of the Republic BRUNETTO LATINI, after having written a tract in French, wrote one in Florentine, entitled the *Tesoretto*.

Around him were gathered the young men of letters of the city, and the poets, who later formed the group of the « Sweet New Style ». They were called GUIDO CAVALCANTI, LAPO GIANNI, GIANNI ALFANI, DINO FRESCOBALDI, and above all their friend DANTE ALIGHIERI promised well.

Briefly summing up, in the thirteenth century civil struggles between Guelphs and Ghibellines were contested in the city. Society was expressed in the rough civil architecture of the tower-houses. Art was reserved for religious buildings which continued in the Romanesque style of architecture, in the Byzantine style for painting, in the Pisan style for sculpture. In literature there appeared the first manifestations, both literary and poetic, in the vulgar tongue.

In this period the first Florentine personalities became known. In the field of architecture and sculpture, Arnolfo di Cambio, in the field of painting Cimabue, in the field of culture, Brunetto Latini, in that of poetry, Guido Cavalcanti. And the universal geniuses of Dante and Giotto announced themselves.

Grain merchants in 14th cent. Florence (Codex of the « Biadaiolo ». Laurenziana Library).

THE FOURTEENTH CENTURY

In the period of industrial prosperity and mercantile fervour, renewing itself after the Guelph victory in the ordering of the arts, the old political hatreds were calmed. Instead, there were born contrasts in social character, at first between the major arts, who took the part of the wolf, and the minor arts, who felt themselves sacrificed; then between the so-called « popolo grasso » (fat people) and the so-called « popolo magro » (thin people). The qualifying adjectives united to the generic term people, clearly tell what was the nature of the conflict.

The city remained under the title of Guelph; but the ancient qualification had even lost its original significance of fidelity to the Papal politics. Not a few times the Commune found itself in diplomatic conflict and also in war with the Popes.

The Guelphism of Florence became the standard in the struggles of communal interests with the neighbouring cities which opposed its expansion. With the battle of Campaldino (1289), in which Dante also took part, Florence subdued Ghibelline Arezzo, on the side of which many of the Florentine exiles had come to fight.

The greatest rival of Florence remained the Ghibelline Pisa, most gravely weakened by the Genoese in the battle of the Meloria (1284)

In 1293 the government of the Florentine Republic was reformed with the **Ordinamenti di Giustizia** (Justice provisions). They were so called because they promised a more equal social justice. With the new arrangements the government in fact took on a completely democratic character. Former magistrates were maintained but a **Gonfaloniere di giustizia** was also created, who governed for two months, together with the **Priori delle arti e della libertà** (Seniors of the Guilds and of Liberty) and the **Consiglio dei Buono-mini** (Council of Good Men). The Gonfaloniere later gradually became the real head of the Republic.

In this period of great prosperity the city flourished and expanded, beginning to develop in the way which it was to follow throughout all the fourteenth century.

In the old centre of the city, there stretched and grew up two types of construction which formed the two poles of the republican, Guelph life: the religious pole, being the House of God, called automatically *Domus* or *Duomo*; the civil pole, being the House of the People, called *Palazzo della Signoria*.

In the precincts of the Duomo, which was later dedicated to *Santa Maria del Fiore*, that is, to the Madonna, protectress of Florence, (begun in 1294), there grew up one by one other religious buildings, such as the *Campanile of Giotto* (begun in 1334), the *Loggia del Bigallo* (begun in 1352), *Or San Michele* (renewed in 1337).

Near to the Palazzo della Signoria (begun in 1298), were built other civil buildings, such as the *Loggia della Signoria* also called *dell'Orcagna* (1376-82), the *Palazzo del Podestà* also called *del Bargello* (begun in 1254).

It has already been mentioned that outside the city gates the popular « borghi » (suburbs) were formed, which radiated like a star, along the lines of communication. To include these suburbs, together with the quarter on the left bank of the river, they thought of enlarging the city walls, and so was built the third circle, very wide, the construction of which diminished the coffers of the Republic.

In the suburbs, in the middle of the working people, the friars of the two mendicant orders, Franciscan and Dominican, established themselves. Their convents had grown up in view of the old circle of walls, but were still on the edge of the country, with two great popular churches, whose façades looked from two opposite points, towards the « nest of malice », that is towards the centre of the city. The great religious reawakening brought by the two orders, the success of their new piety, counselled the enlargement of the convents and the churches. So, the Dominican one, called *Santa Maria Novella*, was rebuilt from 1278 onwards; the Franciscan one, called *Santa Croce*, was refounded in 1295.

We must think that this enormous work was carried on almost all at the same time and was protracted from early in the thirteenth century for the better part of the fourteenth century: the Duomo with its dependencies; the Town Hall with its dependencies; the third circle of the walls with its seven principal gates; Santa Maria Novella, Santa Croce; a mass of works, carried on at the expense of the people, with free offerings, legacies, and fiscal taxes, which employed for a very long time architects, sculptors, painters, gold-smiths, glass-workers, inlayers.

Over the architectural renewal of the city there presided the genius of ARNOLFO DI CAMBIO, who gave the designs for the Duomo, the Palazzo and the Walls. Due to him, the Gothic style, uniformly diffused all over Europe by the Cluniac order, lost in Florence its northern angularity and its excessive ornamental carving. The upward thrust was withheld, the round arch was not conquered by the pointed arch, and so we have an example, unique in the world, of a Gothic style, reposing and solemn, firm and gentle, of great balanced masses.

In civil architecture the tower-houses were succeeded by houses with a more open and serene façade, with double arched windows and covered terrace under the roof, with the great, jutting-out gutter.

In religious architecture, the new structure served to cover great spaces, to give the doors a spaciousness for gathering the crowds of the faithful.

And as the new mendicant orders usually addressed the people at whose imagination they wanted to strike, painting became the most powerful ally of their preaching.

On the vast walls stretched the great pages of the « Bible of the Simple » that is great frescoed paintings, where a strong and candid art, dramatic and plastic, rapid and efficacious is intentionally moving and instructing the people, that they should marvel and be edified. One name above all, GIOTTO (1266-1336), with his numerous followers, from his nephew STEFANO FIORENTINO to TADDEO GADDI (1330?-1366), to PUCCIO CAPANNA (around 1350), to GIOTTINO (1324-1369?), to BERNARDO DADDI (1317-1350).

Giotto was not only a painter, but also the architect of the Campanile and perhaps the sculptor of various panels of the Campanile itself.

To the great names of Arnolfo di Cambio and Giotto was to be united also the very great name of DANTE, who with his *Divine Comedy* consecrated the vulgar tongue with an unparalleled poetic work and made Florentine a national language.

But the pride of power and riches had once more aroused political discords, and the same Guelphs were divided between two tendencies: that of the NERI, very faithful to the Pope; that of the BIANCHI, who nostalgically inclined to the imperial institutions, and who ended by mixing themselves with the remnants of the Ghibelline exiles.

Pope Boniface VIII had sent to Florence, as peace-maker between the two factions, CHARLES OF VALOIS, brother to the king of France (1301). Charles partially favoured the Neri, who, guided by the fierce and ambitious CORSO DONATI, made themselves lords by force, imposing vendettas. Six hundred. Bianchi were condemned to exile, and among them, the poet Dante Alighieri (1302), and the father of Francesco Petrarca. Corso Donati, drunk with success, tried to rule the city and was killed in 1308. A merchant related the happenings of these years in his *Chronicle*. He was called DINO COMPAGNI and was the father of Italian prose history.

The Hospital of the Innocenti by Brunelleschi.

The white Guelphs, united with the surviving Ghibellines, hoped, as usual, for the assistance of the Emperor, and, when HENRY VII came down into Italy, their hope was revived. The Emperor neared Guelph Florence, which closed its gates (1312). The imperial army encamped itself under the unfinished walls, and a street in the suburbs is to this day called the Via del Campo d'Arrigo (Henry's camp). An astrologer had predicted that the emperor would arrive at the end of the world. The place where he encamped was called Capodimondo (Head of the world) (there still exists the street with this name). In fact he did not go much further. The inglorious siege being raised, Henry unexpectedly died of malarial fever at Buonconvento, in 1313. With him died the last hopes of the exiles in the imperial forces. Dante, seing himself prevented from returning to his land, thought only of his poem, which was to be his great revenge.

One could say that the struggle with the Empire had ended. But as much could not be said regarding those Tuscan cities which had declared themselves Ghibelline, being rightly jealous of Florence, whose predominating purposes were quite evident. Pisa fought Florence for the rule over the sea, Lucca for the rule over the mountains. For ten years Florence had to battle with these cities, now carrying the war under their walls, now being subjected to it under its own. UGUCCIONE DELLA FAGGIOLA and CASTRUCCIO CASTRACANI were adversaries more alarmful than the Emperor. And Florence had known the hard routs at Montecatini (1315) and at Altopascio (1325). She endured them better than in the times of Montaperti, and by perseverance continued the struggle. Her enemies kept her at bay. If anything, it was really her so-called protectors, the Guelph King Robert of Anjou and his son Duke Charles of Calabria, who exhausted the Republic's coffers with the excuse of defending it.

Not even great public calamities, such as the flood of 1333, which carried away all the bridges including that called the Old Bridge, and the plague of 1340, halted the city's growth which always enriched itself by means of the textile industries and banking undertakings.

The Florentines, always more busy and rich, even disdained the career of arms. An unhappy experiment to give the charge of the armed defence to a foreigner, GUALTIERI DI BRIENNE, Duke of Athens, and to make him lord of the city, ended in less than a year in his expulsion (1343).

Wealth was not distributed in an equal way in all classes in the city, on the contrary, immense deposits were formed in the hands of a few able merchants. The so-called **magnates**, that is the powerful men in industry and commerce, made the interests of the Republic correspond with their private interests, and in part they were right, because in reality their interests were also the interests of the Republic. But the poor people, discontented, became troublesome. The so-called « ciompi » (woolcarders) rebelled. In the tumult which followed, and which was called the **Tumulto dei Ciompi** (1378) their chief MICHELE DI LANDO was set up as Gonfaloniere di Giustizia. He governed with wisdom and equity, but the triumph of the « ciompi » did not deeply modify the economic composition of society. Industry and commerce had created the so-called « banks » where capital was gathered. These banks were in the hands of a few, powerful bankers, who, as we shall see, fatally took in hand the city politics.

Meanwhile the great artistic works, begun in the last years of the thirteenth century were carried on, even in face of wars and struggles, plagues and famines. To artists such as Arnolfo di Cambio and Giotto, there succeeded ANDREA DI CIONE called ORCAGNA (1308?-1368), FRANCESCO TALENTI (c. 1300-c. 1369) and a band of master-artists not all identified, among whom were NICCOLÒ and PIERO LAMBERTI, FRANCESCO DI NERI, GIOVANNI DI FETTO. Supervising the architectural work, were the so-called MASTERS OF SANTA REPARATA who were the Civil Engineers of the period.

In the field of literature, to Dante there succeeded FRANCESCO PETRARCA, the greatest lyric poet and most erudite man, and GIOVANNI BOCCACCIO, also a scholar and the father of prose narrative. A third was GIOVANNI VILLANI (c. 1276-1348), author of a great *Chronicle*, which is the first example of communal history taken from the documents.

Wedding procession in 15th cent. Florence (Gallery of the Accademia).

COATS-OF-ARMS OF THE GUILDS

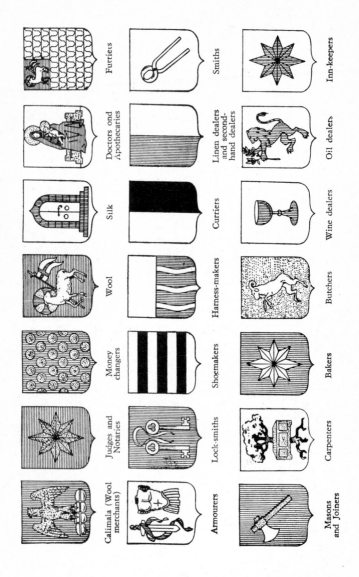

Furriers

Smiths

Inn-keepers

Doctors and Apothecaries

Linen dealers and second-hand dealers

Oil dealers

Silk

Curriers

Wine dealers

Wool

Harness-makers

Butchers

Money changers

Shoemakers

Bakers

Judges and Notaries

Lock-smiths

Carpenters

Calimala (Wool merchants)

Armourers

Masons and Joiners

In the heart of the century there extended also to Florence the influence of the international Gothic style. Architecture became more ornamented, sculpture more sentimental, painting more linear. At the time it seemed that Florentine art would lose its character of classical composure.

In architecture Orcagna could not resist the seduction of the over-ornamented Gothic, and his celebrated tabernacle in Or' San Michele is enough to show it.

In sculpture one felt the influence of Giovanni Pisano, dramatic but weak. In painting, that of the Sienese Simone Martini, ornamented and gentle. ANDREA DI BONAIUTO (c. 1338-1377), AGNOLO GADDI (1333-1396), SPINELLO ARETINO (1333-1410), LORENZO MONACO (1370-1425) complicate the straight-forward and strong Florentine painting with arabesques of line, preciousness in colour, searchings after sentimental effect.

But this wandering was brief. Humanism was at the door, with its return to serene, harmonious traditions.

THE FIFTEENTH CENTURY

The industry, and especially the trading, or what is now called commerce, brought the monopoly of wealth into the power of a group of men who administered the bank of commerce, from which was later born the exchange bank.

This group of merchants, who were called Strozzi, Pitti, Pazzi, Albizi, Antinori, Peruzzi, Rucellai, Tornabuoni, Sassetti, had the government of the city practically in their hands. It was natural that the reappearance of rivalries was no longer by family, nor by party, but by bank. About some of the strongest banks there was gathered a sort of company which gravitated within the orbit of its own bank. The greater banking companies, early in the fifteenth century, were those of the Albizi, Pitti, Strozzi and **Medici**.

Of the latter, the head was the most able and resolute COSIMO DE' MEDICI (1389-1464), who had come to have such power that it was a real danger to the republic and principally to his opposing bankers.

The head of another financial group, RINALDO DEGLI ALBIZZI, succeeded in having him arrested in 1433 as a danger to liberty. (We must bear in mind that when we speak here of liberty, we mean freedom to break the economic power of one's adversary, because the political struggle is continually fed by the financial struggle of the various banks contesting their interests).

Saved from death, Cosimo was condemned to five years' confinement at Padua, but the year after, by mutation of the Signoria, he was recalled to his country, and acclaimed by the people as the true lord of the city. In fact, for thirty years he was the arbitrator of the political destinies of the city, but had the wisdom to take no title of command. They continued with the republican arrangements, but they decided and did nothing without his counsel or his wishes.

Cosimo, later called « il Vecchio » (the Elder) to distinguish him from the other Medici of the same name, and honoured with the classic title of « Pater patriae », wisely conducted the finantial politics of his bank and the diplomatic policy of the republic. The alliances with the Duchy of Milan, with the Republic of Venice, with the King of Naples, with the Pope, manoeuvred with the utmost ability, had already brought about the conquest of the very proud city of Pisa (1406). The sea ways were at last open, and Cosimo thought of sending the Florentine ships against the Byzantine and Mussulman merchants. The gold was accumulating more and more in the coffers of the Republic and in the Medici bank. The cities of Prato, Pistoia, Arezzo, Livorno, which the arms of the Commune had not been able to make submit effectively to the wishes of Florence, were conquered by that gold.

In 1464 Cosimo was succeeded by his son PIERO IL GOTTOSO (the Gouty) (1416-1469), who, despite various initial errors, governed with wisdom, though only for five years. On his death the reins of Florence were taken up by his son, LORENZO, the lettered patron. Saved from the **Pazzi conspiracy** (April 26th, 1478), in which his brother Giuliano was killed, he continued the skilful conduct of Cosimo, surrounding himself however with a real court of poets, artists and philosophers. He had no titles except that of Magnificent, which was due to all persons of great regard. He was the Magnificent Lorenzo, and not Lorenzo the Magnificent as is wrongly written and repeated. His politics, of an unequalled intelligence, secured peace for the city for thirteen years, which had its effects all over Italy.

When he died (1492) in his villa of Careggi, all Europe mourned his departure. There had, however, already grown up in Florence an opposition to his form of domination, occult, but most sound. The opposition had as their head a Dominican from Ferrara, GIROLAMO SAVONAROLA, who rekindled the old republican spirits, and at the same time the Christian spirit of morality and sacrifice.

But foreign policy could no longer be restrained to the remaining Tuscan states, nor to those of Italy. Two colossi had arisen in Europe: France and Spain. The king of France, CHARLES VIII, moving against the Kingdom of Naples, came down into Italy without striking a blow (1494). PIERO IL FATUO, the unhappy son of Lorenzo, succeeded to his father at a very difficult moment, hastily ceded to the King the fortresses between Sarzana and Livorno, which were the key of the defence of Florence. This rash act was the spark of the revolt. While the Pisans rebelled against the Republic and acquired again their liberty, in Florence, the people, aglow with Savonarola's preaching, reinstalled the republican arrangements.

Charles VIII, coming into Florence as a conqueror, had to leave it as an ally, owing to the firm behaviour of PIER CAPPONI, who threatened to ring the bells to call the people to arms.

They hoped that Florence would be able to return to its fourteenth century state. But the times were changed. Florence indeed entered into a political game too much beyond its city walls. The leading spirit was no longer of local diplomacy. The Savonarola Republic failed. The city divided itself between the followers of the friar called « piagnoni » (weepers), and the Medici partisans, called « palleschi » (from the balls on the Medici coat-of-arms). The friar was taken by the « palleschi » and after an iniquitous process was hung and burnt in the Piazza della Signoria (1498).

The funeral pyre of the heroic antagonist of the Magnificent Lorenzo illuminated in a sinister way the end of the Florentine Republic guided by the interests of the bank and the shrewdness of the bankers. During the next century Florence was to become a pawn in the political game of Europe, and it was already much if its moves were not to be brutally imposed by the great powers.

In the fifteenth century in Florence, the most important cultural fact was constituted by Humanism, that is that research and study from ancient and Greek texts which made Florence a « second Athens ».

In the society of the period, in which everyone was worth for his intelligence and capacity, Humanism, which exalted the human personality, had a great reception. In the philosophical field Plato came again to be honoured, and under the protection of Cosimo de' Medici, MARSILIO FICINO renewed at Careggi the Platonic Academy. In the literary field, there was great zeal shown, in finding ancient codices, for their interpretation and copying. In this we must distinguish humanists such as COLUCCIO SALUTATI, POGGIO BRACCIOLINI, NICCOLÒ NICCOLI, GIANNOZZO MANETTI. In poetry, impeccable Latin verses were composed, and elegant little poems in the vulgar tongue. An example of this was the lord of the city himself, LORENZO DE' MEDICI, and his friend AGNOLO POLIZIANO, consideret the most refined lyrical poet of the century.

In architecture the genius of FILIPPO BRUNELLESCHI found again the serene harmony of the ancient forms, without coldly imitating them, giving instead to his compositions marvellous elegance and grace.

The real impress of the fifteenth century society was upon the civil architecture. To the Society of Towers, already expressed in severe and closed Romanesque; to the Communal society which had been manifested in the light, pointed Gothic, there now succeeded the mercantile society, which revealed itself in the elegant, charming and solid architecture of the lordly palace.

In the Florence which had, before every other city in Europe, its roads and its two squares paved, in the Florence where the elegance of the women and the culture of the men amazed the foreigners, every banker wanted to build an airy and commodious palace, worthy of his fortune.

The Duomo and Palazzo Comunale, collective works affirming the city's unity, were followed by the affirmation of private wealth and power. So

Michelangelo: Battle of Centaurs and Lapites (Casa Buonarroti).

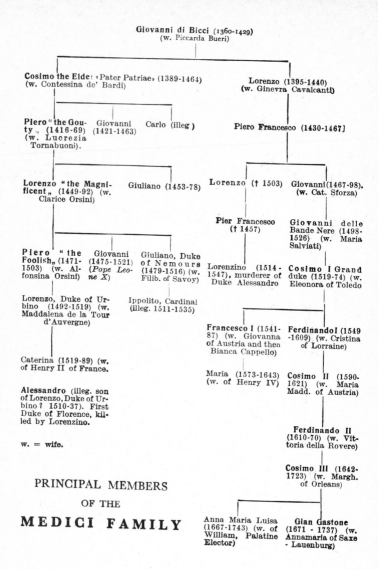

Giovanni di Bicci (1360-1429)
(w. Piccarda Bueri)

Cosimo the Elder «Pater Patriae» (1389-1464)
(w. Contessina de' Bardi)

Lorenzo (1395-1440)
(w. Ginevra Cavalcanti)

Piero "the Gouty" (1416-69) (w. Lucrezia Tornabuoni).　　Giovanni (1421-1463)　　Carlo (illeg.)

Piero Francesco (1430-1467)

Lorenzo "the Magnificent" (1449-92) (w. Clarice Orsini)　　Giuliano (1453-78)

Lorenzo († 1503)

Giovanni (1467-98). (w. Cat. Sforza)

Piero "the Foolish" (1471-1503) (w. Alfonsina Orsini)　　Giovanni (1475-1521) (Pope Leone X)　　Giuliano, Duke of Nemours (1479-1516) (w. Filib. of Savoy)

Pier Francesco († 1457)

Giovanni delle Bande Nere (1498-1526) (w. Maria Salviati)

Lorenzo, Duke of Urbino (1492-1519) (w. Maddalena de la Tour d'Auvergne)　　Ippolito, Cardinal (illeg. 1511-1535)

Lorenzino (1514-1547), murderer of Duke Alessandro

Cosimo I Grand duke (1519-74) (w. Eleonora of Toledo

Caterina (1519-89) (w. of Henry II of France.

Alessandro (illeg. son of Lorenzo, Duke of Urbino ? 1510-37). First Duke of Florence, killed by Lorenzino.

Francesco I (1541-87) (w. Giovanna of Austria and then Bianca Cappello)

Ferdinando I (1549-1609) (w. Cristina of Lorraine)

w. = wife.

Maria (1573-1643) (w. of Henry IV)

Cosimo II (1590-1621) (w. Maria Madd. of Austria)

Ferdinando II (1610-70) (w. Vittoria della Rovere)

PRINCIPAL MEMBERS
OF THE
MEDICI FAMILY

Cosimo III (1642-1723) (w. Margh. of Orleans)

Anna Maria Luisa (1667-1743) (w. of William, Palatine Elector)

Gian Gastone (1671 - 1737) (w. Annamaria of Saxe - Lauenburg)

the typical building of the fifteenth century was the palace, where external magnificence corresponded with interior comfort.

Between the old tower-houses of the thirteenth century, and the house-workshops of the fourteenth century, there broadened out the palaces of the enriched merchants: the *Medici palace*, the *Pazzi palace*, the *Pitti palace*, the *Strozzi palace*, the *Rucellai palace*, square palaces with internal columned courtyard. On the ground floor were rough blocks, with small, barred windows which had still something of the fortres in them; but on the upper floors the palace was lighter and more serene, and there were most elegant double-arched windows. While the towers were embattled, and the Gothic houses had the jutting-out roof, the fifteenth century palace ended with a bracket cornice, which gave great nobility and elegance to the whole building.

The harmonious division of the spaces, the soberness of the various architectural elements, the sensible distribution of rooms round the sunny courtyard, the charm of the stone bench which usually ran round the base, gave to the fifteenth century palace an air of welcoming hospitality and dignified decorum.

Also religious architecture renewed itself, becoming more elegant and harmonious. From the ancient plans there grew up slender columns upon which rested light rounded arches.

The decorations too changed in style, and the bare, trestle roofing was substituted by very rich boxed ceilings, the bronze doors were finely carved, the marble tabernacles were ornamented with very beautiful sculptural reliefs. So the austere aspect of the mediaeval church changed into a serene expression of joy. The new religious buildings, rather than the drama of expiation, expressed the calm certainty of redemption.

So there grew up, in new clothing, the Brunelleschian churches of *San Lorenzo*, *Santo Spirito*, *San Marco*, and the *Hospital of the Innocenti.*

But humanist architecture, more than the traditional Latin Cross plan, preferred the buildings with square or polygonal plan, more regular and perfect. So the true master-pieces of religious architecture of the period were the private Brunelleschian Chapels: the so-called *Old Sacristy* in San Lorenzo and the *Pazzi Chapel* in Santa Croce.

The genius of this architectural renewal was FILIPPO BRUNELLESCHI (1377-1446), followed by MICHELOZZO MICHELOZZI, (1396-1472), LEON BATTISTA ALBERTI (1404-1472), BERNARDO ROSSELLINO (1409-1464), GIULIANO DA MAIANO (1432-1490), BENEDETTO, his brother (1442-1497), GIULIANO DA SAN GALLO (1445-1516), CRONACA (1454-1508).

In the new architectural style, painting gave up its task of narration and instruction, assuming that of a pure element of beauty, expressed in luminous compositions, mostly executed on wood.

Painting showed, in the powerful personality of MASACCIO (1401-1428) sorrowing humanity, in that of BEATO ANGELICO (1387-1455) humanity transfigured by grace, in that of PAOLO UCCELLO (1397-1475) humanity halted in its plastic appearance, in that of ANDREA DEL CASTAGNO (1423-1457) humanity shown ·in its vigourous expression.

The evolution towards the profane and pleasing was accentuated by FILIPPO LIPPI (c. 1406-1469), BENOZZO GOZZOLI (c. 1420-1497) and SANDRO BOTTICELLI (1444-1510).

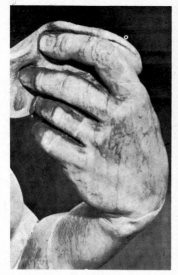 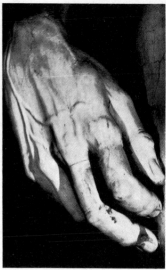

Michelangelo: details from the David (Gallery of the Accademia).

Sculpture, which in Florence had not yet had a great manifestation, with Humanism gained great importance. It seemed almost that the exaltation of man had found its most adequate means in sculpture. Many of the appointed architects were also sculptors: LORENZO GHIBERTI (1378-1455), and the very great Donato di Betto called DONATELLO (c. 1382-1466), NANNI DI BANCO (c. 1383-1421), the DELLA ROBBIA family, LUCA (1400-1482), ANDREA (1435-1525) and GIOVANNI (1469-1529), ANTONIO ROSSELLINO (1429-1479), DESIDERIO DA SETTIGNANO (1428-1464), MINO DA FIESOLE (1430-1484), BENEDETTO DA MAIANO (1442-1497), and finally the sculptor of energy and movement, ANTONIO DEL POLLAIOLO (1433-1498) and the master of Leonardo, Andrea de' Cioni called VERROCCHIO (1435-1488).

No other city, in no other epoch, ever had such an intense flowering of art. This extraordinary fertility culminated, in the moment of political and spiritual crisis in the city, in two sublime geniuses in their almost superhuman power: LEONARDO DA VINCI (1452-1519) scientist and artist; MICHELANGELO BUONARROTI (1475-1564), architect, sculptor, painter and poet. With the former, painting came to the borders of the ineffable. With the second, sculpture touched the height of its expressive power.

It seemed that Florence, before losing its own political liberty wished to completely experience what was allowed to the human spirit in the realm of art.

The imperious instructions of the two supreme masters was to carry away in an irresistable current a crowd of imitators, even in Florence where great, significant personalities were not lacking, such as FRA BARTOLOMEO (1475-1517) and ANDREA DEL SARTO (1486-1531), who by their spirituality, stand between the Renaissance painters and the so-called Mannerists.

THE SIXTEENTH CENTURY

The new century opens with the tragedy of the **Siege**. The reconquest of Pisa, in 1509, had drained the already exhausted finances of the Republic. In 1512 the Medici returned, acclaimed by the people who hoped for new prosperity through them. Piero, called the Fatuo, was not able to return, having drowned in a tragic accident. The last of Lorenzo's sons came back, Giovanni (b. 1475), a Cardinal, who the year after ascended the throne of Saint Peter with the name of Leo X (1513-1521). From then on the Medici considered Florence as a family lordship. Leo X disposed of it, nominating there as a Captain of the Militia his nephew Lorenzo (1492-1519), son of Piero, and creating Archbishop his cousin Giulio (1478-1534), the natural son of Giuliano, the brother of the Magnificent Lorenzo, killed in the Pazzi conspiracy.

In 1523 also Giulio was elected Pope, with the name of Clement VII. He continued to treat the government of Florence as an affair of personal interest. His faithful instrument was Cardinal Passerini of Cortona who did not even take care to hide the Medicean despotism. Republic government was now reduced to a ghost, and the Florentine people, in whom the Savonarola ferment still lived, felt the humiliation of it.

At the news of the Sack of Rome (1527) the Florentine again sent away the Medici, reinstalling the authority of the Republican magistrates. As a sign of their irrevocable, extreme decision no more to submit to the game of dominators, they elected Jesus Christ King and the Virgin Mary Queen of the Florentine people. The powerful men, gathered round the old standards, again took up their abandoned arms. They renewed the unhappy alliance with Francis I, King of France, against the Emperor Charles V.

The challenge provoked the concentration of a powerful army, formed by Germans, Spaniards and Italian mercenary troops. To about 40000 trained soldiers, with heavy artillery, Florence opposed a maximum of 14000 poorly-armed citizens and its walls which Michelangelo had reinforced.

From the end of Summer of 1529 until August 1530, the city was sub-

Vasari: the Siege of Florence (Palazzo Vecchio).

jected to a siege, which was the only effective one in its history. It was a legendary, glorious year, living in the heart of the people. The merchant FRANCESCO FERRUCCI who commanded the troops operating outside the city with the ability of a professional condottiere and with the heart of a classical hero, overcome by his enemies at Gavinana (August 3rd, 1530), was killed in the attempt to break the blockade of the city. Florence, starving, pest-ridden, betrayed, had to capitulate to the imperial troops. So ended its secular liberty. And with this liberty went the singularity of its political system, the original character of its mercantile and artistic civilization, which had given it an unparalleled individuality for more that three centuries. It was beginning to become the capital of a dynastic state, not unlike the other Italian ones.

The Medici came back, no longer as ordinary nobles, but with the official title of **Dukes of Florence**. The first (1531) was ALESSANDRO, a natural son of Lorenzo, son of Piero il Fatuo, son of the Magnificent Lorenzo. A decree of Charles V nominated him head of all the offices. Dissolute, overbearing, but not deprived of a certain awkward talent, he was stabbed by his cousin Lorenzino de' Medici, making himself a Florentine Brutus (1537). With Alessandro and his cousin Caterina, married to King Henry of France, the branch of the Medici descended from Cosimo il Vecchio became extinct.

Among the descendants of a collateral branch of the family, there was now chosen the son of Giovanni delle Bande Nere, the eighteen years old Cosimo (1519-1574). Nominated Duke of Florence, he took the name of COSIMO I, which distinguished him from Cosimo « il vecchio ».

Cosimo I governed for thirty-six years with great capability and firmness, making himself respected by both the French and the Spaniards.

He finally overcame Siena (1555), and extended his rule over almost all Tuscany being given by the Pope, and confirmed in it by the Emperor, no longer the title of Duke of Florence, but of **Grand Duke of Tuscany**. He widened the field to real politics also on the seas, by the creation of the military order of the Knights of St. Stephen (1561) which also had the task of policing the Tyrrenian Sea, which was infested with Turkish corsairs. This order, ambitious to equal the Knights of Malta, and the navies of Venice and Rome, in a series of wonderful exploits, succeeded for three centuries in fighting against the Mediterranean expansion of the Ottoman Empire.

Under Cosimo I, Tuscany knew a prosperous period, and Florence one of new splendour. He was succeeded, in 1574, by his eldest son FRANCESCO I (1541-1587), a strange person, an inventor and collector, who gave himself up with equal enthusiasm to study and debauch. On his sudden death, the lot of the Grand duchy was again raised up by his brother FERDINANDO I (1549-1609), who continued and even surpassed his father's work, giving new impulse to politics, commerce and the arts. To him is due the development of Livorno as a Tuscan port, the improvement of the Val di Chiana, the beginning of the work of draining the Maremma and the marshes of Fucecchio. He had as his emblem a queen bee in the middle of her swarm, wishing to signify that he governed with persuasion and not by force, in the love and not in the fear of his subjects.

About the Grand ducal Court were gathered, now calm and ordered, the city aristocracy, who no longer had reasons for struggling as all the favours and positions were now given from above. As commerce no longer rendered the fruits it once did, and as Florence was no more at the centre of the world market (other roads being opened over the Atlantic Ocean), the riches were becoming invested in land. So came about the development from a merchant to a land-owning nobility. The more enterprising took to the seaways for the great powers, such as AMERIGO VESPUCCI (1454-1512), who gave, by his own continued exploration, his own name to the New World, and GIOVANNI DA VERRAZZANO who by his navigation (1523-1527) discovered for King Francis I what was later to be New York bay.

The city, extended itself in the more quiet areas. The same Grand Duke, who at the first moment, to affirm his sovereignity had installed himself in the Palazzo della Signoria, now retired to the edge of the country, in the Pitti Palace, bought by the wife of Cosimo I, Eleanor of Toledo, progressively enlarged and provided with a splendid garden, the Boboli.

The Grand Duke elected himself a trustworthy artist, which became a sort of superintendent of monuments. During the first years of the Grand duchy, the trustworthy artist of Cosimo I was GIORGIO VASARI from AREZZO (1511-1574), fervid, untiring, and often genial organizer of artistic works, passionate enquirer and historian of artistic events. His task, fully accomplished, was to change the severe republican Palazzo della Signoria into a proud court. With originality and wisdom he solved the difficult problem of adding there a building to house the Offices of the State, making a structure of clear, dignified usefulness. Less happy, even harmful, were his alterations of churches, which he was under the illusion of making more sumptuous, adding large altars and monuments which broke up the harmony.

His aim was more than anything one of praise, of spectacular decoration, as was shown also in his bombastic and hasty paintings. He had as collaborators ingenious architects such as GIOVAN BATTISTA DEL TASSO (d. 1553) and BACCIO D'AGNOLO (1462-1543); emphatic, heavy sculptors such as BACCIO BANDINELLI (1487-1559), BARTOLOMEO AMMANNATI (1511-1592), VINCENZO DE' ROSSI (1525-1587), FRANCESCO DA SAN GALLO (1494-1576), and, more animated and original, the goldsmith-sculptor BENVENUTO CELLINI (1500-1571); painters of formal wisdom but with little inspiration such as AGNOLO BRONZINO (1503-1572), SANTI DI TITO (1538-1603), BATTISTA NALDINI (1537-c. 1600) and GIOVANNI STRADANO (c. 1556-1605).

Under the guidance of Vasari and with, as head, Michelangelo « father and master of the three arts », there was instituted the **Academy of Design**, in which were gathered the greatest artists of the three figurative arts, simbolised by three crowns of oak, olive and laurel intertwined. On the inspiration of the sculptor Giovannangelo da Montorsoli (c. 1507-1563), friar of the Servites of Mary, the **Compagnia di San Luca** was founded, a religious-artistic confraternity.

Consideration of the tragic events of the country brought out the greatest political and historical writers of any epoch. NICCOLÒ MACHIAVELLI (1469-1527) considered the founder of political science, JACOPO NARDI (1476-1563), FRANCESCO GUICCIARDINI (1483-1540), sharp, wise investigator into historical facts, BERNARDO SEGNI (1504-1558), G. B. ADRIANI (1513-1579).

The lettered men, gathered in the famous **Accademia della Crusca**, learnedly discussed under the guidance of the erudite historian BENEDETTO VARCHI (1503-1565). Others, not having great themes to discuss gave themselves

Zocchi: the Lungarni in the 18th cent.

to the care of the beautiful form of the language, and so came about the splendid prose of AGNOLO FIRENZUOLA (1493-1548), and the lively fantasies of FRANCESCO VETTORI (1474-1539), of FRANCESCO BERNI (1497-1535), of ANTON FRANCESCO DONI (1513-1574), of Anton Francesco Grazzini called the LASCA (1503-1584).

In the second half of the century, the architect who knew how to intepret the spirit of Grand ducal Florence war BERNARDO BUONTALENTI (1536-1608), of an exuberant and original temperament, but sober in the breadth of his style, who gave to architecture an easy, wide development with spacious intervals between the large windows. With him the horizontal rhythm had a definite advantage over the vertical one. The palaces took on that air of comfortable and peaceful living, in their bright, warm façades, where the golden sunlight spread out without heavy shades.

This architecture harmonized with the painting of the so-called « mannerists », painters of great charm, easy designers, notable colourists, who put the value of painting itself before that of iconography: such as Jacopo Carrucci called the PONTORMO (1494-1557), the ROSSO FIORENTINO (1494-1541), ALESSANDRO ALLORI (1535-1607). In decoration there excelled the fantastic BERNARDINO POCCETTI (1548-1612).

Sculpture sought in bronze the warm plastic quality of GIAMBOLOGNA (1524-1608), and later of PIETRO FRANCAVILLA (1553-1615), two Florentinized Frenchmen, and of PIETRO TACCA (1577-1640), in whom the mannerism derived from Michelangelo gathered very lively expression of a compromise between the naturalistic and the fantastic.

The Grand ducal Court was cultivating a new form of art: the music of the melodrama, born from the experiences of the **Camerata dei Bardi**. Indeed one can say that it was really music, more than the three arts of design, the interpreter of the magnificent, fantastic life of the sixteenth century Florence.

THE SEVENTEENTH AND EIGHTEENTH CENTURIES

To Ferdinand I succeeded his son Cosimo II (1590-1621) and his grand son Ferdinando II (1610-1670). If they could not direct great policy in their relations with the European powers, they protected and encouraged science, particularly in the person of Galileo Galilei (1564-1642), who dedicated to them the most lasting of monuments, calling the satellites of Jupiter, in their honour, « Medici Stars ».

Under the protection of Ferdinando II and thanks to the great Evangelista Torricelli, there was founded in Florence, by Cardinal Leopoldo de' Medici, in 1657, the first Academy for scientific research and experimental physics, called the **Accademia del Cimento** (attempt, risk), which was the model of every other European academy.

To his son and successor, Cosimo III (1642-1723), unhappy through a badly chosen dynastic marriage, but a most just sovereign with a pious spirit, was given the thankless task of submission to the politics of the powers who ever more endangered the independence of the small state. Yet he ably knew how to baffle attempts at annexation, preserving a certain autonomy, at least in law, in Tuscany. He reigned long, and when, already old, he realised that his dynasty was becoming extinct, he thought of giving back to Florence its Republican arrangement, to save its independence.

Detail of the Baroque Church of San Firenze.

His son, GIAN GASTONE (1671-1737), also the victim of an unhappy dynastic marriage, had no successor. Discouraged, he let himself be carried away by scepticism and an excessive laxity, deeming useless every resistance to the adverse destiny which he thought conspired for the extinction of the Grand duchy.

His sister, ANNA MARIA LOUISA (1667-1744) married to the Elector of Saxony, bequeathed all the family artistic patrimony to Florence, and wished that the treasures should become the inalienable property of the citizens, so repairing, in one generous act, all the injustices which her house had perpetrated during the centuries of rule.

It was the merit of the last Medici that they put in order and enlarged the collections of art in the *Gallery of the Uffizi* and made the *Pitti Palace* a marvellous museum of paintings.

The wave of the Baroque, which after the Gothic, starting from Rome, became established as a universal style, acclaimed everywhere with enthusiasm, met a strong resistance in Florence. For the Baroque also happened just what had already taken place for the Romanesque and the Gothic. Accepted with a certain reserve by the Florentine artists, it underwent a process of elaboration and adaptation according to the local tendencies. The sense of measure, which dominated by secular tradition, calmed its rhetorical thrust, and breaked its exuberant eloquence, gathering it in wide, solemn divisions.

The most famous architect of this period was MATTEO NIGETTI (1560-1649) author of the grandiose and powerful mass of the *Chapel of the Princes* in San Lorenzo, which was to be the impressive and a little laborious mausoleum of the Medici sovereigns.

The extreme developments of Florentine Baroque were characterized by two buildings anything but noisy: one religious, the *Convent of San Firenze*, the other civil, the *Capponi palace*, and both are balanced examples of plastic decoration well contained in buildings which are firm and bright in their architectural mass.

Sculpture produced few experiments, with GHERARDO (1579-1675) and PIER FRANCESCO (1620-1685) SILVANI, later with GIOVAN BATTISTA FOGGINI (1652-1725).

But painting had the exuberant geniality of a real, and most learned artist, GIOVANNI DA SAN GIOVANNI (1590-1636), the colourful richness of Baldassarre Franceschini, called the VOLTERRANO (1611-1689), the exquisite luminosity of FRANCESCO FURINI (c. 1600-1646), the easy vein of PIETRO DA CORTONA (1596-1669), the delicate sensualism and flowing sentimentalism of CARLO DOLCI (1616-1686).

Literature celebrates international enterprises with the poetry of VINCENZO DA FILICAIA (1642-1707).

Despite these artistic manifestations upon which recent art history has passed too summary a condemnation, the expression of the Florentine society of the epoch could not be given either in architecture, or literature, or sculpture, or painting.

The aristocratic society which lived around the Grand Duke, showed two profound passions: that for science, and that for music. Of science we have already spoken. We must add that the love for botany brought about the creation of large gardens, in which were acclimatized exotic plants and flowers, uniting the usefulness of scientific experience to the beauty of garden architecture.

Music then, with the theatrical spectacles, in which architecture and scenographic painting was greatly employed, was very greatly honoured and one can say that the most important musical operas of the epoch were baptized in Florence.

So, the real masterpieces of that time now remaining, are a garden and a theatre: the *Garden of Boboli*, continually enlarged and embellished with plants and statues, and the *Theatre of the Pergola*, which was the model for all the other theatres in Europe. In the first the green scenery, with marble groups, had architectural, plastic and pictorial effects. It offered at the same time possibility for botanical experiments, arbours for social meetings, places for theatrical spectacles. In the second the succession of boxes, from which the society of the period looked out and put themselves on view, formed a sight even more suggestive than a stage.

In 1737 the Grand duchy of Tuscany passed to the **Princes of Lorraine,** foreign but not harmful sovereigns, and to them Tuscany owed a new period of prosperity.

FRANCESCO II (1737), later raised to the Imperial throne of Austria (1745) left Florence in the mercy of an unhappy regency Council, until his death (1765). He was succeeded by his brother PIETRO LEOPOLDO (1765), who ruled Tuscany in an exemplary way, undertaking great and bold reforms, carrying ahead the drainage of the Maremma, executing important public works, until he renounced the Grand duchy (1790) to take up the empire.

FERDINANDO III, his son, followed more weakly the example set by his father. In 1799 the French under Napoleon expelled him from the Grand duchy ruining the state exchequer and reducing Tuscany to a field of provision.

The rationalism of the Lorraine Grand dukes who were pleased to be « illuminated princes » was not the most adapted for the artistic life of the city. The only problems deemed worthy of an illuminated sovereign regarded economic reforms. Tuscan agriculture took advantage of this and the nobility set an active example, guiding the rural reforms of the country which lay at the head of agricultural progress. He was not noble who did not pass many months in his country villa, in contact with his tenants, under that form of collaboration which expressed itself in the « mezzadria ». The great agricultural undertakings and the drainage absorbed the best energies and the most enormous capitals. There remained hardly anything for art, and in fact, the eighteenth century was for Florentine art a period of almost complete lethargy.

To solve the modest problem of the urgent building of a triumphal arch, in front of Porta a San Gallo, they had recourse to the direction of a mediocre foreign architect (1739), and the Florentine executors of the statues showed only a meagre and flat workmanship.

The weak artistic production of almost all the century was accompanied by the decadence and the end of the precious artistic industries, once most flowering, such as that of silk-weaving, of tapestries, of silver-work, of embroidery, of velvet and of tipography.

The only sign of happy activity was the initiative of the Marquess CARLO GINORI, who founded, at his own expense, with adventurous happenings, the *Factory of china-ware of Doccia* (1735), competing with those of Meissen, Vienna, Sèvres, Capodimonte, attaining success with original products, which still today are a part of the boast and wealth of Florence.

Pietro Leopoldo, always with illuminated sufficiency, wanted to reform the glorious Accademia del disegno, making it a State school with the name of **Accademia delle Belle Arti**, (1785) and calling to teach there, according to didactic, well determinated rules, cold artists directed by the engraver RAFFAELLO MORGHEN (1794) who suggested models in clay or etchings to the pupils. Since then, the term « academic » has become the synonym of pedantry, coldness, lack of fire and phantasy.

Signorini: Carnival celebrations on Piazza Santa Croce (19th cent.).

FROM THE NINETEENTH CENTURY TO OUR DAYS

Napoleon's politics, by which he made and unmade kingdoms at his pleasure, brought to life the ephemeral **Kingdom of Etruria,** with LODOVICO I of Bourbon (1801) and later with his widow MARIA LUIGIA (1803), regent for her son Carlo Ludovico.

In 1807, Tuscany became part of the French Empire, but for a short time, because the sister of Napoleon, ELISA BACIOCCHI, had the ambition to become, in 1809, Grand duchess of Tuscany.

During this period even Florentine art valued the theory of the « Neoclassicism » which had become the official style of the empire. So, in architecture, the old GASPARE MARIA PAOLETTI (1727-1813), GIUSEPPE CACIALLI (1727-1828) and PASQUALE POCCIANTI (1774-1858) were inspired by cold but dignified classical canons. Some work of neoclassic architecture, such as *Palazzo Borghese*, *Villa Demidoff*, the refacing of *Villa di Poggio Imperiale*, are not void of a certain beauty.

In sculpture, the style of CANOVA dominated also in Florence, and the greatest event of the day was the inauguration of the *Monument to Vittorio Alfieri* by this artist (1810) in the Church of Santa Croce. STEFANO RICCI (1765-1837) was responsible, in Santa Croce still, for the Cenotaph dedicated to Dante Alighieri.

In painting the rules of David became interpreted with a certain grandeur by PIETRO BENVENUTI from Arezzo (1769-1844) and made warm by the Florentine LUIGI SABATELLI (1772-1850).

On the fall of Napoleon in 1814, Ferdinando III came back, acclaimed, and was succeeded in 1824 by LEOPOLDO II, a kind-hearted sovereign, a lover of peace, an excellent administrator. Under him Tuscany passed now years of prosperity, after the Napoleonic disorder.

The great artists reacted to the cold neoclassicism: the sculptor LORENZO BARTOLINI (1777-1850) in whom Canovian purity was enlivened with a breath of healthy naturalism; the painter GIUSEPPE BEZZUOLI (1784-1855), in whom the mannerism of Benvenuti was conquered by cordial sensibility. Meanwhile the first impulses of the national « Risorgimento », encouraged « Romanticism », which instead of being inspired by the Greek and Roman world, discovered again the Middle Ages.

So began the renewed love of restorings and renewals which brought about the alteration, first of the *Castello di Vincigliata* (1855), then of the *Torre del Gallo* (1906), and of the *Casa di Dante* (1910). An Englishman was collecting arms, works of art, and mediaeval costumes in the *Villa Stibbert*.

The rediscovery of the Giottesque frescoes in Santa Croce and at the Bargello, the theories of Ruskin, brought the primitives into idolatry, and there was not a painter who was not a little bit of a restorer. They felt the need of, and presumed themselves capable of finishing the façades of Santa Maria del Fiore and Santa Croce, and they studied the actuation ot it, analysing the Gothic style on the Academy's tables. In literature the so-called « Purism » had the merit of exuming fourteenth century texts.

Romanticism brought the great love for historical subjects among which we can distinguish, apart from the aforesaid Luigi Sabatelli and Giuseppe Bezzuoli, ANTONIO CISERI from the Ticino (1821-1891) and STEFANO USSI (1822-1901).

In these times the city filled itself with statues representing historic personages, statues due to the chisels of LUIGI PAMPALONI (1791-1847), ARISTO-DEMO COSTOLI (1803-1871), ODOARDO FANTACCHIOTTI (1809-1877), PASQUALE ROMANELLI (1812-1887), PIO FEDI (1816-1892), VINCENZO CONSANI (1818-1887), ENRICO PAZZI (1819-1899), and, more justly praised, for his honest naturalism, GIOVANNI DUPRÈ (1817-1882).

City culture gathered itself round the historian and lettered man GINO CAPPONI (1792-1876), the satiric poet GIUSEPPE GIUSTI (1809-1850), and the educator PIETRO THOUAR (1809-1861). At the centre of a fervid editorial activity, GIAMPIETRO VIEUSSEUX (1779-1863), showed the boldest initiatives and founded a public library, which is still flourishing today.

As much as the Grand duchy was a guarantee of a relative well being and Leopoldo II, happily called « Canapone », came to be loved and valued, the national unity required the sacrifice of regional and local interests. In 1848, during the first War of Independence, the Grand duke was forced to flee. He returned in 1849 and reigned for ten years among the difficulties which the patriots brought him, until, during the second War of Independence in 1859, a peaceful and respectful revolution made him leave Florence for good.

So disappeared from the map of Italy a state which for three centuries had brought to Tuscany, in the middle of international political complications, happiness, dignity and a certain independence.

United to the **Kingdom of Italy**, Florence was chosen in 1865 as the provisory **capital**. The Ministeries took up residence in the finest palaces, disfiguring them with alteration works, which were not always made good again after the transfer of the capital. The most lovely convents were transformed into uncomfortable and gloomy barracks, or into dark and sad schools, or dirty offices, or unhealthy hospitals, with enormous waste and disorder, which lasts until today on account of laziness, ill-will and the idea of misunderstood economy.

In the name of hygiene and decency, they inconsiderately and unfortunately cleared out the centre of the town. Under the growth of the population, the third circle of walls was pulled down and bourgeois constructions sprang up everywhere outside the isolated gates. So came about the vulgar triumph of the so-called « Eclecticism », a stupid mixture of historic styles.

Fortunately Florence also had at this moment a talented architect, GIUSEPPE POGGI (1811-1901). He knew how to keep the true eclecticism within the limits of a certain stylistic nobility, and above all revealed his geniality in the tracing of an intelligent regulated plan, which however, the short-sightedness of technical officials did not allow to be completely carried out. On the perimeter of the pulled down walls he made the *Viali di Circonvallazione* and he continued them on the left bank of the Arno, with the very beautiful *Viale dei Colli* (1865-1870). Through the merit of this ample urban solution, the olives and cypresses of the hills made a background to the plane-trees in the avenues and the flowers of the gardens.

There were already interpreters of the love for the country and for nature, the so-called « *Macchiaioli* », that is those painters who made their pictures with splashings of colours, like TELEMACO SIGNORINI (1835-1901), SILVESTRO LEGA (1826-1895), GIOVANNI FATTORI (1825-1908). Their movement determined itself in a spontaneous and original manner, contemporaneous to the French Impressionism, had accents of greater gravity, and left a tradition alive until today, after two generations.

Fattori: Midday rest (Gallery of Modern Art).

To the vivacity and originality of the Macchiaioli corresponded the sculpture of ADRIANO CECIONI (1838-1886), who gave to his small plastic works the breath of Impressionism.

Almost at the same time, the group of the « Amici pedanti » formed itself, from which came the greatest poet of united Italy, GIOSUÈ CARDUCCI (1836-1907).

When, in 1871, the capital left Florence to be fixed in Rome, the city remained upset and impoverished. However, from the exhausted land of literature there came out, in 1882, another masterpiece, and it was the *Pinocchio* of Carlo Lorenzini called COLLODI. A small book, which has travelled the world over and which has been justly considered an absolute masterpiece of children's literature.

In the first years of the twentieth century, Florence again became a most lively centre of culture. With the review *Leonardo* (1903) was initiated a series of Florentine publications which was to arouse the whole nation. They were, successively, *La Voce* (1908), *Lacerba* (1913), *Il Selvaggio* (1924), *Solaria* (1925), *Il Frontespizio* (1929).

One of the city cafés, called, after the waiters' jackets, *Le Giubbe Rosse*, became the general quarters of national culture, enlivened by two Florentines, GIOVANNI PAPINI and GIUSEPPE PREZZOLINI. The former (died in 1956) is one of the most famous Italian writers.

In literature are outstanding the personalities of ALDO PALAZZESCHI, EMILIO CECCHI, BRUNO CICOGNANI, FERDINANDO PAOLERI, DOMENICO GIULIOTTI, NICOLA LISI, ARTURO LORIA, CARLO BETOCCHI, ALESSANDRO BONSANTI, MARIO LUZI, ROMANO BILENCHI, VASCO PRATOLINI.

In the theatre those of SEM BENELLI and GIOVACCHINO FORZANO.

In painting, those of ARMANDO SPADINI, ARDENGO SOFFICI, OTTONE ROSAI, PRIMO CONTI, GIANNI VAGNETTI, BACCIO MARIA BACCI, ARTURO CHECCHI, GALILEO CHINI, EDOARDO GORDIGIANI, ALBERTO CALIGIANI, GUIDO FERRONI, ENNIO POZZI, ENZO PREGNO, UGO CAPOCCHINI, RICCARDO MAGNELLI, DILVO LOTTI, GUIDO PEYRON, FRANCO DANI, SILVIO PUCCI, SILVIO POLLONI.

In sculpture, those of LIBERO ANDREOTTI, EVARISTO BONCINELLI, VALMORE GEMIGNANI, ITALO GRISELLI, ROMANO ROMANELLI, ANTONIO BERTI, BRUNO INNOCENTI, CORRADO VIGNI, MARIO MOSCHI, QUINTO MARTINI.

In engraving, the best are BRUNO BRAMANTI and PIETRO PARIGI. In illustration PIERO BERNARDINI.

So we see that the artistic vitality of Florence is anything but exhausted, and we still await from Florence much artistic and cultural rebirth, after the last destructive war which badly hit the city.

In vain one hoped that Florence, the city of beauty, would be declared an « open city » or at least a « white city ». Bombardments, at least on the periphery, damaged it. In August 1944, attacked in front by the allied troops, the bridge area was stupidly and barbarically mined by the German troops. No strategic reason demanded this sorrowful happening, because the almost dry Arno was easily fordable, neither on the other hand was there great need to brake the allied advance which was proceeding slowly. But despite this, the Germans blew up the city bridges; they made an exception for the Ponte Vecchio, but created much more serious ruins than would have resulted from its destruction, because, with the end of preventing passage at that point, the Germans did not mind blowing up all the adjacent streets for a radius of two hundred metres. Thus was destroyed the core of the mediaeval city, and the most ancient streets on the other side of the Arno.

Like this, there disappeared the very ancient, characteristic street of Por Santa Maria, with its immediate adjuncts; part of Via Guicciardini; a large part of the very fine Borgo San Jacopo and of Via de' Bardi looking over the Arno, with their houses grown up on corbels, with smalll loggias and most gracious balconies. An irreparable loss for which no rebuilding can compensate.

The incomparable Santa Trinita bridge has been integrally rebuilt on the existing designs, with a part of the recovered materials; but Borgo San Jacopo, Via de' Bardi remain phantasms of nostalgia for whoever knew Florence before Mars, her old betrayed god, vindicated himself upon her beauty.

THE POLITICAL CENTRE OF THE CITY

Piazza della Signoria - Loggia della Signoria
Palazzo della Signoria - Uffizi Palace and
Gallery - Palazzo del Podestà or del Bargello
(National Museum) - Church of Badia - Tower
of the Castagna - House of Dante - Orsanmichele.

Palazzo Vecchio lighted up to celebrate a Feast Day.

PIAZZA DELLA SIGNORIA

We shall take as our starting point the Piazza della Signoria, centre of the political life of the city and of the history of Florence. It was once the site of the tower-houses of the Degli Uberti. This was a Ghibelline family to which belonged Farinata degli Uberti whom Dante condemned as a heretic (Inf. X) but extolled as the man who saved his native city from the destruction then threatened by his own victorious party. The square was made so that these houses, razed to the ground when the Ghibellines in their turn were defeated by the Guelphs, should never rise again. Then, on the margin of the accursed site, rose the palace, the seat of the municipal government. The square was enlarged for the people's « parliaments » and the *Loggia* was built for public ceremonies. The *Palazzo del Popolo e del Comune* or *dei Priori*, later called the *Palazzo della Signoria*, took on its present name of **Palazzo Vecchio** only after 1550, when Cosimo I left it to establish himself and his court in the Palazzo Pitti. It seems that its architect was ARNOLFO DI CAMBIO from Colle di Val d' Elsa (1232-1301), who took as his model the castle of the Counts Guidi at Poppi. It was begun on the 24th of February 1299 on the site of the Foraboschi houses, behind the church of *San Pietro Scheraggio*, and shortly after was occupied by the Gonfaloniere di Giustizia (Chief Judge) and the Priori delle Arti (Heads of the Guilds); which means that, virtually, it was occupied by the « Signoria ». Dante Alighieri, among the first of the « Priori », resided there from June 15th to August 14th 1300, when the nucleus of the building was still unfinished. It is a solid cube of stone quarried in the caves of Boboli, with narrow windows on the ground floor and a door to one side to which today we have immediate access but which, during the short tyranny of Gualtieri, Duke of Athens (1342-1343), had in front of it a fortified door, the work of Andrea da Pontedera, called Andrea Pisano. The first and second floors have elegant mullioned windows. The whole is crowned with an embattled and machicolated gallery. The *tower* too, built on that of the Foraboschi, called *della Vacca* (of the Cow), which juts out boldly from its base, the highest tower of the city and symbol of the supreme authority of the Commune, is crowned with a battlemented gallery. Its summit ends in a copper ball surmounted by a lion rampant with the Lily, the emblem of the city. Here and there throughout the interior we shall come across more of these lions, sometimes carved, sometimes painted. The lion was the symbol of the sovereignity of the Commune and from the early fourteenth century to the end of the eighteenth century, the governors of the city always kept one or more pairs of lions in a cage called the « stia ». Another lion, seated, called the « Marzocco » (a reproduction of the original by Donatello, now in the National Museum of the Bargello), with the coat of arms, emblazoned with the Lily, under its paw, is placed at the foot of the Palazzo, on the left, where once stood the *Aringhiera*, or platform from which orators used to speak to the people gathered in the square. Everything surrounding the Palazzo spoke of liberty: on the right of the Marzocco, the very beautiful *Judith* (c. 1460) by DONATELLO, represents the Hebrew woman who liberated her people from the tyranny of Holophernes, as the inscription on the base tells us; on the left of the door the superb *David* (1503), masterpiece of the twenty-eight year old MICHELANGELO (the original has been in the Gallery of the Accademia since 1873) was the young hero who confronted and conquered a giant who was threatening the liberty of his country; on the right of the door the mediocre group of *Hercules killing Cacus* (1534) by BACCIO BANDINELLI, represents the allegory of the antique seal of the Florentines,

The tower of Palazzo Vecchio.

The copy of the David by Michelangelo seen from the courtyard of Palazzo Vecchio.

the victory of the demigod over the thief who was impoverishing the countryside. On the door an inscription under St. Bernardino's monogram of Christ « *Rex Regum et Dominum Dominantium* » (*King of Kings and Lord of Lords*), records the last years of the liberty of the Republic (1528-1529), when the Florentines elected Christ as their king. At the sides of the door two marble « *terminals* » by VINCENZO DE' ROSSI and BANDINELLI which used to hold up the chain barring the entrance to the Grand Duke's residence. Cosimo I took the palace as his seat and enlarged and embellished it, to make it like a royal palace.

Cosimo I (GIAMBOLOGNA'S *equestrian statue* of him, 1594, stands in the Piazza on the left side of the Palazzo) considered transforming the Piazza as well, and Michelangelo advised him to continue the Loggia dei Priori right round it; it would thus have gained architectural unity, but the enormous expense which it would have involved made him renounce the project. In the years 1560-1575 BARTOLOMEO AMMANNATI completed the **Neptune Fountain**, called of the « Biancone » (the big white man) because of its badly sculptured marble colossus. The rhythmic composition, inspired by a drawing of Leonardo da Vinci, is adorned with bronze statues of nymphs and fauns, also by Ammannati and his assistants and collaborators. A little in front of the fountain, in the paving of the Piazza, is a marble disc, marking the spot where, with his companions Domenico Buonvicini and Silvestro Maruffi, the Dominican monk, GIROLAMO SAVONAROLA, proud opposer of the Medici, was hung and burnt on the 23rd of May 1498. Every year on this day the stone is covered with flowers.

Detail of the Neptune fountain on the Piazza della Signoria.

The winged putto by Verrocchio and a detail of Judith by Donatello.

LOGGIA DEI PRIORI or DELLA SIGNORIA

On the right of the Palazzo della Signoria stands the **Loggia dei Priori** or **della Signoria,** also called the Loggia of **Orcagna** (d. 1368), after a supposed design by that master, but built by the architects who were also working at the construction of Santa Maria del Fiore (the Cathedral) during the period 1376-1382. It consists of three great arches, under which the Chief Magistrate of the City and the Priori used to sit during public gatherings and ceremonies, which had previously been held on the « Aringhiera » or in the church of St. Pietro Scheraggio. In the panels are allegorical figures of the *Virtues* (1383-1386) carved from designs by Agnolo Gaddi. On either side of the steps are placed two lions, one of the classical period, the other by Flaminio Vacca (1600). When the city lost her liberty the Loggia was occupied by the Duke's guard and German Halberdiers, called Lanzichenecchi, from whom it took the name of *Loggia dei Lanzi* (Lancers).

Later it was peopled with statues, some of them (those in the background) Roman; in the foreground are the famous *Perseus* (1553) by CELLINI on the left, and the *Rape of the Sabine Women* (1583) by GIAMBOLOGNA on the right. In the middle, *Hercules and the Centaur* (1599) by GIAMBOLOGNA, *Ajax lifting the corpse of Patroclus*, a Hellenistic work restored by Stefano Ricci, and the *Rape of Polissena* by PIO FEDI (1866).

Among the buildings which surround the Piazza is the palace of the **Tribunale di Mercanzia** (1358), (Mercantile Court), left of the Palazzo Vecchio, near the site of the old Roman theatre, with the heraldic arms of the various Guilds on the front. On the left side of the Piazza, facing the Loggia, is the 16th century **Palazzo Uguccioni**, built on a design brought from Rome and of which a wooden model was made by Mariotto Folfi, c. 1550. Opposite the Palazzo Vecchio, where the « Tettoia dei Pisani » and the ancient church of St. Cecilia used to stand, the *Palazzo delle Assicurazioni di Venezia* was erected in 1871 by the architect Landi, a cold imitation of the Renaissance style.

INTERIOR OF THE PALAZZO DELLA SIGNORIA

In the interior of the Palazzo, little of the original aspect has survived. In the **Courtyard**, only the plan is original; the columns, the arches, the walls up to the roof are by MICHELOZZO MICHELOZZI, who reconstructed it throughout on the model of the courtyard of the Palazzo Medici between 1439 and 1454. On the occasion of the marriage of his son Francesco to Giovanna of Austria in 1565, Cosimo I gave GIORGIO VASARI the task of modernising the courtyard. The columns were duly faced with stucco decoration and the walls covered with frescoes of views of Austrian cities, in honour of the bride. On the porphyry fountain by Battista del Tadda, is a little winged *Genius with a Fish* (1476), by ANDREA DEL VERROCCHIO, which was previously in the villa at Careggi. Under the portico was placed *Samson and a Philistine* a sculptured group by PIERINO DA VINCI (d. 1554). The only part restored in its original form was the *Armoury*, reached by a door in the corner on the left.

As we pass out of the Courtyard, on our right and left are the two flights of stairs constructed by Vasari when Cosimo took over the Palazzo (1555-1561). They lead to the **Salone dei Cinquecento** (Hall of the Five Hundred) constructed by Simone del Pollaiuolo, called CRONACA, in the days of Savonarola's Republic.

It was built for the great Council, which was constituted in December 1494, on the Venetian pattern, of relays of five hundred citizens in their twenty-ninth year, summoned for the election of the Council of Eighty which was intended to assist the Signoria. The first convocation of the Council was held in the Salone dei Cinquecento on February 25th 1496. In the same hall, the following August, the voice of Savonarola was heard, urging the cause of liberty; and here his death sentence was read on April 19th 1498. After the fall of the Republic, Cosimo I had it altered and embellished to make it into an audience and reception hall. From November 1865 to 1871 it was the seat of the House of Commons of the United Kingdom of Italy. The decoration of the Hall as it is today, is all an exaltation of the House of Medici and especially of the Grand Duke Cosimo I.

GIORGIO VASARI, architect, painter and art historian, on receiving the task of « overhauling » the whole palace so that the Duke's family could take up residence there, chose a team of painters, decorators, wood-carvers and sculptors, almost all from the Academy of Drawing (*Accademia del Disegno*) and began, on December 15th 1555, the long series of works which were only finished in 1572. The « inventions », that is to say the choice and distribution of historical and allegorical sujects and instructions for details of execution, were provided by three very erudite literary men, Don

The rape of the Sabine women by Giambologna under the Loggia of Orcagna.

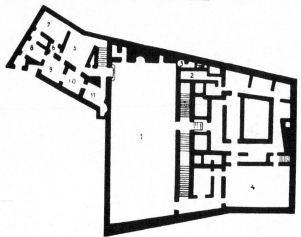

I FLOOR. — 1. Salone dei Cinquecento. - 2. Studying-room of Francesco I. - 3. Treasury-room of Cosimo I. - 4. Sala dei Duecento. - 5. Room of Leone X. - 6. Chapel. - 7. Room of Clemente VII. - 8. Room of Giovanni dalle Bande Nere. - 9. Room of Cosimo the Elder. - 10. Room of Lorenzo the Magnificent. - 11. Room of Cosimo I.

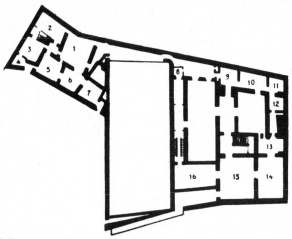

II FLOOR. — 1. Room of the Elements. - 2. Terrace of Saturn. - 3. Room of Hercules. - 4. Room of Juno. - 5. Room of Jupiter. - 6. Room of Cybele or Opis. - 7. Ceres Room. - 8. Chapel of the Duchess. - 9. Room of the Sabines. - 10. Room of Esther. - 11. Room of Penelope. - 12. Room of Gualdrada. - 13 Chapel of the Signoria. - 14. Sala dell'Udienza. - 15. Room of Lilies. - 16. Wardrobe.

Vincenzo Borghini, head of the Foundling Hospital, Giovan Battista Adriani and Cosimo Bartoli.

The analytical examination of the complicated decorative scheme created by one of the greatest known decorators, can be made with the help of the guide to it which Vasari himself left in his « Ragionamenti » to Prince Francesco de' Medici. If one has time to dedicate more than one day to it, one can follow here in the most unexpected aspects the life of the historical, artistic and literary thought of one of the greatest centres of 16th century civilisation. There is no other example in the history of art of a great complex of this importance and extent presented by its own author, who was moreover the first, and is even now among the greatest of art historians. In the 14 « Ragionamenti », which are divided into three days, he himself explains, in the form of a dialogue with the Prince, the subjects depicted by him and his assistants in the rooms already built and in the ones which he constructed. He is principally concerned with the value of the contents, substantially political, of the work, the pictorial value of which is almost always negligible, because of the haste with which the work was done and the scanty talent of its authors.

The ceiling of the Salone dei Cinquecento describes, in scenes grouped round the central picture of the *Triumph of Duke Cosimo I*, the organisation and prosperity of Florence and Tuscany, traced through the legendary and historical changes in the Republic, up to the events of the conquest of Siena and the battle of Marciano.

There are in all 39 pictures, representing in allegory the *four quarters of the city* (circular paintings at the two ends of the ceiling), *sixteen cities and dependencies of the Duchy* (square pictures in the four corners), *six outstanding scenes of the history of Tuscany*, from the foundation of the city to the disembarking of Eugenius IV at Leghorn (rectangles and squares in the central part), *seven episodes in the wars for the conquest of Pisa* (rectangular, octagonal and square pictures on left), *seven incidents in the war against Siena* (corresponding pictures on right). In the picture to the left of the central one, which represents the *Return of the Marquis of Marignano to Florence*, after the capture of Siena, are the portraits of Vasari's counsellors as well as his own.

The two largest walls were to have been decorated with frescoes by Michelangelo Buonarroti and Leonardo da Vinci, after 1503, but as a result of political developments and the indifference of the two artists they got no further than the preparation of a few cartoons and an unhappy experiment in fresco by Leonardo; few drawings and sketches of this work remain.

Entrance wall. Above to the left: *Cosimo I founds the order of the knights of St. Stephen*, by Domenico Cresti, called PASSIGNANO. Below: three large scenes of the conquest of Pisa, corresponding to those on the ceiling, by Vasari and assistants: *the Florentines defeat the Pisans at the Tower of S. Vincenzo; the Emperor Maximilian attempts the conquest of Leghorn; Antonio Giacomini leads the Florentine troops to the assault of Pisa.* Above, on right: *Twelve nations are represented at the court of Pope Boniface VIII by ambassadors, who are all Florentines* (Jacopo Ligozzi). Three marble groups representing *three of the Labours of Hercules* (Vincenzo de' Rossi). *Statue of Cosimo I* (Baccio Bandinelli). Below the frescoes, on this wall and on the opposite one, are hung **tapestries** made in the Medici factories, with *scenes from the life of St John the Baptist*, which take the place of ten frescoes which Vasari had planned, to complete the decoration.

The **end wall** (raised floor) was transformed by Baccio Bandinelli into a stage to form the background of the solemn ceremonies in the midst of which the Grand Duke was accustomed to give public audience and which therefore came to be called the « Udienza ». Central niche with statue of *Leo X* (B. Bandinelli and V. de' Rossi), lateral niches with statues of *Giovanni delle Bande Nere* (of the Black Bands) and of *Alessandro de' Medici* (B. Bandinelli). On right: niche with statue of *Charles V crowned by Pope Alexander VII* (B. Bandinelli and G. Caccini). Another niche with statue of *Francesco I* (G. Caccini).

Wall opposite entrance. Above, on left: *Cosimo receives the title of Grand Duke from Pope Pius V* (Lodovico Cardi, called il Cigoli). Below, three large scenes of the conquest of Siena: *the Marquis of Marignano enters Siena, Taking of Porto Ercole, Victory of Marciano* (G. Vasari). Above, on right: *Cosimo acclaimed Duke of Florence by the Florentine Senate* (Cigoli). Three other groups representing three other *Labours of Hercules* (Vincenzo de' Rossi).

Right end wall. - Unfortunate decoration of 1874: Loggia linking the State Apartments. Below: *Genius overcoming brute force* (MICHELANGELO). This group, intended to decorate the tomb of Pope Julius II, was placed in the Hall very much later, in 1921, in memory of the Italian victory of Vittorio Veneto in 1918. In the niches, antique statues of *Ganymede, Mercury, Apollo and Bacchus.*

Through a small door on the extreme left of the entrance wall, we go into the **Small Studying-room of Francesco I**. It is a beautiful little room by Vasari, constructed between 1570 and 1572, as a retiring room for the eccentric prince, an investigators of the mysteries of nature and a passionate lover of beauty. It is a strange complex unified by the « inventions » of Vincenzo Borghini, the sections of which painted by lively mannerists (Angelo Tori called BRONZINO, Battista Naldini, Santi di Tito, Girolamo Macchietti, Giovanni Stradano, Mirabello Cavolori) record the myth of the conquests of Prometheus, human activities, the progress of the sciences, the mysteries of magic and alchemy, which fascinated the future Grand Duke no less than continual indulgence in the pleasures of the senses. The elegant bronze statues are by GIAMBOLOGNA, Bartolomeo Ammannati, Stoldo Lorenzi, Domenico Poggini, Vincenzo de' Rossi, Elia Candido, Andrea Calamech, Giovanni Bandini; the carvings by Dionigi di Matteo; the stuccoes and frescoes of the ceiling by Francesco Morandini, called il POPPI, are all dominated by the two admirable *portraits of the Grand Duke Cosimo I* and of *Eleonora di Toledo,* the Prince's parents, painted on slabs of slate by BRONZINO. A small stairway takes us to the « **Tesoretto** » of **Cosimo I**, another fanciful creation of Vasari, decorated by his assistants: it was the secret writing room of the Grand Duke who hid his most precious possessions in the carved cupboards.

Coming back to the Hall of the Five Hundred from the platform of the « Udienza » we go through a corridor decorated in the grotesque style by Lorenzo Sabatini (1565), into the **Sala dei Duecento** (Hall of the Two Hundred) constructed for the meetings of the military council, created in 1441 and comprising two hundred citizens whose business it was to deliberate on all alliances, wars and military matters. The decoration of the Hall was taken up with fervour by GIULIANO and BENEDETTO DA MAIANO (1475-80). The very beautiful carved coffered ceiling in white on a blue ground is attributed to MICHELOZZO. On the walls, *tapestries* from the Medici factories, with *scenes from the Life of the Patriarch Joseph,* designed by Bronzino, Salviati and Pontormo.

The small Studying-room of Francesco I.

Retracing our steps back to the Hall of the Five Hundred, through a door in the wall opposite the entrance we come to the **State Apartments** now occupied by the Mayor and the Municipal Council. Dedicated to various personalities and decorated once again by GIORGIO VASARI and his assistants, they too glorify the fame of the Medici. We begin with the *Room of Leone X*, previously Cardinal Giovanni de' Medici, now the ante-room of the Mayor's Rooms; it is decorated (1560) with scenes from this Pope's life, full of portraits reproduced very faithfully from carefully chosen prototypes, in landscape settings reconstructed or taken straight from nature, and therefore of exceptional documentary interest. Of particular iconographic interest is the *Creation of 21 Cardinals*, where, among the portraits are those of Leonardo and Michelangelo. In the scene of the *Journey through Florence* is a reconstruction of the Piazza della Signoria, with the church of St. Pietro Scheraggio which was destroyed by Vasari to make room for the « Uffizi ». The *Chapel* nearby formerly contained the *Madonna dell'Impannata*, by Raphael, which was later replaced by a copy. In the *Room of Clemente VII*, formerly Cardinal Giulio de' Medici, is the great panoramic *view of Florence besieged in 1529-30*, with the positions of the Imperial troops, as seen from the hills of the Pian de' Giullari. The adjacent *Room of Giovanni delle Bande Nere*, father of Cosimo I, decorated in 1559, exalts the war-like qualities of the great soldier. The decoration of the *Room of Cosimo il Vecchio* (Cosimo the Elder), of 1558, records the political and mercantile activity of the great founder of the Medici family fortunes; there are portrayed the chief artists and political and literary men of his time. In the *Room of Lorenzo the Magnificent* (1559) is depicted the assembly of literary men and scholars who were the chief title to glory of the most representative figure of the Renaissance. In the decoration, executed in the same year, of the *Room of Cosimo I*, the iconographic interest is especially great because the personalities and places represented are taken directly from nature: near the military and literary men who lived under the protection of the Grand Duke's court we recognise the extremely life-like faces of Cellini, Bandinelli, Ammannati, Tribolo, Giovan Battista del Tasso, Nanni Unghero and Camerini, whom Vasari knew and used as models.

We go up a stairway to the second floor (on the first landing a strange fresco of the 16th century: *St. John's day bonfires*) and enter the **Quartiere degli Elementi** (Apartment of the Elements) built by the architect BATTISTA DEL TASSO, once again by order of Cosimo I, who took possession of the Palazzo in 1537 and established himself there with his family in 1540. The name derives from the allegories in the first room, painted by VASARI who also altered and decorated the ceiling, with the help of his assistants, especially of Cristoforo Gherardi, called DOCENO. On the walls, *Allegories of Earth, Air, Water and Fire* with scenes and mottos exalting the house of Medici. The apartment continues in a series of small rooms all decorated on the ceilings and on the friezes with mythological and allegorical scenes. In succession we see: the *Terrace of Saturn* (1558) affording a fine view; the *Hercules Room* (1557); the *Terrace of Juno* (1557); the *Jupiter Room* (1556); the *Room of Cybele or Opis* (1557; the *Ceres Room* (1556) and the *Calliope Room* (1556), where Cosimo I arranged his first collection of statuettes, coins, miniatures and antique cameos, only part of which has remained intact, and is now in the Palazzo Pitti. These rooms have also lost the tapestries, stained-glass windows, sculptures and the original furnishings which completed their decoration.

We pass across the gallery which crosses the Hall of the Five Hundred, into the **Apartment of Eleonora of Toledo**, prepared in 1562 by Vasari for the beautiful bride of Cosimo I. The *Chapel* reserved for the Duchess, decorated throughout with frescoes by AGNOLO BRONZINO (1564) is a derivation from the work of Raphael. Beyond it are four rooms with ceilings of Tasso and lively frieze decorations with scenes of female life by VASARI and STRADANO (1562). The first called the *Room of the Sabines*, used to be assigned to the ladies of the court. The second, the *Room of Esther*, was the dining room. The third, the *Penelope Room*, was the work room, and lastly, the *Room of Gualdrada* with eight lively scenes of fifteenth century Florence, was the Duchess's private chamber.

Until now we have been dealing with quarters either constructed or transformed by Cosimo I, which make of the Palazzo della Signoria a Medici palace created from the old Palace of the People. The rooms which follow, with the Hall of the Two Hundred, are all that remains of the **Quarters of the Priori**, and here we have to go back almost a century to a form of art and mode of life considerably more austere, as it was under the influence of Savonarola. Crossing the **Chapel of the Signoria**, with frescoes by RIDOLFO GHIRLANDAIO (1514) and an altar piece of the *Holy Family* by MARIANO DA PESCIA, we enter the rooms decorated during the time of the Republic, where the lion is the main decorative and simbolic element. We go into the **Sala dell'Udienza** (Audience Hall), the marble sculptured entrance-door of which has the composed severity of republican taste; the dedicatory inscription to Christ, above it, « Sun of Justice », sounds as a last invocation (1529) to the old Faith before the invasion of the conquering courtly paganism. It has a magnificent *carved ceiling* and *architrave with frieze* by GIULIANO DA MAINO and his assistants (1478). The *portal* at the exit, by the brothers GIULIANO and BENEDETTO DA MAIANO (1475-81), frames an inlaid door of wood with figures of Dante and Petrarch, by Francione and Giuliano da Maiano (1480). On the walls, late fifteenth century frescoes by SALVIATI with scenes from the *life of Camillus*. Next is the **Room of the Lilies** so-called from the decoration of gold fleur-de-lys on a blue ground, which has strangely survived to record the illustrious alliance of the Republic with the royal House of France. The *portal* by BENEDETTO DA MAIANO is very beautiful, as is the *ceiling* by GIULIANO DA MAIANO and his assistants. On the walls, *allegorical frescoes* by DOMENICO GHIRLANDAIO (1481-85) with large figures of the patron saints of the city, together with Roman models of heroic virtues. From this room there is access to the **Segreteria,** which was used as an office by Niccolò Machiavelli, who is here portrayed in a polychrome sculptured bust and in a painting by SANTI DI TITO. In this room, we can also see a fine basrelief of *St. Giorge,* a work from the Pisan school of the 14th cent., which was formerly on the Porta San Giorgio where it has been sustituted by a copy. In the next room, the **Guardaroba** (Wardrobe), is a collection of 53 maps by FRA IGNAZIO DANTI (1563-75) and DON STEFANO BONSIGNORI (1575-84), painted on the doors of the cupboards, of extreme interest in the history of map-making and geography through the centuries. In the centre of the room, the large *mappamundi* by Danti. From the Guardaroba, we enter the **Terrace of Eleonora** with a small sewing-room delightfully

Portal in the Audience Hall and statue of Genius overcoming brute force by Michelangelo.

Room of Esther in the Apartment of Toledo.

decorated; here a small latticed window allowed the women of the court to look into the Sala dei Cinquecento without being seen.

A narrow staircase leads to the **Mezzanine**, which Cosimo I had arranged for his mother Maria Salviati, the widow of Giovanni delle Bande Nere. It now houses the very interesting collection of antique furniture and objets d'art donated by the American art collector Charles Loeser.

From the Room of Lilies we come to the staircase which takes us to the **Battlements**, the fortifications crowning the Palazzo, from the parapet and machicolations of which the square could be dominated in safety and the approaches to the Palace defended, making it the fortress and defence of the Florentine Signoria before the use of field artillery. From the Battlements, we go up to the **Tower**, passing before the cell euphemistically called the « *Alberghettino* » (the Small Inn): it was a secure prison for important prisoners arrested for political reasons. In it Cosimo the Elder was imprisoned (1438) before his exile, as he was rightly considered to be a danger to the safety of the Republic, and there it was that Savonarola passed the last days of his life (1498), before being hung and burnt in front of the Palazzo. From the top of the tower we have a view over the whole of Florence in its magnificent shell-like valley that stretches from the ridges of the Appennines to the river Arno which flows down to the sea at Pisa.

The Perseus by Cellini; in the background the Uffizi Palace.

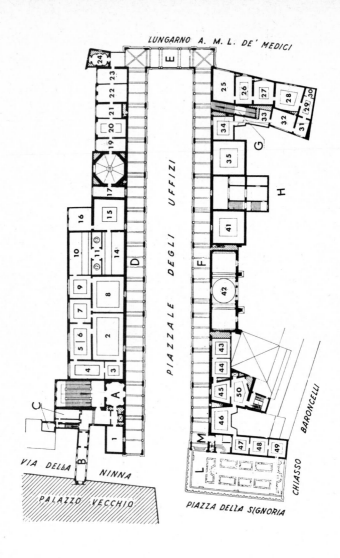

PLAN OF THE UFFIZI GALLERY

A. Vestibule.
B. Corridor leading to Palazzo Vecchio.
C. Office of the Director
D. First corridor.
E. Second corridor.
F. Third corridor.
G. Stairway leading to Vasari's corridor.
H. Exit stairway.
I. Bar.
L. Terrace on Loggia dei Lanzi.
M. Entrance to toilets.

1. Ancient sculptures.
2. 13th and 14th cent. Tuscan school.
3. 14th cent. Sienese school.
4. 14th cent. Florentine school.
5/6. International Gothic style.
7. 15th cent. Florentine school.
8. Paintings by Filippo Lippi.
9. Paintings by Pollaiolo and Botticelli.
10. Paintings by Botticelli.
11. Paintings by Botticelli and Filippino Lippi.
12. Flemish painting of the 15th cent.
13. 15th cent. Florentine school.
14. Flemish and Florentine painting of the 15th cent.
15. Umbrian and Tuscan painting of the late 15th cent.
16. Paintings by Leonardo and Lorenzo di Credi.
17. Umbrian painting of the late 15th cent.
18. (Tribune). Florentine portraits of the 16th cent.

19. Umbrian and Ferrarese painting of the 15th cent.
20. Venetian and German painting of the 15th and 16th cent.
21. Venetian painting of the 15th and 16th cent.
22. German and Flemish painting of the 16th cent.
23. 16th cent. painting of Emilia, Lombardy and Flanders.
24. Room of miniatures.
25. Paintings by Raphael and Michelangelo.
26. Paintings by Andrea del Sarto and Tuscan painters of the 16th cent.
27. Paintings by Pontormo and Tuscan painters of the 16th cent.
28. Paintings by Titian and Venetian painters of the 16th cent.
29. 16th cent. painting of Emilia.
30. 16th cent. painting of Emilia.
31. Venetian and Ferrarese painting of the 16th cent.
32. Venetian painting of the 16th cent.
33. Tuscan and foreign painting of the late 16th cent.
34. Paintings by Veronese.
35. Paintings by Tintoretto.
41. Paintings by Rubens.
42. Room of Niobe.
44. Paintings by Rembrandt, Caravaggio and Italian and Dutch masters of the 17th cent.
45. Paintings by Italian masters of the 17th and 18th cent.

THE « UFFIZI »

On the right flank of the Palazzo della Signoria opens the long, closed and silent **Piazza degli Uffizi.** When Cosimo I made the Palazzo della Signoria his ducal mansion he ordered the administrative and judiciary offices, the archives and collectors' offices to be cleared away and planned to gather them together in a single vast building. He gave the task to his trusted architect, GIORGIO VASARI, who built (1560-70) beside the ducal residence the new « Fabbrica dei Magistrati » (Building of the Magistrates) to which he suceeded in giving a character of unity and ordered tranquillity as had been intended by the new dynasty.

Under the surrounding arcade easy access was afforded to the various offices on the ground and first floors. The upper part of the building was provided with an airy loggia or gallery, joined by a passage over Via della Ninna to the Palazzo della Signoria. Subsequently (1565) Duke Cosimo I ordered Vasari to construct a « corridor » which passing over the Ponte Vecchio linked it up with Palazzo Pitti, bought by his wife Eleonora da Toledo to be the ducal residence. By this corridor, from the Palazzo della Signoria, called from that time the Palazzo del Duca, one could pass under cover the whole way from the new buildings to Palazzo Pitti. From the use made of the lower part, the whole building came to be called the « Uffizi » (Offices). The Medici family was in possession of many works of art collected by Cosimo the Elder,

Madonna Enthroned by Cimabue and Madonna Enthroned by P. Lorenzetti.

Lorenzo the Magnificent and other members of the family: works of art scattered throughout their various palaces and villas, and plundered more than once in time of political upheaval. When at last there was no longer risk of these depredations being repeated, the Grand Duke Francesco I planned to bring them together in a single place and to this end ordered BERNARDO BUONTALENTI, Vasari's successor (1574), to transform the loggia of the Uffizi Palace in such a way that it would be suitable for a museum of sculpture, and to construct a number of rooms in which the other works of art could be arranged and in which could be gathered workshops for every kind of artistic or scientific activity to which the strange Prince applied himself. Thus the top floor of the building took on the exotic name of « gallery » which subsequently became the usual name for a collection of works of art.

To the already existing works of art the Grand Duke Ferdinand I added a great many more which he acquired in Rome while he held the office of Cardinal, and it was he who ordered Buontalenti to build the *Tribune*. Under Ferdinand II the precious objects had already been distributed in the loggia overlooking the Arno and in part of the right wing. To these collections was added the *Cabinet of Gems* and the nucleus of the *collections of Drawings and Self-portraits* which we owe in particular to Cosimo III, who had brought hither from the Villa Medici in Rome the wealth he inherited from his uncle Cardinal Leopold, including medals, coins and classical works, among them the famous Venus which became known as the *Medici Venus*.

Anna Maria Louisa, the last of the Medici, who married the Elector Palatine, enriched the gallery with German and Flemish paintings. With singular understanding of the importance acquired by the Museum which is indeed unequalled throughout the world, she insured by the «Family Compact» of 1737 that all the works of art collected by her family should remain the inalienable property of the city of Florence. In this way grew up, increased and finally became the definite patrimony of the city, the famous *Uffizi Gallery*, which even the Grand Dukes of the Lorraine dynasty cherished and amplified. Napoleon's representative, ignoring the provision of Anna Maria Louisa, plundered the collections as unscrupulously as the churches and convents. The greater number of works of art were restored later but not a few remained unlawfully in the Louvre.

Simone Martini and Lippo Memmi: Annunciation.

Detail from the Madonna Enthroned by Duccio di Buoninsegna.

The building used also to contain the *Medici Theatre*, which Francesco I had ordered to be built (1586) and in which the Italian Senate sat when Florence was capital of Italy (1865-71). In 1890 this theatre was dismantled to make new rooms for the Gallery on the upper floor where more works of the Tuscan primitives were arranged in chronological order, so that today the Uffizi presents an unbroken sequence of works of art up to the end of the eighteenth century.

About the middle of the nineteenth century the niches already provided by Vasari in the colonnade were filled with statues of the greatest figures in Tuscan history, whose names can be read on the pedestals. The artistic value of these statues is negligible but they have the merit of recording, in a superb and by no means exhaustive survey, seven centuries of the prodigious civilization of Tuscany.

The Uffizi Gallery. - As regards the inside of the Gallery, in consideration of the wealth of exhibits, we shall limit ourselves to indicating the works of major importance and universal fame — a thankless and difficult task since frequent re-arrangements have already produced a most selective display. All the works exhibited in the Gallery are of great value. For those whose visit need not be too hurried we advise a special catalogue. For those who cannot stay long we give here a very brief account of the great masterpieces.

Entrance Hall. - *Tapestries* on the walls and busts of members of the Medici family who contributed to the formation of the collections: *Lorenzo the Magnificent, Cosimo I, Francesco I, Ferdinando I, Cosimo II, Maria Maddalena,* the wife of Cosimo II.

Corridor. - *Tapestries* on the walls and busts of other benefactors of the Gallery: *Ferdinand II, Cardinal Leopold,* son of Cosimo II, *Gian Gastone,* last of the male line of the Medici family, *Ferdinando III of Lorraine, Leopold II of Lorraine,* the last Grand Duke of Tuscany. In the wall can be seen two columns with traces of decoration, remains of the **Church of San Pietro Scheraggio,** pulled down to make room for the Uffizi palace.

The numerous Roman busts which decorate these rooms, like the ones we find in public and private houses, gardens and courtyards throughout the city, are largely reconstructed with fragments discovered in all parts of Italy, chiefly in Rome, but also in Greece and Egypt. One of the chief occupations of the regular court sculptors of the Medici was the fixing of heads of Greek and Roman statues to mannerist half-busts of their own fabrication, after which operation the literary men added names of antique personalities, albeit arbitrary, to the « finished » product. It is not difficult to distinguish the original fragment and appreciate its beauty, detaching it mentally from the conventional addition.

On the first floor three doors mark the entrance to the former *Medici Theatre,* constructed in 1585 by Buontalenti and first used in the following year during the Carnival in which was celebrated the wedding of Virginia de'

Domenico Veneziano: Madonna Enthroned and Saints.

Medici and Cesare d'Este, for a representation which was the beginning of a long series of splendid Autumn and Carnival theatrical seasons.

Turning left off the great stairway we go into the **Cabinet of Prints and Drawings**, one of the richest and most important of such collections in the world. In the first room are exhibited collections of works by a single artist or a group of related artists. They are changed periodically, thus giving the public access to important documents and discoveries usually reserved for the student.

At the top of the stairway, in the **Vestibule**, are classical statues. And finally, we enter the beautiful lightfilled **Gallery** itself, its ceiling decorated with « grotesque » frescoes by the sixteenth century artists Allori, Butteri, and Bizzelli. On the walls are 16th cent. tapestries of Flemish and Florentine manufacture. Along the Loggia are arranged classical statues. It is advisable before going into the separate rooms, to go slowly along the whole loggia to appreciate the unity of its architectural elements and decorations, and the harmonious distribution of the sculptures and tapestries. From the south side of the Loggia we enjoy the beautiful view of the river, the hills, and the « Oltrarno ». From the opposite windows, thanks to the art of Vasari who framed them to noble effect between the two wings of the building, we have an unparalleled view of the distant buildings dominated by the superb tower of the Palazzo della Signoria.

Giotto: Madonna Enthroned (detail).

Gentile da Fabriano: Adoration of the Magi (detail).

69

Room I - *Ancient sculptures.* Notice the *Hermaphrodite,* a Roman replica of a Hellenistic original; a Roman *Torso;* and the Hellenistic relief of a *Wayfarer resting.*

Room II - *Thirteenth and Fourteenth Century Tuscan School.* The paintings in this room represent two aspects of the Tuscan character: one powerful, architectural and solemn, embodied in the works of the Florentines CIMABUE (active 1272-1302) and GIOTTO DI BONDONE (1266-1337); the other full of grace and musical quality, represented by the Sienese DUCCIO DI BONINSEGNA (active 1278-1318). Three large panels of the same subject, *The Madonna Enthroned,* give us the possibility of comparing and admiring these three great masters in their different style and characters: we can notice in them the passage from the rhythmical Byzantine quality of Cimabue and Duccio to the truly humanistic style of GIOTTO, precursor of the Renaissance.

Room III - *Fourteenth Century Sienese School.* The subtle and sinuous grace of this school of painting is represented by the *Annunciation* by SIMONE MARTINI (1333) and by various *Scenes in the Lives of Saints* by PIETRO and AMBROGIO LORENZETTI.

Room IV - *Fourteenth Century Florentine School.* Some of the most representative masters of this flourishing school are grouped in this room, among which we should notice the highly dramatic GIOTTINO, the lyrical BERNARDO DADDI, the delicate GIOVANNI DA MILANO.

Room V-VI - *The International Gothic Style* was followed more by the artists of North Italy (and here we may see a delightful *Madonna and Child*

Sandro Botticelli: The birth of Venus.

Two portraits by Antonio and Piero del Pollaiolo.

by the Venetian IACOPO BELLINI, still reminiscent of Byzantine schemes), less by those of Tuscany and especially of Florence, who were influenced by the naturalistic art of Giotto. There were, however, some noteworthy followers of this style in Florence, such as LORENZO MONACO, GHERARDO STARNINA, GENTILE DA FABRIANO (born in the Marches and active in North Italy before he came to Florence), represented in this room by fine examples of their painting rich in arabesques and jewel-like colours.

Room VII - *Fifteenth Century Florentine School.* Having their roots in the powerful, naturalistic style of Giotto and taking their inspiration from the philosophical humanistic movement, the Florentine painters develop an art of solid strength and profound human feeling. And so we have the *St. Anne with the Virgin and Child* by the great MASACCIO (1401-28), the *Battle of San Romano* by that passionate explorer of the third dimension, PAOLO UCCELLO (1396-1475), the *Madonna with Child and Saints* by DOMENICO VENEZIANO (active 1438-61), a master who joins strength to a refined handling of light and colour. Native of Sansepolcro, on the border of Tuscany and Umbria PIERO DELLA FRANCESCA is in many ways connected with the Florentine School, but stands alone in his perfection; these *Portraits of Federico da Montefeltro* and *his Wife Battista Sforza* well represent the lyrical and abstract quality of his art.

Room VIII - The pleasing sweetness and superficial sensuality of FILIPPO LIPPI (c. 1406-1469) is represented here by several panels of the *Madonna and Child* and by the *Coronation of the Virgin* full of portraits of unknown contemporaries and beautiful ladies.

Piero della Francesca: Federico di Montefeltro, duke of Urbino.

Paolo Uccello: The battle of San Romano.

Room IX - ANTONIO (1429-98) and PIERO (1443-96) DEL POLLAIOLO who were also famous as sculptors, introduced in the Florentine style, a dynamic impulse, a nervous linear elegance which had far-reaching influence. Together with the six panels of *Virtues* and some other works by these artists we may see in this room several examples of the youthful production of SANDRO BOTTICELLI (1444-1510), that most original Florentine painter, that melancholy dreamer, creator of a languid, musical beauty unreached in its harmonious grace.

Room X - Here are exhibited the greatest masterpieces of BOTTICELLI: the *Primavera* (c. 1478) and the *Birth of Venus* (c. 1482), which were among the first pictorial representations of that trend of neo-paganism originated in the literary field among the Humanists of the « Studio Fiorentino », the *Minerva and the Centaur*, and allegory justified by the civilizing function which the Humanists claimed for themselves, and the two round panels with the *Madonna of the Magnificat* and the *Madonna of the Pomegranate*.

Room XI - Here are some small paintings of BOTTICELLI, among which *Calumny*, a complex allegorical composition inspired by the dialogues of Lucian, and the exquisite *Madonna adoring the Child* by FILIPPINO LIPPI (son of Filippo) a youthful work much influenced by Botticelli.

Room XII - The works of some Flemish artists of the 15th cent. who worked in Italy or for Italian patrons of the arts have been gathered in this room. We can see the *Entombment* by ROGIER VAN DER WEYDEN, a dramatic subject interpreted with melancholy and serene composure, a *Madonna* and some beautiful *portraits* by HANS MEMLING.

Room XIII - Two Florentine masters influenced by Botticelli and Ghirlandaio, JACOPO DEL SELLAIO and BARTOLOMEO DI GIOVANNI, are here represented by some panels of pleasing anecdotical quality. Notice also a robust *Venus* by LORENZO DI CREDI, a *Self-portrait* and a *Portrait of an old Man* by FILIPPINO LIPPI.

Sandro Botticelli: Primavera.

Room XIV - This room is dominated by the *Adoration of the Shepherds* by HUGO VAN DER GOES, painted in Bruges (1476) by order of Tommaso Portinari who is represented in it with his wife and children. This great painting, which was intended for the Florentine church of St. Egidio attached to the Hospital founded by Folco Portinari, was of great importance for the local school, stimulating the love of beautiful decorative details and the faithful portraying of patrons. Around this masterpiece are gathered the works of several Florentine painters who were, more or less, influenced by it: FILIPPINO LIPPI, LORENZO DI CREDI (1459-1537), DOMENICO GHIRLANDAIO (1449-1494), FRANCESCO BOTTICINI (died 1498). A follower of the Flemish school is also NICOLAS FROMENT from Avignon whose harsh style is represented here by a triptych with the *Resurrection of Lazarus*.

Room XV - The *Umbrian School* appears here with the monumental and dramatic works of LUCA SIGNORELLI (1441-1523) (*Madonna and Child, Holy Family, Crucifix with Mary Magdalen*) and with the *Madonna between St. Sebastian and St. John the Baptist* by PIETRO PERUGINO (1446-1523) sweet and languid as the atmosphere of Umbria. In this room we can also admire the unfinished *Adoration of the Magi* in which LEONARDO DA VINCI (1452-1519) shows, barely sketched in, yet still revealing, the complete conception and all the characteristics of his art. This work, unfinished like Michelangelo's « Palestrina Deposition », is an expression of the final conclusion which two great artists reached by the same path of indefatigable labour: the incapacity of human means to fully render the conception of the intellect. By ANDREA DEL VERROCCHIO, Leonardo's master and an artist better known as a sculptor, we see the *Baptism of Christ*.

Room XVI - This is called the Map Room from the decorative maps of Tuscany painted on the walls by the Olivetan monk Stefano Bonsignori (1586), one of the first trustworthy cartographers. Here are exhibited: the serene *Annunciation*, an exquisite work from the youthful period of LEONARDO, and a fine *Portrait of a Young man with a red cap* attributed to LORENZO DI CREDI.

Room XVII - The Umbrian School of the 15th cent. is here represented by minor artists and by some small paintings by LUCA SIGNORELLI among which is an interesting *Allegory of Fecundity*.

Room XVIII (Tribune) **-** This room shaped like a small temple, was designed by Bernardo Buontalenti (c. 1588), to give a suitable setting to the pagan statues destined to be placed in it. The decoration of polychrome marbles, the mosaics of the drum and the lining of the small dome with mother-of-pearl shells are the scenographic apparatus for the so-called *Medici Venus*, the original work, very little retouched, of an artist of the 3rd cent. B. C., derived from Praxiteles, who undertook to present the goddess as the epitome of beauty, at the moment of her rising, newly created from the foam of the sea. We should here recall to mind that this same idea was rendered in a not dissimilar way by Sandro Botticelli almost a century and a half before this work was brought to Florence. The realistic school of Pergamus is represented in the *Knife-grinder* (3rd cent. B.C.) or more exactly the *Flayer*, intended to stand at the foot of another figure representing Marsyas flayed, of which we shall see two copies on the west loggia. Of the Hellenistic school there is the *Music playing Faun* (3rd cent. B.C.) still admirable, despite

Sandro Botticelli: The Madonna of the « Magnificat ».

Sandro Botticelli: Minerva and the Centaur (detail).

restorations, in its pose and in the play of the muscles. From the Greek school there is the small statue of *Apollo*, a very graceful representation of the god of light (4th cent. B.C.).

On the walls are hung very beautiful portraits, chiefly of the Medici family, by AGNOLO BRONZINO (*Eleonora of Toledo with her son Giovanni, Maria de' Medici* as a child, *Garzia de' Medici* as a child, *Lucretia Panciatichi, Bartolomeo Panciatichi*), by PONTORMO (*Cosimo the Elder*), by GIORGIO VASARI (*Lorenzo the Magnificent*, probably painted after the death-mask of Lorenzo and labouriously enriched with allegorical details).

Room XIX - PERUGINO is here represented by some excellent *portraits*. Some more fine *portraits* are by FRANCESCO FRANCIA and LORENZO COSTA, two painters of the school of Ferrara (end of the 15th and beginning of the 16th cent.) who, more or less directly, came under the influence of Perugino.

Room XX - ANDREA MANTEGNA (1431-1506) is the founder of the Venetian School of the Renaissance; his powerfully dramatic and sculpturesque style is here well represented by the triptych with the *Adoration of the Magi, Circumcision* and *Ascension*, and the beautiful *Madonna of the Caves*. ALBRECHT DÜRER, the great German artist of the early 16th cent. spent a long time in Venice where he studied the painting of Andrea Mantegna; this is the reason why his dramatic and luminous works have been hung in this room: the *Adoration of the Magi* and the *portrait of the artist's father*. LUKAS CRANACH is contemporary of Dürer and a follower of him but his style is more nervous and subtle as can be seen from his *Adam* and *Eve* which are a replica of the same subject painted by Dürer.

Room XXI - A beautiful *Allegory of Purgatory* and a monochrome *Pietà* well represent the art of GIOVANNI BELLINI, who added to the plasticism of Mantegna a subtle lyrical feeling and a warmer colour. The two small paintings: *Moses as a child at the trial of gold and fire in the presence of Pharaoh* and *Solomon's Judgment*, after many controversies, have been definitely attributed to GIORGIONE (1478-1511) who, starting from the style of Giovanni Bellini, reached a sublime lyricism and foreran the style of Titian in his luminous colours.

Leonardo da Vinci: Annunciation.

The « Tribuna » with the Medici Venus.

Room XXII - The two German painters HANS VON KULMBACK (1476-1522) and ALBRECHT ALTDORFER (1480-1538) have been indirectly influenced by the Venetian school while HANS HOLBEIN (1497-1543) learnt in Lombardy his clear plasticism. He is famous especially for his portraits which he mostly painted in England; here we see the wonderful *Portrait of Sir Richard Southwell*. Two panels by GERARD DAVID (*Deposition* and *Adoration of the Magi*) show the monumental yet simple and serene compositions of this Flemish master.

Room XXIII - Antonio Allegri called CORREGGIO (1489-1534) is one of the outstanding Emilian artists of the 16th cent. His *Virgin adoring the Child* is a refined innovation in its childlike grace, the use of a very vivid blue and the supernatural light emanating from the figure of the Child; in his *Rest in Egypt* he abandoned the traditional schemes of composition and introduced a diagonal scheme. Correggio started under the influence of the Emilian painters Francia and Costa but was later influenced also by Leonardo. The other painters of Lombardy who are represented in this room were also under the influence of Leonardo (notice the exquisite *Narcissus* by G. A. BOLTRAFFIO) as, indirectly, were also the Flemish QUENTIN MASSYS and JOOS VAN CLEVE.

Room XXIV - Miniatures of Italian and foreign artists from the 15th to the 18th cent.

Room XXV - Here we find two masterpieces by RAPHAEL (1483-1520): *Pope Leo X with the Cardinals Giulio de' Medici* (the future Pope Clemente VII) and *Cardinal Luigi de' Rossi*, one of the finest portraits which were ever painted, and the *Madonna of the Goldfinch*, painted in Florence and revealing the teachings of Leonardo, by virtue of which the delicacy of the colouring, of light and shade effects and soft atmosphere of the landscape confer on the geometrical composition the spirituality demanded by the suject. By MICHELANGELO (1475-1564) we see the round painting of the *Holy Family*, also called the *Doni Madonna*, after Angelo Doni who ordered it, and for whose wedding it was to be executed. It is one of the very few paintings on wood by Michelangelo and it is conceived in masses, like sculpture, in which both colour and light and shade are used to render a depth which stretches back gradually to the bare horizon in the distance. The few inches accorded to this landscape are almost the only concession Michelangelo ever made

Bronzino: Eleonora of Toledo with her son Giovanni.

towards the decorative in painting. In this room are also some paintings of Roman and Florentine « Mannerists », that is those painters who worked in the « manner » of Raphael and Michelangelo. Among these notice a very moving *Pietà* by BRONZINO whose work as a portraitist we have already seen in the Tribune.

Room XXVI - Some more works by Florentine « Mannerists »; the refined colourist ANDREA DEL SARTO (1486-1531), called the « faultless painter », with his *Madonna of the Harpies, Four Saints, Portrait of a young Lady with a Book*; ROSSO FIORENTINO (1494-1541) with a delicate *Portrait of a Girl*, a youthful work under the influence of Raphael and Andrea del Sarto, and *Moses defending Jethro's daughters* in which Michelangelo's sculptural style is interpreted with a very original technique and personal feeling.

Room XXVII - PONTORMO (1494-1557) is the most original artist of the « mannerist » school of Tuscany. Here we see several of his works, most interesting of which is the *Supper at Emmaus*, a powerful, dramatic piece of painting. Among the other works by Pontormo notice the *Portrait of Francesco dell'Ajolle* and the *Madonna between St. Jerome and St. Francis*. Another noteworthy Tuscan « mannerist » is BACHIACCA (1490-1557) by whom is to the seen here a delightful predella with the *Stories of St. Acacius*.

Room XXVIII - Here are the famous works of TITIAN (1477-1576): *Flora*, the synthesis of the pictorial ideal of the great Venetian, with magnificent gradations of tone from pale yellow to gold; *Venus with the little*

Raffaello: The Madonna of the Goldfinch (detail).

Dog, one of the most beautiful interpretations of this subject; *Venus and Cupid*; a *Knight of Malta*. Among other Venetian masters of the 16th cent., in this room, is to be noticed PALMA IL VECCHIO (1480-1528) with a *Judith* very rich and original in colour.

Rooms XXIX and XXX - The Emilian School of the 16th cent. is here represented by several interesting artists among which most noteworthy: PARMIGIANINO (1505-1540), a very original, although mannered, innovator (*Madonna « of the long neck »*, *Portrait of a Man*, *Madonna of St. Zacharias*) and DOSSO DOSSI (1489-1542) from Ferrara but who followed the richness of colour and composition of the Venetian School (*Portrait of a Warrior*, *Rest on the Flight to Egypt*).

Room XXXI - Notice some more, larger paintings of DOSSO DOSSI and a beautiful, moving *Portrait of a Man*, called *The sick Man*, which is uncertainly attributed to SEBASTIANO DEL PIOMBO (1485-1547), a Venetian master with the characteristic qualities of colour and light effects and romantic feeling of the painters of the Laguna, although he spent many years in Rome and studied Raphael and Michelangelo.

Room XXXII - Here can be seen the works of some masters either Venetian or under the influence of the Venetian school. Notice LORENZO LOTTO (1480-1556) (*Holy Conversation*), a romantic artist, also influenced by the German school of painting of the period; PARIS BORDONE (1500-1571) who excels in his *Portraits*, rich and decorative; ROMANINO (1485-1566) full of poetic and dramatic vein (*Portrait of a child*, *Portrait of Teofilo Folengo*).

Room XXXIII - In this passage room have been gathered several works — mostly of small size — of the late 16th cent. from various parts of Europe. There is a good number of very decorative works of the Florentine school of that period. Among the foreigners are to be noticed: a *Portrait of Francis I of France* by FRANÇOIS CLOUET, a *Christ bearing the Cross* by the Castilian LUIS DE MORALES, a *Self-portrait* of the Flemish ANTHONY MOR.

Titian: Venus with the little dog.

Room XXXIV - Here can be seen the works of PAOLO VERONESE (1528-1588), one of the most famous Venetians of the 16th cent. His compositions, rich, luminous and full of movement well represent the opulence of Venetian life at that period. His *Holy Family with St. Barbara* and the *Annunciation* are to be especially noticed. GIOVAN BATTISTA MORONI (1525-1578) from Bergamo and GIULIO CAMPI (died 1572) from Cremona both follow the Venetian style and excel in their rather grave and melancholy *portraits*.

Room XXXV - TINTORETTO (1518-1594) is, together with Veronese, the most out-standing master of the second half of the 16th cent. in Venice. But Tintoretto brings into his style a restlessness which makes it very dramatic. Here are to be seen his *portrait of Jacopo Sansovino, Leda and the Swan* and *Christ and the Samaritan Woman*. Another Venetian, JACOPO BASSANO (1515-1592), famous for his night scenes, has here a very original and powerfully painted composition of *Hunting-dogs*. Near these two Venetian masters we see BAROCCIO (1528-1612) from Urbino, a follower of Correggio but also influenced by the Venetians, with the large canvas of the *Madonna del Popolo* and a good *portrait of Francesco Maria della Rovere*.

Rooms XXXVI, XXXVII, XXXVIII, XXXIX, and **XL** have been closed as on their area a new exit stairway has been opened. The most important paintings of these rooms have been temporarily transferred to rooms XLII, XLIV and XLV, until new rooms will be available in which the rich collection of 17th and 18th century works, both of Italian and foreign schools, owned by the Uffizi Gallery, will be definitely exhibited.

Room XLI - Here are gathered precious masterpieces of RUBENS (1577-1640), the exuberant lord of official painting: *Henry IV at the Battle of Ivry* and *Entry of Henry IV into Paris,* the first of a series of paintings executed for the widow of the French King, Maria dei Medici, who had herself been glorified by the painter in the superb Louvre series. Notice also the lovely *Portrait of Isabella Brant,* first wife of the painter. In this room are some *portraits* by ANTHONY VAN DYCK (1559-1641) and a good *Portrait of Galileo* by JUSTUS SUSTERMANS (1597-1681) a Flemish artist who lived many years in Florence as official portraitist at the court of the Medici Grand Dukes.

Rooms XLII - The Grand Duke Pietro Leopoldo of Lorraine had this room made at the end of the 18th cent. to house the great collection of the 14 statues of *Niobe and her children struck by Apollo and Diana*. Excavated in 1583, in Rome, where they probably stood in some sylvan setting and not, as is sometimes held, in front of the temple of Apollo Sosianus, they were transported to the Villa Medici and thence, in 1775, to Florence. They are considered to be the work of the Greek Scopas (c. 400-350 B. C.), the solemn and dramatic sculptor of the Bacchante in the Capitol Museum and of the Apollo playing the Lyre in the Vatican.

In this room are temporarily exhibited some paintings of the Italian and French 18th century among which the beautiful Venetian landscapes by GUARDI and CANALETTO, the exquisite *Flute Player* by WATTEAU and the delightful pictures of a *Boy playing with cards* and *Girl with a shuttlecock* by CHARDIN.

Room XLIV - In this room are gathered the masters of the Baroque style. The great innovator CARAVAGGIO (1573-1610) created a very original style especially in the field of light effects and had a flock of pupils and followers (notice the *Head of Medusa* and *Bacchus*). ANNIBALE CARRACCI (1560-1609) also created a new school of painting in Bologna, reacting to the « mannerism »

Michelangelo: Holy Family.

Correggio: Virgin adoring the Child.

of the late 16th century. Works of some followers of Carracci (GUIDO RENI FRANCESCO ALBANI, GUERCINO) are also to be seen here, while the influence of Caravaggio can be noticed in some Dutch « genre » paintings by FRANS VAN MIERIS, JAN STEEN, GABRIEL METZU. Some masterworks by the great, dramatic Dutch painter REMBRANDT VAN RJIN (1606-1669) are also exhibited here: two *Self-portraits* and the wonderful *Portrait of an old man*.

Room XLV - Here we can see the paintings of some Neapolitan followers of Caravaggio: BATTISTELLO, BERNARDO CAVALLINO, MATTIA PRETI, all belonging to the 17th century. To the same period belong the Roman DOMENICO FETI, BERNARDO STROZZI from Genoa and the German JAN LYS, who all worked in Venice. The painting style of GIUSEPPE MARIA CRESPI (1664-1747) belongs instead to the 18th century and was influenced by the Bolognese masters of the 17th century as well as by the contemporary Venetian painting. Crespi painted mostly « genre » scenes (*Fair at Poggio a Caiano, The Flea*) but also some religious subjects as the beautiful *Massacre of the Innocents* exhibited here.

Coming to the end of the west wing, one should go out on the terrace on the roof of the Loggia della Signoria from which one can enjoy a new and very impressive view of the Palazzo Vecchio.

Returning, between the entrance doors of rooms 34 and 25, a stairway leads to **Vasari's Corridor** linking the Uffizi Gallery to the Pitti Palace. This corridor was severely damaged and partly destroyed by the German mines in 1944. It was again badly damaged by the flood of Novembre 1966. It has now been reconstructed and restored but only the first part is yet open to the public. Here have been temporarily exhibited some of the finest and most interesting pieces of the very famous *Collection of Selfportraits*, among which those of Raphael, Titian, Rubens, Corot, Ensor.

Guardi: Landscape with a canal.

Between the Palazzo Vecchio and the Uffizi runs *Via della Ninna* and here we see the remains of the church of *San Pietro Scheraggio*, so-called from the « schiaraggio » i.e. clearing trench made for the first city walls founded in 1066, and which, in spite of the glorious memories of the Commune with which it abounded, was not saved from gradual destruction from the time when the Palazzo della Signoria was built, to when the Uffizi were completed. Via della Ninna leads to the *Loggia del Grano* designed by Giulio Parigi (1619), and transformed into a theatre (1867) by the famous actor Tommaso Salvini.

Through the *Via dei Leoni* (so-called because until 1550 the lions regarded as the symbols of the Commune's sovereignty were kept there), we come to the exceptionally varied and picturesque **Piazza S. Firenze,** nearby. On the left is the 15th cent. *Palazzo Gondi,* by GIULIANO DA SANGALLO (1494-1576), a typical example of civil architecture of the time, with a very beautiful courtyard; on the right the harmonious building of San Firenze, a convent of the Order of Filippo Neri, comprising the façades of the church dedicated to San Fiorenzo, on the left, by FERD. RUGGERI (1725), of the abolished church of S. Apollinare, on the right, and of the convent-palace, by ZANOBI DEL ROSSO (1772). The Tribunal is uncomfortably installed in this palace which is functionally unadapted to its needs. The majestic flight of steps and the severe interior of the church by ANTONIO FERRI (1668) merit special attention as a practically unique example of the moderately restrained Baroque architecture and the sober taste which obtained in the region of Florence in the 17th century. From the steps we have an extremely beautiful scenographic view of the massive structure of Palazzo Vecchio, the attractive façade of Palazzo Gondi, the group of the Badia, with its elegant Gothic tower and the strong rugged bulk of the **Palazzo del Podestà,** later called the **Bargello,** which, in political importance and architectonic grandeur, rates as the second civil building of the medieval city. It has the decided character of a small fortress, with its high embattled tower called « la Volognana », because when it was built the Commune still had to defend itself against enemies from outside, and still more against those from

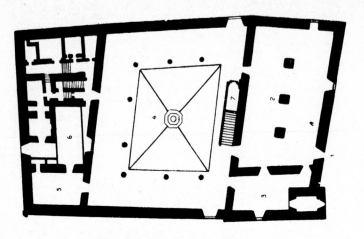

BARGELLO - PLAN OF THE GROUND FLOOR.

1. Entrance - 2. Entrance Hall (Michelangelo sculpture and Armory) - 3. Room of the Tower - 4. Courtyard - 5. Room of Trecento Sculpture - 6. Room of temporary exhibitions - Stairway to the 1st floor.

inside. The front part was completed in 1255, 43 years before the Palazzo della Signoria, as the seat of the Capitano del Popolo, the magistrate instituted in 1250 with the special office of supporting the interests of the people against the Ghibelline nobles; the person who took this position had to be a noble, but was attended by the Council of the Commune. From 1261 this palace was the seat of the Podestà, the foreign magistrate (whose office had been created at least 68 years previously) whose business it was to maintain a reasonable equilibrium between the parties. In the last years of the Republic the Judges of the « Tribunale di Rota » were accomodated there and after 1574 it gave quarters to the Capitano di Giustizia or Bargello, in other words the Chief of Police. Over a period of almost three centuries it was continually more and more cut up to make prison-cells; finally in 1857 it was liberated from tens of thousands of tons of material added to the original building and restored with considerable faithfulness. In 1859 the provisory Government of Tuscany chose it as the seat of the National Museum, which had to be made to house sculpture and objects of art, but

Donatello: David (detail).

only on the occasion of the celebration of the sixth centenary of the birth of Dante (1865), after laborious restorations, was it declared open.

To the various blocks of the building correspond the several purposes of their erection, not all recognisable with certainty. Originally the tower and front part of the palace were destined for the Capitano del Popolo; they were, at least in part, the work of FRA SISTO and FRA RISTORO, the Dominican architects of Santa Maria Novella. The part behind, lower and more approachable, which grew up round the main courtyard, formed the Podestà's quarters; NERI DI FIORAVANTE (1331-1345) and other masters were responsible for it.

Interior - The National Museum - At the moment of the publication of this guide-book (1969) a thorough new arrangement of this Museum has been planned. However, as the changes will be done gradually and will take a long time, we can only give a description of the various rooms and collections as they are at present.

The vast entrance hall with its pillars and sturdy vaults, gives an immediate impression of force and grandeur. The heraldic decoration of the walls with crests of the Podestàs (Mayors) of the end of the 13th and 14th

Courtyard of the Palazzo del Bargello.

Michelangelo: Bacchus (detail).

century, number among the parts of the building which have been restored; of the remains of frescoes which have survived, only the *Madonna and Child*, of the 14th cent. is in its original location. This great room and the smaller adjoining one harbour now a wonderful résumé of half a century's sculptural work by MICHELANGELO: the *Drunken Bacchus* (1496), the *Madonna teaching the Child Jesus and the little St. John to read* (c. 1504), *David* (c. 1530), *Brutus* (c. 1540), the *Martyrdom of St. Andrew*. Around these masterworks are grouped some sculptures by artists which were influenced by Michelangelo, amongst them BARTOLOMEO AMMANNATI, NICCOLÒ TRIBOLO, VINCENZO DANTI and PIETRO FRANCAVILLA. To these we can add the *bust of Michelangelo* by DANIELE RICCIARELLI, a work of powerful realism.

In the great entrance hall there are a few pieces of the immensely rich **Medici Armory.**

The irregular scenographic **Courtyard** is an unforgettable sight for the visitor. The spacious court is overlooked by an elegant balcony, reached by an open staircase which is interrupted in its course by a 14th cent. portal with a 16th cent. gate. In this courtyard the instruments of torture were burnt,

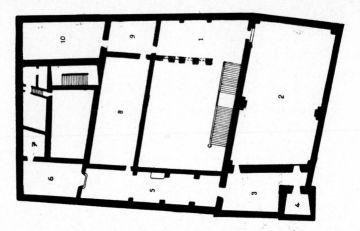

BARGELLO - PLAN OF THE FIRST FLOOR.

1. Balcony. - 2. General Council Hall (or of Donatello). - 3. Tower Room. - 4. - Tower. - 5. Hall of the Podestà (Carrand Collection). - 6. Chapel. - 7. Sacristy. - 8. Room of the Ivories. - 9. Room on the left of the balcony. - 10. Room of the Majolicas.

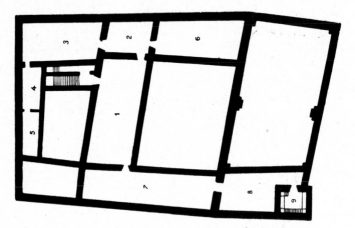

BARGELLO - PLAN OF THE SECOND FLOOR.

1. Cellini Room. - 2. Room of the Fountain. - 3. Verrocchio Room. - 4. First room of the Collection of Medals. - 5. Second room of the Collection of Medals. - 6. Room of the Chimney piece. - 7. Hall of Small Bronzes. - 8. Tower Room (Franchetti Collection). - 9. Little room of the Plague.

Andrea della Robbia: Madonna and Child.

after the first abolition of the death penalty was decreed by the Grand Duke Pietro Leopoldo in 1782. In olden times every Podestà and every Giudice di Rota used to have his crest, in stone or terra-cotta, attached to the walls of the courtyard, and the remains of all these crests now form the most original and interesting part of the decoration which lightens the severe and powerful architecture. Below the arcade are the picturesque signs of the different quarters of the town. Along the walls stand *statues* by BACCIO BANDINELLI, BARTOLOMEO AMMANNATI, GIAMBOLOGNA, and, a little out of its elements, both in the matter of style and of subject, the *Little Fisher* by VINCENZO GEMITO (1917).

Trecento Sculpture (14th cent.) - Through a door in the corner opposite the entrance we go into a room in which are gathered together a number of examples of 14th cent. sculpture, some also earlier than this, and various specimens which have survived the fanatic destruction of the art of the past which began in Florence in the time of the capital (1865-1871) and went on until the end of the nineteenth century.

Noteworthy are: the *Madonna and Child* and the *Angel with praying Man* by the plastic TINO DI CAMAINO; the exquisite *Madonna and Child* of the Venetian school; the base of a holy water well with *three acolytes* by the school of Nicola Pisano; the three monumental statues of a *Madonna with Child, St. Peter and St. Paul* by PAOLO DI GIOVANNI, once on the Porta Romana.

We go back to the courtyard and up the steps to the **Balcony** where there are a number of pieces of sculpture, those by GIAMBOLOGNA being most noteworthy. They include the very famous *Mercury* who launches into flight borne on a breath of wind, Caduceus in hand and finger raised; the extremely beautiful decorative bronzes: the *Turkey*, the *Eagle*, the *Goshawk*, a *Satyr*, two *Putti* and the marble figure of *Architecture*.

From the Balcony we enter the majestic **Salone del Consiglio Generale** (General Council Hall) which since 1887 has housed a group of works by DONATELLO and other 15th century artists. The little group of Donatellian works would suffice to make this collection an incomparable treasure. In the centre of the end wall is the figure of *St. George* (1416), which used to be in one of the niches of Or San Michele where its place is now filled by a copy; on the right is the polychrome head of *Niccolò da Uzzano*, of doubtful attribution and mistaken identity; to the left is the so-called head of *Giovanni Antonio da Narni*. In the centre of the room sits the fine *Marzocco* (Donatellian only by tradition) which used to be on the « aringhiera » of Palazzo Vecchio, surrounded by the bronze *David* (1430), taken from the courtyard of Palazzo Medici; the marble *David* (1415) which used to be in the Palazzo Vecchio; the *Little St. John*, from the house of the Martelli family. In front, the bronze *Cupid* and *Athis*. And, as if all this wealth were not enough, other works extremely important for the history of Florentine sculpture have been put with them: works by DESIDERIO DA SETTIGNANO, MICHELOZZO, BRUNELLESCHI, GHIBERTI, BERTOLDO, AGOSTINO DI DUCCIO, and VECCHIETTA and many beautiful pieces by LUCA DELLA ROBBIA, the famous creator of exquisite glazed terracotta works. Luca was the first to render terracotta more durable by coating it with a layer of coloured glazing. His invention immediately had so great a success that the workshop which he opened flourished for more than a century and produced innumerable works, whose author it is not always possible to identify. In this room are also several very beautiful *marriage chests* of the 15th cent. and of

Young St. John by Desiderio da Settignano and Mercury by Giambologna.

the end of the 14th cent., some of which are painted with scenes very interesting for the study of the life of that period.

Through a door at the end we pass into the **Sala della Torre** (Tower Room) the walls of which are hung with rich stuffs and tapestries.

In the adjoining **Hall of the Podestà** is arranged the extremely rich collection bequeathed to the city by the French antiquarian Louis Carrand (d. 1888), including wrought gold objects, enamels, iron work, and glass, while the bronzes, arms and ivories which were part of this collection are now in the Hall of Small Bronzes (2nd floor), in the Armoury (ground floor) and in the Hall of the Ivories (1st floor). This collection is altogether a treasure of inestimable value.

In the **Chapel**, dedicated to the repentant sinner St. Mary Magdalen, prisoners who had been condemned to death used to be comforted in their last hours by the brothers of the « Compagnia dei Neri ». Early restorations (1840) brought to light there the remains of frescoes in the manner of Giotto, among them the consoling *scene of Paradise* with the famous *portrait of Dante*, which, as literary tradition would have it, was painted from nature by GIOTTO, the poet's friend.

In the little **Sacristy**, altarpieces, sacerdotal raiments and a collection of « paxes » in niello work, fifteenth century masterpieces of Italian metal work.

Leaving the chapel, we go into the **Hall of the Ivories**, where is exhibited one of the richest collections of ivories known to us.

Luca della Robbia: Madonna and Child.

We now pass into the **Room on the left of the Balcony** where are exhibited some church goldsmith's pieces and vestments of the 15th cent. and then into the **Hall of the Majolicas** in which are gathered the remains of the splendid collection of ceramics owned by the Medici family and which for a great part were collected and then bequeathed to the Museum by Luigi Pisa.

A flight of stairs leads us to the second floor, where we find the **Cellini Room**, dominated by the great *bust of Cosimo I*, flanked by the lively little wax and bronze *models of the Perseus.* By Cellini are also the low-relief of the *Liberation of Andromeda*, formerly on the base of the Perseus, a small low-relief of a *Greyhound* and the statue of *Ganymede*.

In this room are also works by artists of the DELLA ROBBIA workshop, from GIOVANNI DELLA ROBBIA (1469-1528) to SANTI BUGLIONI (1494-1576) the last representative of this famous school.

Left we pass into the **Room of the Fountain** where are exhibited various fine works by ANDREA DELLA ROBBIA (1435-1525), nephew of Luca.

In the **Room of the Chimney Piece**, so-called from its chimney-piece by BENEDETTO DA ROVEZZANO, are gathered works of sculpture of the 16th and 17th centuries, among them the *bust of Costanza Bonarelli*, by BERNINI.

David by Verrocchio and Young St. John by Donatello.

The Lady with a nose-gay by Verrocchio and Costanza Bonarelli by Bernini.

In the **Verrocchio Room** we find works by this master (Andrea de' Cioni, called Verrocchio, 1435-88) including the bronze *David;* the polychrome terracotta of the *Resurrection*; two *Madonnas*, one in marble, the other in terracotta; the *portrait of Piero di Lorenzo dei Medici*; the *bust of a Lady with a nose-gay*; and the low-relief of the *Death of Francesca Pitti Tornabuoni* (1477). With them are other extremely beautiful works by ANTONIO DEL POLLAIOLO, MINO DA FIESOLE, BENEDETTO DA MAIANO, ANTONIO ROSSELLINO, FRANCESCO LAURANA, MATTEO CIVIDALI and others.

Rooms of the Collection of Medals. - In these two rooms we find the Medici Collection rich in medals of the 15th and 16th cent., among them specimens of exceptional importance by PISANELLO, MATTEO DEI PASTI, BERTOLDO and B. CELLINI.

Going back into the Cellini Room, we pass into the **Hall of Small Bronzes**, which contains some very fine works by RICCIO, GIAMBOLOGNA and other masters famous in this field of sculpture. Next comes the **Tower Room** with a valuable collection of textiles, a donation of Baron Giulio Franchetti, and finally the **Little Room of the Plague** which contains pieces modelled in wax, among them a realistic representation of revolting pestilence scenes, a work of monstrous skill by the Syracusan GAETANO ZUMBO (d. 1701).

Here we end our visit of the **National Museum of the Bargello** with its great review of Tuscan masters of sculpture from the 14th to the end of the 16th century which in this field is of an importance equivalent to that of the Uffizi Gallery in the sphere of painting.

Donatello: St. George.

THE CHURCH OF BADIA

Facing the Bargello is the church of the Benedictine Abbey, founded by the Countess Willa, which underwent continual transformation up to the 17th, century, and was of great importance (from 978) in the political life of the city at the time of the marquessate and of the first republican « Priori » who took up residence there. The *portal* was designed by BENEDETTO DA ROVEZZANO (1495) and has a *Madonna* by BENEDETTO BUGLIONI, a pupil of the Della Robbia school. The extremely beautiful *campanile*, the lower part of which is in Romanesque style (1310), subsequently completed in the Gothic manner (1330), its slender form contrasting with the rugged tower of the Bargello, can be admired only from the Piazza San Firenze or from the door of the great cloister in the via dei Magazzini nearby.

The interior of the church is a veritable little museum of Renaissance sculpture. On the right, the *tomb of Giannotto Pandolfini* (d. 1456), from the workshop of Bernardo Rossellino; *the Madonna and Child with St. Lawrence and St. Leonard* (1464-69), low-relief by MINO DA FIESOLE, is dedicated to the devotion of the first patron of the church and the cult of the protector of the prisoners; next the *tomb of Bernardo Giugni*, by Mino da Fiesole (1469-1481). On the left, the *tomb of Count Ugo, marquess of Tuscany* (d. 1006), also by Mino da Fiesole, before which, for nine and a half centuries, and still in our own time, the colourful obsequies are celebrated every year on the anniversary of the Count's death. On the wall left of the entrance, the *Madonna appearing to St. Bernard* (1480), masterpiece by FILIPPINO LIPPI. The *ceiling*, designed by Matteo Segaloni is a magnificent example of Florentine carving of the Baroque period (1625). In the small **cloister** near the apse, called **of the Orange-trees**, is a series of fifteenth century frescoes depicting the *life of St. Benedict*, the work of an unknown 15th century artist of outstanding vivacity and iconographical interest (at the present moment they have been detached in order to be restored and they are exhibited at the Forte di Belvedere).

A few steps along *via Dante Alighieri*, on the right, we come to the so-called **house of Dante**, a deplorable, mannered restoration (1875-1910) on the ruins of some antique houses, which, it seems, were the property of the Alighieri family. A little further on, near an arch, on the right is the ancient **church of Santa Margherita**, where the Portinari tombs used to be, and where it is believed that Dante was married to Gemma Donati.

Opposite the presumed house of Dante, is the old **Torre della Castagna** (Tower of the Chestnut), the first residence of the «Priori delle Arti» (1282). In the small *square of San Martino* is the **Oratory of the «Buonomini»** where, since 1478 has been the seat of the Company of the Purveyors of the Poor, called the «Buonomini» (Good Men), founded in 1442 by St. Antonino to give secret help to those of fallen fortune. In the interior is a series of ten frescoes with *scenes from the life of St. Martin*, and representations of *Works of Mercy*, attributed to a «Buonomo» miniaturist, FRANCESCO D'ANTONIO, of great interest for the history of 15th century costume. From the *via dei Magazzini* we turn right into the *via dei Cimatori* the name of which recalls the working or shearing of the bales of imported raw wool often brought from England. We pass the remains of ancient *tower-houses*: of particular note are those of the *Cerchi family*, to whom belonged the walled *Loggia* in the next street, named after them. Coming out into *via Calzaioli*, we turn right. A few steps bring us, on the right hand side, to the **church of San Carlo,** begun in 1349 by NERI DI FIORAVANTE and BENCI DI CIONE, completed in 1384 by SIMONE TALENTI; on the high altar is a picture of the *Burial and Ascension of Christ*, by NICCOLÒ GERINI.

The Church of Orsanmichele.

Opposite this church is **Orsanmichele** which has a strange history. Its name means San Michele in Orto (in the Garden), and derives from the fact that on its site, until 895, stood a church, dedicated to the Archangel Michael, near the garden of a convent. In 1290 ARNOLFO DI CAMBIO built on this site the *Loggia del Grano*, below which the grain market was held, and in the storehouses above it were kept the reserve supplies of grain, to be distributed to the people in time of war and famine. The construction of this majestic semi-ecclesiastical, semi-agricultural building was ordered in honour of the miraculous painting of *Our Lady of the Pillar*, and for the better conservation of the grain. It was begun in 1337 and completed in 1404, by the same master-builders who were working on the construction of the Cathedral, the Loggia dei Priori and the fortifications: FRANCESCO TALENTI, BENCI DI CIONE, NERI DI FIORAVANTE and SIMONE TALENTI. In 1349 the People's Signoria discussed the construction of a chapel in honour of St. Anne, to whose intercession was attributed the expulsion of Gualtieri di Brienne, Duke of Athens, happily secured on July 26th, 1342, through the direct intervention of the armed forces of the Art Guilds. In honour of the Virgin, protectress of the Florentine people, the great arcades were closed with a light screen by SIMONE TALENTI (1387), on the pilasters of which, in a number of tabernacles, were placed statues of the Patron Saints of the Major Arts, to whom the task of maintaining the cult was assigned. Thus Orsanmichele became one of the most curious and interesting buildings in the city, both in its architectural structure, half-civil, half-ecclesiastical, and for the collection of sculptures, which represented an epitome of the development of art from the late 15th to the early 17th century.

This is the order of the statues on the exterior, beginning in **via Calzaioli**, from left to right: I) Guild of Calimala (Foreign Wool merchants): *St. John the Baptist*, by GHIBERTI (1414-16). II) Tribunal of the Merchants: *Tabernacle* by DONATELLO and MICHELOZZO (1425) with group of the *Incredulity of St. Thomas* (1464-83), by VERROCCHIO. III) Guild of the Magistrates and Notaries: *St. Luke* (1601), by GIAMBOLOGNA. In **via Or San Michele.** IV) Guild of the Butchers: *St. Peter* (1408-1413), by DONATELLO. V) Guild of the Tanners: *St. Philip* (1405-

Verrocchio: The Incredulity of St. Thomas.

1410), by NANNI DI BANCO. VI) Guild of the Forgers, Joiners and Masons: *Four crowned Saints* (1408), by NANNI DI BANCO. VII) Guild of the Armourers: *St. George* (1416), by Donatello (bronze copy; we have seen the marble original in the Bargello). In **via dell'Arte della Lana.** VIII) Guild of the Money Changers: *St. Matthew* (1420), by GHIBERTI. IX) Guild of the Wool workers: *St. Stephen* (1426-28), by GHIBERTI. X) Guild of Farriers: *St. Eligius* (1415), by NANNI DI BANCO. In **via dei Lamberti.** XI) Guild of the Linen dealers and Old-clothes men: *St. Mark* (1411-13), by DONATELLO. XII) Guild of the Furriers: *St. James*, by a pupil of Ghiberti. XIII) Guild of the Doctors and Apothecaries: *Madonna and Child* (1399), attributed to Simone Talenti. XIV) Guild of the Silk workers and Goldsmiths: *St. John the Evangelist* (1515), by BACCIO DA MONTELUPO. The medallions in terra-cotta are by LUCA DELLA ROBBIA; among them, that of the Guild of the Butchers is a modern work from the Ginori factory.

In the **interior** constructed with the most ingenious technical devices (on the left hand pillars can be seen the trap-doors for emptying the grain from the store-room above, and above the small entrance-door, a model of a bushel-measure), is a series of frescoes and pictures dedicated to the Patron Saints of the Minor Guilds, dating from the 14th to the 16th century, and an altar dedicated to St. Anne (who liberated the city from the tyranny of

Andrea Orcagna: The Death of the Virgin.

the Duke of Athens) surmounted by a solemn marble group by Francesco da Sangallo, the *Virgin and Child with St. Anne* (c. 1526). But all these works of art are dominated by the **Tabernacle** of Andrea Orcagna (1335-59), an example of the highly decorative Gothic style which was in favour even in Florence in the middle of the 14th century. Architecture, sculpture and polychrome mosaics merge to create a whole which no longer follows the composed rhythm of Romanesque art, but a complicated and most erudite fantasy. The panels represent scenes, in low relief, of the *Life of the Virgin*; in the large relief, in the back, of the *Death and Assumption of the Virgin* is a portrait of Andrea (last figure on top right). The *painting* framed by the tabernacle is attributed to Bernardo Daddi. In Republican Florence the Madonna came to be considered as the « Lawyeress of the city » and before her image the Company of the « Laudesi » (praise singers) sang her daily praises.

Joined to Or San Michele by an overhead bridge, is the **Palazzo dell'Arte della Lana** (Palace of the Guild of Wool workers). Once the property of the Compiobbesi family, later it belonged to one of the richest Guilds, which had as its emblem the Lamb of God and ordered work in some twenty factories and commerce in more than two hundred shops. The building is of the 14th cent., spared from the destruction of the old centre, and restored with too much liberty (1905), while on the North side was reconstructed the *Tabernacle of Santa Maria della Tromba* (Bugle) formerly in the Piazza del Mercato Vecchio (Square of the Old Market), removed to make room for the modern Piazza della Repubblica. The fine painting is by Jacopo Landini, called del Casentino (d. 1349).

In the interior are various rooms formerly occupied by the Consoli (Councillors) of the Guild, with interesting remains of decorative frescoes of the 15th cent. Through the overhead bridge we reach the old Granary of the Republic. The two great halls, one above the other, have been recently restored and are architecturally very beautiful and interesting; art exhibitions are often held there.

Our first itinerary may be concluded with the nearby *Piazza della Repubblica*, formerly Piazza Vittorio Emanuele II. It used to be the centre of the Roman city, with Forum and Capitol. From medieval times, for centuries, it was the so-called Old Marked, round which ran a close network of extremely narrow streets in which stood the houses of the oldest families of the city (Medici, Brunelleschi, Sacchetti, Castiglioni, etc.) with 24 towers, ancient churches, Guildhalls tabernacles and loggias, some of them very beautiful. Shortly before 1890 everything was pulled down without discrimination, when for reasons of hygiene and, even more, from the desire for novelty the ancient centre was gutted to construct a quarter in an eclectic style devoid of character. The Ghetto disappeared, but with it were lost numberless buildings which could have provided successful contrast to the triumphant criteria of rectilinear symmetry. An airy « Loggia del Pesce » (Loggia of the Fish) by Vasari and the « Colonna dell'Abbondanza » (Column of Plenty) having been pulled down, the crossing of the Roman « cardi » was marked out and the plans made for the vast square with colonnades and the « Arcone » (Great Arch) on which a triumphant inscription was placed to record the transformation. Relics of the devastation are harboured in the Museum of San Marco and the works of art distributed in the other museums. The *Colonna dell'Abbondanza*, with its fine statue, was set up again in 1956 in the north-east corner of the Piazza.

Andrea Orcagna: The Assumption of the Virgin (Orsanmichele).

THE RELIGIOUS CENTRE OF THE CITY

Piazza del Duomo - Baptistery - Cathedral of Santa Maria del Fiore and Giotto's Campanile Museum of the Opera del Duomo - Church of San Lorenzo and Medicean Chapels - Laurenziana Library - Church of Santa Maria Maggiore.

PIAZZA DEL DUOMO

This time we will start the excursion from Piazza San Giovanni, religious centre of the city.

The **Baptistery,** or **Basilica of St. John the Baptist** is one of the most ancient sacred buildings in this centre, even if it did not arise, as the chronicles relate, on the ancient temple of Mars. Begun about the year Thousand, perhaps a rebuilding of a small pre-existing church of the 4th century, dedicated to the Saviour, it is an admirable and typical example of the Romanesque architecture in Tuscany, octagonal in plan, faced with marble, the white from Lunigiana, the green from Prato, roof like a camp tent. The progressive raising of the piazza, originally sunken, has slightly altered the proportions of the building. Three doors open to the cardinal points, with the rigorous orientation of the Roman street network; the west end of the church is closed by the rectangular apse, called « the pocket », of the 13th century. Considering that Baptism was originally administered only twice a year, one can explain the immense size of the Baptistery and the number of its doors. The lantern or « capannuccio », is thought to have been constructed to shut the opening in the centre of the roof, which is found in similar Roman buildings.

The exterior architecture is greatly enhanced in beauty by three enormous bronze doors, whose gilding lightens up in the exterior the composition and line of the marble, with

The Baptistery from the Campanile.

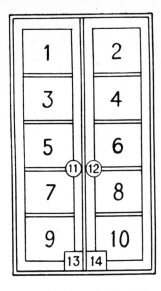

Ghiberti: details of the Door of Paradise: Abraham and the three Angels; the Creation of Eve.

DOOR OF PARADISE

Description of the panels.

1. The Creation of Adam and Eve; the first sin; Adam and Eve driven from the Garden of Eden. - 2. The first house, and the first human family; Cain and Abel offer sacrifices; Abel the shepherd, and Cain ploughing; Cain slays Abel; God rebukes Cain. - 3. The story of Noah: Noah and his family and the animals leave the Ark after the flood; Noah offers a sacrifice of thanksgiving; God sets the rainbow in the sky as a sign of reconciliation; Shem and Japhet leave the drunken Noah. - 4. The story of Abraham: Sarah at the entrance of the tent; Abraham welcomes the three Angels; Abraham sacrifices Isaac; the servants wait. - 5. The story of Jacob: Rebecca talks with God; Isaac sends Esau to the hunt; Jacob receives the blessing in Esau's place. - 6. The story of Joseph; at the top of the door he is drawn up from the pit and sold to the slave-merchants; he interprets Pharaoh's dream; he gathers in a supply of wheat against the threatened famine; the gold cup is discovered in Benjamin's sack; Joseph upon his throne makes himself known to his brothers; their departure; the meeting of Joseph and Jacob. - 7. The story of Moses: Moses receives the tables of the Law on Mount Sinai; the Israelites encamped at the foot of the Mountain. - 8. The Story of Joshua: Joshua at the taking of Jericho; the people pass the river Jordan dryfooted; they take up twelve stones in memory of the event; the hosts of Israel with the Ark of the Covenant and seven trumpeters compass the walls of Jericho for six days, the walls fall down on the seventh. - 9. The Story of Saul and David: fights with the Philistines; David cuts off the head of Goliath; he carries it, with the giant's arms to Jerusalem. - 10. Solomon's Temple; the Queen of Sheba visits Solomon. - 11. Portrait of Lorenzo Ghiberti. - 12. Portrait of Ghiberti's stepfather. - 13. 14. Young mother who leans out to kiss her son.

the same criterion as the internal gilding and the mosaics in the cupola.

The oldest *door* is the *south* one, by ANDREA DA PONTEDERA, called PISANO (1330-36), with the twenty condensed *stories of St. John the Baptist*, and the allegories of eight of the *cardinal and theological Virtues*. It was the first great monument of sculpture in Florence, and had an exceptional importance, for having excited the emulation of the city artisans, founding a local school which later flourished marvellously. The very rich doorposts, with branches and foliage, animals and angel's heads of refined workmanship, are by VITTORIO GHIBERTI, son of Lorenzo (1452-62). On the architrave, *St. John the Baptist, Herodias, and Carnifex* by VINCENZO DANTI (1571).

The *north door*, in compartments, is by LORENZO GHIBERTI (1403-24), and his wonderful assistants, Donatello, Bernardo Ciuffagni, Paolo Uccello, Bernardo Cennini, with *stories from the New Testament, Evangelists and Doctors*. The designing of this door was given to the very young master after an open competition (1402), in which Brunelleschi, Jacopo della Quercia and Niccolò d'Arezzo took part. It is an evident evolution from the lines and criterions of Andrea Pisano with a clear tendency towards a free naturalism. The doorposts are also by the same artist, the self portrait of whom can be seen in the central head of the left side of the door. On the architrave, *St. John the Baptist disputing with a Levite and a Pharisee*, by GIOVAN FRANCESCO RUSTICI (1506-11), under the influence of Leonardo da Vinci. Not far off, the **Columm of St. Zenobius,** in memory of an elm-tree which is alleged to have burst into flower as the body of the Saint passed by (429). Opposite, the little palace of the **Opera di San Giovanni**, with fifteenth century *doorway* and *statue of the Infant St. John* attributed to Michelozzo or Rossellino.

The *east door*, panelled, which Michelangelo said was worthy of Paradise, is the masterpiece of LORENZO GHIBERTI who flaunted there all his skill as a goldsmith and a pictorial and perspective sculptor (1425-52). Here are ten *Scenes from the Old Testament*, grouped according to the themes given by Leonardo Bruni, chancellor of the Republic. Between the panels, 24 statuettes of *Prophets* and *Sybils*, of most lively expression, and 24 *portraits*, among which that of the artist (fourth from the top in the middle band, to the left) and of

MOSAICS OF THE CUPOLA

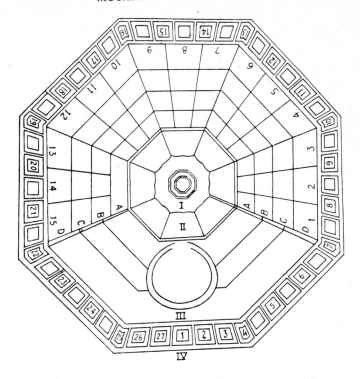

I - Decoration of vine branches and small heads.
II - God the Creator and the Celestial Hierarchies.
III - Universal Judgment. In the centre: *Christ the Judge.*
    Upper band: *Angels of the Judgment.*
    Middle band: *The Madonna, St. John the Baptist, Apostles and Saints.*
    Lower band: *Resurrection of the Dead*; on the left, *Paradise* (Cimabue); on the
    right, *Hell.*
A - Stories from the Genesis: from the Creation to the Flood.
B - Stories of the Patriarch Joseph.
C - Stories of Mary and Jesus.
D - Stories of St. John the Baptist.
IV - Panels of the band between the matroneum and the cupola (1-27): Saints and
    Deacons.

his step-father, and his assistants, who were Michelozzo, Benozzo Gozzoli, Bernardo Cennini. Doorposts by the same Ghiberti, very fine, ornamented with flowers, branches and animals. On the architrave, *Baptism of Jesus* by ANDREA SANSOVINO (1502) with an *Angel* by INNOCENZO SPINAZZI. At the sides of the door, two porphyry columns taken by the Pisans from the Saracens of the Balearic Isles, and given to the Florentines who had guarded their city (1117), object of pleasing legends about the secular battle for the conquest of Pisa.

Inside - Above an order of Corinthian columns of oriental granite, with gilded capitals, runs a double arched balcony. In the floor, embellished with a variety of intarsia, we must notice a square compartment with the signs of the Zodiac. Against the walls, the *Magdalen*, by DONATELLO (about 1460), the *Sepulchre of the Antipope John XXIII*, who died in Florence shortly after his resignation of the triple crown (1419), by DONATELLO with the help of Pagno Portigiani and Michelozzo (1420-27).

The **Cupola**, all splendidly decorated in mosaic, in horizontal bands, with the *celestial Hierarchies, Stories from the Genesis, Stories of the Patriarch Joseph, Stories of Mary and Jesus, Stories of St. John the Baptist*, all depicting to human kind the trial of the *Universal Justice* imparted by *Christ the Judge*. For this work, Venetian-byzantine mosaic-workers were called to Florence, and further generations of artists worked there: BROTHER JACOPO DA TORRITA (1225-28), ANDREA DI RICCO, called TAFO, GADDO GADDI, CIMABUE, APOLLONIO GRECO, AGNOLO GADDI, etc. The iconography of Florentine painting had in these mosaics the prototypes which were followed for more than two centuries.

Interior of the Baptistery.

Mosaic of the Baptistery: Joseph meeting his Father.

THE DUOMO or SANTA MARIA DEL FIORE

The city cathedral until the middle of the 11th cent., was San Giovanni, which later became the Baptistery. In the 10th century, there was built, opposite San Giovanni, the church of Santa Reparata, cathedral of the city, but the church proved inadequate when the Republic flourished under the Guelph regime. For that reason, in 1294 they thought of making a new church, on the site of the old one, but much larger and more splendid. The work of it was entrusted to ARNOLFO DI CAMBIO, who demolished houses, as had been done for the Palazzo della Signoria, and laid the first stone on the 8th of September 1296. The construction of the great church proceeded slowly. Thirthy-three years after the death of Arnolfo (1301), the direction of the work was taken by GIOTTO (1334-37), then ANDREA PISANO (1337-48), then FRANCESCO TALENTI, first alone (1349-59), and later together with GIOVANNI GHINI (1360-69), and only in this period a definite model of the construction was approved (1368), which was executed by successive master-masons with fidelity, notwith-

Detail of the right side of the Cathedral.

standing tempestuous changes, wars, plagues and the subsequent endless famines. In 1420 BRUNELLESCHI gave the designs for the execution of the cupola, and finally, on the 25th of March 1436 the temple could be consecrated, even before the closing lantern was built. The construction of the church had occupied, then, a good 140 years, and the various phases of its development can be followed on the exterior proceeding from the façade towards the apse. But the façade, begun by Arnolfo di Cambio and carried on by Talenti, was left unfinished. The existing part (about a third of the height from the ground) was demolished in 1588 and for centuries there were proposed and repeated attempts to solve the difficult architectural problem. Only in 1875 was the present design of EMILIO DE FABRIS approved, coldly imitating in laudable measure the 14th century style, but with the fatal, mannered carvings of the 19th century taste. To date the Gallery of the drum of the Cupola remains incomplete. BACCIO D'AGNOLO (1506-15) had begun the construction of it, which was later letf off, because, they believe, of a judgment of Michelangelo, who likened it to a « cage of crickets ».

Proceeding to the right of the Campanile, around the great structure, to admire the sides of the Cathedral, we have a view which allows us to appreciate the complex of harmonious majesty, of the apse and the cupola above it.

Nanni di Banco: St. Luke and Arnolfo di Cambio: Boniface VIII (Museum of the Opera del Duomo).

Opposite the right side, on the *Palazzo della Canonica* two statues were placed in 1830, representing the two greatest architects of the Cathedral: *Arnolfo di Cambio* and *Filippo Brunelleschi*, by LUIGI PAMPALONI. A little further on, a stone, called *Dante's Stone*, marks the place where popular tradition says Dante sat watching the construction works, just begun (1294-1302). Passing into *Via dello Studio*, one can see the façade of the *Casa di Sant'Antonino*, where the popular Archbishop of the city was born (1st March 1389), and further on the old seat of the *Studio*, or the glorious theological University of Florence, dependent upon ecclesiastical authority (1348). Behind the apse of the Cathedral, opens the **Museum of the Opera del Duomo** with a bust on the door, which is the best portrait of *Cosimo I* (1572) by GIOVANNI BANDINI, called DELL'OPERA.

In this Museum, which it is advisable to visit before the interior of the Cathedral, are gathered remains of Romanesque sculpture, statues and architectural pieces coming from the old façade and the structure of the Cathedral and the Baptistery. On the ground floor, of great interest are the statues by ARNOLFO DI CAMBIO, the first master-mason of the Cathedral (d. 8th March 1301), or from his workshop, among which the great figure, with arm raised in blessing, of *Boniface VIII*, the Pope fervently opposed by Dante, who announced the first regular Jubilee in 1300. Here is also to be seen the magnificent statue of *St. Luke* by NANNI DI BANCO formerly in the Cathedral. In the adjoining room on the right were exhibited some beautiful illuminated *liturgical books* most of which were badly damaged by the flood of November 1966 and are being restored at present. From this room there is access to a small chapel containing the most precious *Reliquaries* from the Treasury of the Cathedral.

On the first floor, in the large central room, are the two *Choir-lofts* which until 1688 were over the doors of the two Sacristies in the Cathedral: the one by DONATELLO (1433-38) with its most lively dancing children, and the other by LUCA DELLA ROBBIA (1431-38) with its graceful, serene singing youths. Here are also the statues which were formerly in the niches on the Campanile, among which the magnificent ones by DONATELLO, representing *Habakkuk*, *Jeremiah* and two other *Prophets*.

In the room on the right may be seen the very precious *Altar of St. John the Baptist*, in silver and enamels, for the making of which there worked for more than a century (1367-1480) about ten of the best Florentine goldsmith-sculptors, among whom were MICHELOZZO, VERROCCHIO, ANTONIO DEL POLLAIOLO and BERNARDO CENNINI. On either sides of the altar are two fine 15th cent. statues representing the *Virgin Annunciate* and the *Archangel Gabriel*. Other interesting works of art are exhibited in this room; we should note: the magnificent strips of embroidery representing *twentyseven episodes in the life of the Baptist* which were done by several embroiderers at the end of the 15th cent. on designs of ANTONIO DEL POLLAIOLO; two panels with *Scenes from the Life of Christ and the Virgin*, a rare Byzantine mosaic work of the early 14th cent.; two marble statuettes of the *Redeemer* and a *female Saint* by ANDREA PISANO.

Donatello: detail from the Choir-loft in the Museum of the Opera del Duomo.

In the room on the left we may see the original bas-reliefs of the lower zone of the Campanile which have been brought here to prevent their utter deterioration.

Continuing round the Cathedral, before *Via dei Servi*, a bust records the spot where was Donatello's workshop, together with Michelozzo, after 1443. On the left side of the Cathedral opens the very lovely *Door of the Mandorla,* so called from the almond-shaped glory frame in which is shut the *Madonna taken up into Heaven* who gives her belt to St. Thomas the Apostle, low-relief, left unfinished by NANNI DI BANCO (1414-21), and finished by Donatello (1422), one of the very first expressions of the local sculptural Renaissance. The mosaic in the lunette, with the *Annunciation* is by DOMENICO DEL GHIRLANDAIO.

Interior of the Cathedral (148 × 38 m.; at the transept, 94 m.). The first impression is one of a somewhat squalid majesty. The solemn Gothic construction does not allure with any pleasantness or decorative preciousness. And this is the value of Santa Maria del Fiore; and the merit of the Florentine who wanted to give to, and maintain, in the house of God the bare solemnity of pure architecture, forbidding, after 1440, that sepulchres of laymen should be made there without the deliberation of the Consuls of the Wood Guild and of the « Operai »: an architecture which has the thrust of the Gothic arch, the strength of the pillars and the grandeur of the vaults curved with great boldness, without having however, of the

Gothic, all those decorative trifles — statuettes, tracery, floral motifs — which often makes it tiresome. Here we must admire the pure architectural line, the curves of the arches, the solidity of the pillars, the vast extent of the vaulting on which finally rests Brunelleschi's bold cupola, showing that this is one of the most expressive churches in Christianity. The works of art almost disappear in this majestic and very simple space.

The three round windows piercing the façade were made from cartoons by LORENZO GHIBERTI (1404-13). The clock in the middle, with four heads of *Prophets*, was painted in fresco by PAOLO UCCELLO (1443). In the lunette of the doorway, *Coronation of the Virgin*, mosaic attributed to GADDO GADDI (14th cent.). On the right of the principal door is the fine *tomb of Bishop Antonio d'Orso* (d. 1321), work of TINO DI CAMAINO, Sienese, who erected it in memory of the Commander of the defences against the imperial army of Henry VII, in the Autumn of 1312.

Right aisle, entrance to the vault of the old Cathedral of Santa Reparata of the 4th, 5th century, recently discovered, built on Roman remains, altered during the 8th century, definitely buried afterwards under the present Cathedral. Of great interest are the Roman fragments of decorative marbles, the floors and the decorations painted on plaster which have come to light.

First bay: *Bust of Brunelleschi,* by his disciple and heir Andrea Cavalcanti called BUGGIANO (1447), with inscription by the chancellor Carlo Marsuppini. Wooden tabernacle with statue of the *Prophet Isaiah* by NANNI DI BANCO (1408). Medallion with bust of *Giotto,* by BENEDETTO DA MAIANO (1490), with epigraph by Poliziano. Third and fourth bay: *stained glass windows* from cartoons by AGNOLO GADDI (1395). Bust of the philosopher *Marsilio Ficino* (d. 1499), by ANDREA FERRUCCI (1521).

The interior of the Cathedral.

Michelangelo: Deposition.

Cupola - The prodigious, « terrible » undertaking of the covering of the vast octagon designed in its exterior lines since 1367, together with the final model of all the church, could only have been accomplished by merit of the master-mason Brunelleschi, nominated in 1420. His concept to construct two vaults which would be built without timber-work, was derived from the study of the constructive system of the roof of the Baptistery, genially developed; the outside vault, more sloping, is connected with the inside, rather flatter one, by a most rational system of spurs, vaults and rings, tending to reduce the thrust upon the vertical line. The ascent to the cupola enables one to realize the marvellous solution of a new and very serious technical problem, which is the glory of our architect. The diameter of the drum at the beginning of the curve of the vault is 45 m. 50 cm. and exactly double is the height of the cupola up to the foot of the lantern, which, designed by Brunelleschi, reveals its marvellous architectural and functional perfection, above all when one climbs up to the cupola. The inside surface is covered by the lugubrious fresco representing the *Last Judgment*, after the invention of Don Vincenzo Borghini, on the execution of which GIORGIO VASARI (1572-74) worked for two years, until his death; FEDERICO ZUCCARI with other pupils of his (1574-79) worked for five years to finish it. The merely decorative effect of an exceptionally vast and distant surface, so far away, explains, if it does not justify the dullness of the execution of the work, which, seen closely, is only too easily censurable. The eyes of the drum have windows executed from cartoons of GHIBERTI (*Presentation in the Temple, Prayer in the Garden of Gethsemane, Ascension*, c. 1425), of DONATELLO (*Coronation of the Virgin*, 1434), of PAOLO UCCELLO (*Resurrection, Nativity*, 1444), of ANDREA DEL CASTAGNO (*Deposition*, 1444). Below, marble tabernacles with sixteenth century statues of *Apostles*. In the middle, the marble **Choir** designed by BACCIO BANDINELLI, with *figures in low-relief* by the same artist and by GIOVANNI DELL'OPERA. On the high altar, designed by GIULIANO DI BACCIO D'AGNOLO, is a dramatic *Crucifix* by BENEDETTO DA MAIANO.

Over the doors of the *Sacristies*, lunettes by LUCA DELLA ROBBIA. That of the *Resurrection* (over the door of the *New Sacristy*, on the left) was the first experiment (1444) of sculpture glazed in colours, which was one of the pleasing creations of Florentine Renaissance art. The *bronze door* under this lunette is also a work of LUCA DELLA ROBBIA with the collaboration of Michelozzo and Maso di Bartolomeo. It was in this Sacristy that Lorenzo the Magnificent saved himself, on the 26th of April 1478, escaping from the stabs of the conspirators who assassinated his brother Giuliano.

In the *chapel of the end of the apse*, dedicated to St. Zenobius, *bronze urn* with the relics of the Saint, work of LORENZO GHIBERTI (1432-42) with *Scenes from the Life of the Saint* and, on the back very fine figures of *flying angels*. In all the chapels of the apse as well as in those of the transepts we should notice the beautiful *stained glass windows* made in the 15th century from cartoons by GHIBERTI.

In the first chapel on the right of the left transept is the dramatic, unfinished *Deposition* of MICHELANGELO, the most notable work of art in the whole Cathedral. In the centre of the floor of this transept is the *Gnomon*, the largest and most exact sundial known. It was laid out, about 1468, by the Florentine astronomer and mathematician Paolo dal Pozzo Toscanelli, to show the Summer solstice, with the sun-rays coming from a conical opening in the lantern of the cupola.

Left aisle, fourth bay: *Dante with the Divine Comedy shedding light on Florence; Hell, Purgatory and Paradise*; this painting by DOMENICO DI MICHELINO after a design of Alesso Baldovinetti was the strange monument in honour of the poet — a tardy means to repair the cruel sectarian condemnation — decreed by the Republic in 1465. Among the most outstanding artists of the 15th century are Paolo Uccello, a very fascinating personality who unites the vivacity of the Gothic style to the monumentality of classical art, and Andrea del Castagno, a painter of rather harsh but very powerful and sculpturesque quality. In the third bay we see an *Equestrian statue* painted by PAOLO UCCELLO (1436), to honour the English general *Giovanni Acuto* (*Hawkwood*), bloody and cruel enemy of the Republic, who then passed over to serve it faithfully until 1394; and that of *Niccolò Marrucci da Tolentino* painted by ANDREA DEL CASTAGNO (1456), both frescoes transferred on to canvas. The *stained-glass windows* in the fourth and third bay were made

Andrea del Castagno: Niccolò Marrucci da Tolentino.

from cartoons by AGNOLO GADDI (1395). Second bay: *bust of Antonio Squarcia-lupi*, organ builder, by BENEDETTO DA MAIANO (1490), with epigraph attributed to Poliziano. First bay: Medallion with *bust of Arnolfo di Cambio*, by ULISSE CAMBI (1843), and *bust of Emilio de Fabris*, architect of the façade, by VIN-CENZO CONSANI (1887). In the middle, statue of *Joshua*, the work of Donatello, Bernardo Ciuffagni and Nanni di Bartolo and said to be the portrait of the humanist Poggio Bracciolini.

The *marble flooring* was executed on designs attributed to BACCIO D'AGNOLO and FRANCESCO DA SANGALLO (1520-1526).

Excavations have been recently made under the floor and many remains of the foundations of the old 10th cent. cathedral of Santa Reparata have been found. Visitors will be able to climb down and see them as soon as the works of excavation and restoration will be finished.

It is advisable to climb up (463 steps) and walk round the internal gallery, entering between the two vaults of the *cupola* and coming out on the *Lantern of Brunelleschi* from which one overlooks the most wide panorama of the city and surrounding country.

Nomad pastoral life (relief of the Campanile).

The art of working metals (relief of the Campanile).

Returning to Piazza San Giovanni, we now give our attention to the **Campanile,** called Giotto's bell-tower, (1334-1387), of really marvellous harmony and elegance, conceived in a way that, going from the fulness of the base to the successive bands, always with more windows, the construction seems to become lighter and stretch up, without effort or heaviness. The colourful harmony of the marble, the white from Lunigiana, the red from Siena and the black-green from Prato, accentuates the impression of lightness which rises from the lines of the plan. The base was laid out on the foundations three years before the death of Giotto (1337); it is decorated with hexagonal panels with the representations in fabulous and allegorical symbols of the *Mechanical and Practical Activities of the Work of Man,* following upon the loss of the free idleness of the earthly Paradise: they are by ANDREA DA PONTEDERA and LUCA DELLA ROB-

BIA, probably upon designs by Giotto. The second band is more soberly decorated with rhomboidal panels with symbolic figures of the *Planets*, of the *Virtues*, of the *Liberal Arts* and the *Sacraments*, showing the astral, intellectual and supernatural influences which dominate and regulate human activity, to direct it towards the final end of obedience, and the glorification of the Creator. They were sculptured by various artists of the 14th century. The reliefs we see here, however, are copies of the originals. These have been brought to the Museum of the Opera del Duomo to preserve them from utter deterioration. Above the Giottesque base, fully crowded with decoration, rises the band of TALENTI (1349-59), later (1419-36) decorated with 16 niches, where used to be the *Prophets* and *Sibyls* by DONATELLO, NANNI DI BARTOLO and others, which are now in the Museum of the Opera del Duomo, and which expressed the prophecies, the revelations and the testimonies of the divine Revelation on the destiny of the human race. Here the sculptural decoration ends, and the bands which follow, first with double-arched windows, then with triple-arched ones, the work of TALENTI (1384-1460), give the bell-tower an extreme lightness and finished elegance.

The bell-tower, which in the early project should have ended in a point, is crowned by a balustrade and covered by a flat roof. It is about 82 meters high. One can climb to the top, using 414 marble steps.

Returning to the Piazza, we see on the corner of *Via Calzaioli* the **Loggia of the Bigallo.** Religious piety would be sterile if it did not produce works of mercy. And the name of Santa Maria della Misericordia is that of a Florentine confraternity instituted in 1240 by Saint Peter Martyr, but which legend says was founded by Piero Borsi, porter of the Wool Guild, in 1325, for the assistance of the sick and wounded, and for the burial of the dead. It is, therefore, the prototype of the humanitarian associations for the help of invalids. From this, the international Red Cross had its origin, during the Crimean war, through the initiative of Fiorence Nightingale. The little palace, unique of its kind, with large protruding gutter, charming, double-arched windows and a most elegant *Loggia* in Florentine Gothic style was once the seat of the Misericordia confraternity. It was built between

1352 and '58, perhaps by the painter and sculptor ALBERTO ARNOLDI, master of the Opera del Duomo. By the same artist are the statues of the *Madonna and two Angels* in a large Renaissance tabernacle, behind a railing at the back of the loggia. This was used to expose to the public lost or abandoned children. Since 1425 this little palace was the seat of the *Compagnia del Bigallo*, another charitable association, which takes care of the orphans.

On the façade, three tabernacles with statues of the Pisan school of the 14th cent.: the *Madonna and Child* in the middle, *Saint Peter Martyr* on one side, *Saint Lucy* on the other. Remains of a fifteenth century fresco with *Stories of Saint Peter Martyr*. In the lunette over the door, low relief by ALBERTO ARNOLDI: *Madonna with Child* (1361). Once the loggia was entirely frescoed. To prevent the paintings deteriorat-

Partial view of the church of San Lorenzo.

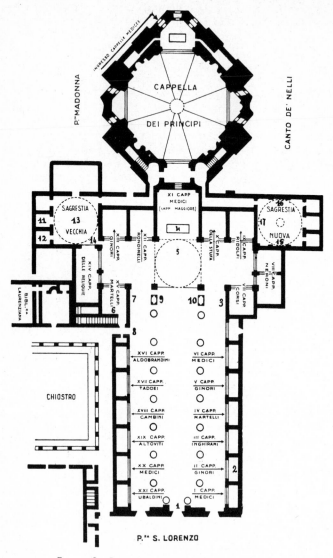

PLAN OF SAN LORENZO AND OF THE MEDICEAN CHAPELS.

ing they were taken down, and can now be seen in the old *Council Hall*. Of particular interest is that of the *Madonna of Mercy*, in which is a synthetic view of the city in 1352.

On the other corner of Via Calzaioli, is the present seat of the **Archconfraternity of the Misericordia**, which for four centuries has exercised its continuous work of Christian charity. There is always there a squad of brothers cloaked in black, ready to rush at any call for help, covered by the hood which hides their piety, being rewarded by the phrase in the ritual: « God give you the merit for it ». It is certainly the most characteristic and the most beloved of all Florentine institutions. In the hall one can admire a very beautiful *Madonna* by BENEDETTO DA MAIANO and *two praying Angels* from the workshop of the Della Robbia. In an adjoining room, another sculpture by BENEDETTO DA MAIANO, the statue of *St. Sebastian*, the patron saint of the confraternity. In the Oratory is a large altar-piece by ANDREA DELLA ROBBIA, the *Madonna with Child and Saints*.

On the other side of the Baptistery is the **Archiepiscopal Palace** with a very fine *courtyard* by GIOVAN ANTONIO DOSIO (1573-84), and behind it is the small façade of **San Salvatore del Vescovo**, one of the typical Romanesque façades of the city, with marble decoration, of 1221.

Near the northern corner of the Archbishop's palace once opened the *Bishop's gate*, or *gate « Contra Aquilonem »*, of the first ring of walls. In fact the houses built along the street which begins here, were called Borgo (suburb) and *Borgo*

Interior of the church of San Lorenzo.

San Lorenzo is still the name of the street. On the corner, remains of a typical civil building of the fourteenth century. Going down the crowded **Borgo**, once full of artisans' workshops, and now with shops, we come to the

CHURCH OF SAN LORENZO

On the piazza surrounded by high *palaces,* among which the *Lotteringhi della Stufa*, with columned loggia, is the ugly *statue of Giovanni dalle Bande Nere*, work of BACCIO BANDINELLI, also author of the fine base (1540).

For long outside the first circle of the walls, like the homonymous Roman basilica, San Lorenzo is of very ancient origin, and is the sacred building of the Christian city of which we have the oldest dated record. It was consecrated by St. Ambrose, Bishop of Milan, in 393. Rebuilt in Romanesque style and reconsecrated in 1060, it was probably the cathedral church for some time. In 1423 Giovanni di Bicci de' Medici, who had his palace near the church, entrusted FILIPPO BRUNELLESCHI with the task of rebuilding it in splendid fashion. The works continued from 1425 to 1446, at the

Tomb of the Duke of Urbino (detail).

expense of Giovanni, and later of his son Cosimo. With the death of Brunelleschi, the direction of the works passed to ANTONIO MANETTI the elder, until 1460, then to his son Antonio. Meanwhile San Lorenzo was becoming almost the Medici family church, in which many members took the name of Lorenzo. And once again by the Medici, MICHELANGELO BUONARROTI was employed to construct the internal façade, the New Sacristy and the Library, besides making a project for the façade, which was never executed. The large and very fine church so became the sepulchre of the Medici family, and the Grand Dukes added there their pompous Cappella dei Principi.

Interior - The three naves, divided by Corinthian columns on which rest delicate arches, are the most perfect result of the serene colourful harmony and of the elegant architectural linear rythm of Brunelleschi. The coffered ceiling on a white background, with gilded rosettes, the transverse vaults, the shallow chapels, the cornices in blue-grey stone give the church a calm and extremely clear tone. We are face to face with one of the master-pieces of Florentine Renaissance architecture, the harmony of which is founded solely upon design and the two elementary colour-notes of the plastering and the stone.

Filippo Lippi: Annunciation.

Donatello: Crucifixion.

The **inside façade** with the balcony and three doors, between two pilasters with festoons of oak and laurel held up by Medicean rings with diamond points, was built from the design of MICHELANGELO to exhibit to the public the relics preserved in the Sacristy.

The works of art are few and well distributed, giving no sense of overcrowding or of confusion. On the altar of the **second chapel on the right** *Marriage of Mary* by ROSSO FIORENTINO (1523), imposing experiment of the local pictorial manner, called the manner of the « cangiantisti », from the use of colours changing and graduating in the stuffs. At the **end of the right aisle,** the very beautiful *tabernacle* by DESIDERIO DA SETTIGNANO, with admirable details, which fixed the liturgical style, and was the sculptural prototype of innumerable tabernacles of the Italian Renaissance from Lombardy to Sicily. Turning into the right transept, we notice in the chapel on the right an early Christian sarcophagus which contains the mortal remains of the 17th century Danish naturalist and anatomist Niels Stensen (called in Italy Nicola Stenone); on the altar, 16th cent. painting with the *Adoration of the Child and Saints.* On the **high altar,** of semiprecious stones (1787), a marble *Crucifix* by the sixteenth century artist BACCIO DA MONTELUPO. In front of the Main Chapel, three gratings with coats-of-arm, mark the place of the crypt beneath where *Cosimo the Elder* (1464) is buried, and the inscription, destroyed and renewed, attributes to him the classic title of « Pater Patriae », officially decreed him. From the steps of the high altar one can see the superb spectacle of the basilica, and the harmony of Brunelleschi's architecture with Michelangelo's façade. In the **left wing,** on the altar of the last Chapel, *Annunciation* by FILIPPO LIPPI, one of the most brilliant and picturesque compositions of its type, with the background of a charming little garden, and predella with very lively *Stories of Saint Nicholas of Bari* (1425). On the wall, the *tomb of Donatello* (buried in the vault), by the nineteenth century artists Guidotti and Romanelli.

Opening the door, one is astonished by the corresponding atmosphere of the landscape in the painting by Lippi with the view of the cloister and its vegetation, in a whole of graciousness and singular solemnity. In the same chapel is a *marble sarcophagus*, attributed to DONATELLO. In this chapel of the Martelli family, the second wife of Cosimo I should be buried whom her step-son harshly kept away from the court, because she was not sufficiently noble.

Left aisle: *Martyrdom of Saint Lawrence*, pompous fresco of AGNOLO BRON-ZINO, which has been much discussed (1569), and which is one of many works badly influenced by the Universal Judgment of Michelangelo; marble *choir-loft* on design by DONATELLO (1443).

Under the two last arches of the **central nave,** the two wonderful, original *Pulpits* with the bronze panels representing *Scenes from the Passion,* begun during DONATELLO's old age, and finished by his assistants BERTOLDO DI GIOVANNI and BARTOLOMEO BELLANO. Coming back to the end of the transept, we enter, on the left, the

Old Sacristy - Three of the greatest artists made of this sacristy per-haps the most precious jewel of the Renaissance. Brunelleschi gave it the original composition of a severe architecture; Donatello decorated it with low-reliefs; Verrocchio completed its beauty.

It is a small place, square in plan, covered by a cupola with a lantern. BRUNELLESCHI, freed from the traditional plan of the Latin cross, then conse-crated for liturgical use, was able to create here, for the first time, his archi-tectural idea of a perfect plan (1420-29). DONATELLO decorated the splays and the

Donatello: Bust of St. Lawrence (detail).

lunettes of the little cupola with medallions of coloured stucco representing the four *Evangelists* and four *stories of St. John the Evangelist*. Donatello also modelled the beautiful terracotta *bust of Saint Lawrence* (about 1440), and over the right door, the *Doctor Saints Cosmas and Damian;* over the left door, *St. Lawrence and St. Stephen*. The two doorways and the bronze door-wings with *Martyrs* (on the left), *Apostles* and *Doctors of the Church* (on the right) are also by Donatello. The little **apse** repeats the architectural motifs of the sacristy; the altar and the fine balustrade were probably made after designs of Donatello; from his workshop, finished by Verrocchio is the *Lavabo* which can be admired in the little room on the left.

We now come to the *Medici tombs*, the first of which were actually built in this Sacristy. Under the marble table in the middle, Cosimo the Elder had a *Sarcophagus* placed, worked by ANDREA CAVALCANTI (1434), for his own parents, Giovanni di Bicci (d. 1428) and Piccarda Bueri (d. 1433). Cosimo the Elder, instead, was buried in the vault under the transept of the church, as we have seen. His sons, Giovanni and Piero lie in the marvellous porphyry *Sarcophagus* worked by VERROCCHIO (1472), placed between the Sacristy and the Chapel of the Relics, under a decorated arch, closed in by a most original bronze tracery. The completely profane phantasy of the various decorative parts, and the perfect execution confirm the supposition that the greater part of the work was imagined and completed by Leonardo da Vinci, charming carver of foliage, who was in Verrocchio's workshop as a pupil and collaborator from 1470 to 77. To contain the bodies of the other members of the Medici family, MICHELANGELO was charged (1520) with the building of the

New Sacristy, which is on the side opposite the Old Sacristy. (Once one could enter it from the church, but now one must go round, outside the right wall of the church, entering by the special entrance). As an analogy it is called a Sacristy, but really it is a sepulchral chapel, square in plan, and covered by a cupola (1524). Comparing the two Sacristies, one can understand the diversity

Donatello: The Apostles (door-wings in the Old Sacristy).

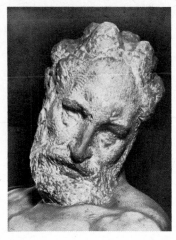

Michelangelo: details from the Madonna and « Twilight » in the New Sacristy.

between two of the greatest architects. Brunelleschi serene and elegant; Michelangelo solemn and tragic. The whiteness of the marble parts contrasts with the vigourous stone framing, and the statues accentuate the shadows, giving it all an austere and melancholic beauty.

In the wall, on the right going in, were interred, in 1495, the bodies of the two brothers, sons of Piero di Cosimo, *Giuliano*, assassinated in the Pazzi conspiracy (1478), and *Lorenzo* called *the Magnificent* (d. 1492). MICHELANGELO did not finish the sepulchre and for them sculptured only the *Madonna with Child* (1521), giving to Brother G. A. DA MONTORSOLI the job of sculpting the *Saint Cosmas* (1533), and to RAFFAELLO DA MONTELUPO the *Saint Damian*. The group of the Madonna shows traces of the uncertain work of the artist who began work on the marble without having taken the exact measurements, and so lacked the material for the right arm of the Madonna. The other two sepulchres were for another two Giuliano and Lorenzo, not to be confused, however, with the famous grandsons of Cosimo. *Lorenzo, duke of Urbino*, (d. 1519) whom Michelangelo has represented in meditative attitude (so called « the Thinker »), was son of Piero the Foolish, son of Lorenzo the Magnificent. (Piero the Foolish, thrown out of Florence, died by drowning in the Liri, 1503, and his tomb was in the basilica of Montecassino). On the sarcophagus of Duke Lorenzo are the two symbolic figures of *Dawn* and *Twilight*. *Giuliano, duke of Nemours*, whom Michelangelo has portrayed with breastplate and baton of command, was the third son of Lorenzo the Magnificent, the Giulianino of the family, tender and poetical, who died young (1479-1515). At his feet are the symbolic figures of *Day* and *Night*. The figure of Night, finished after the collapse of Florentine liberty (1531) provoked the well known verses of praise of the poet G. B. Strozzi, to which Michelangelo answered with a celebrated quatrain in which he alluded to the « damage and the shame » of the country. The significance of the attitude of the allegorical figures is much discussed.

The concept may be that Time, symbolised by the four reclining figures, dominates everything and destroys Thought and Action in men.

After 1568 Cosimo I, Grand Duke of Tuscany, arranged for Vasari to build a new Chapel behind the choir of the basilica, as a sepulchre for the Medici. They were no longer members of a very powerful family, but already rulers of the city: so the great construction added to the apse of the church of San Lorenzo took the name of **Chapel of the Princes**. The design made by the natural brother of the Grand Duke, don Giovanni, was executed and elaborated by the architect MATTEO NIGETTI. It is a large octagon sheathed with precious marbles and semi-precious stones, prevalently dark in tone, and decorated with gilded bronzes. The general effect is of funereal pomp, and of a dead richness. The profusion of precious stones worked in the « Opificio delle Pietre Dure », fully in activity during the Medicean Grand Duchy, makes this architectonic work, only recently finished (1938), a real coffer of jewels. In the plinth of the chapel stand out the *sixteen coats-of-arms of the Grand-ducal Cities*, work done in semi-precious stones, mother-of-pearl, coral and lapislazuli. Round about, six great monuments in Egyptian granite, in green Corsican jasper, in grey oriental granite dedicated to the memory of the Grand Dukes buried in the crypt beneath: *Ferdinando II* (d. 1670); *Cosimo II* (d. 1620); *Ferdinando I* (d. 1609); *Cosimo I* (d. 1574); *Francesco I* (d. 1587); *Cosimo III* (d. 1723). Those of Cosimo II and Ferdinando I are surmounted by gilt bronze statues by PIETRO and FERDINANDO TACCA. The *cupola* was vividly frescoed by the Neoclassical painter PIETRO BENVENUTI (1828), with scenes from the *Old and New Testament* and figures of the *Precursor*, of *three Prophets*, and of the *Evangelists*. In the *small room near the altar*, are precious reliquaries of inestimable value.

Michelangelo: « Dawn ».

Michelangelo: « Night » (detail).

Laurenziana Library. - Through the door on the left of the façade of the church we enter the *Cloister* in the style of Brunelleschi, and ascending a stairway, we come to the Laurentian Library, founded by Cosimo the Elder, enlarged by Lorenzo, from whom it took its name. On the expulsion of the Medici in 1494, the collection of precious manuscript codices bought at a high price all over Europe by Niccolò Niccoli, by Lascaris, by Vespasiano da Bisticci, was confiscated by the Signoria, and was liable to be dispersed. The Dominicans saved it, redeeming it with a large sum of money collected in Florence, and transferred it to the Convent of St. Mark. Cardinal Giovanni dei Medici, later Pope Leo X, bought it back, transferring it to Rome. But another Medici pope, Clement VII, restored it to Florence, entrusting MI-CHELANGELO (1523) to construct the building, which is a most beautiful example of the majestic style, already preannouncing the Baroque, and matching well the lines of the New Sacristy, and in evolutionary harmony with the Basilica and the Old Sacristy of Brunelleschi. In the *Vestibule,* with double, well-bracketed, projecting columns, in the *Staircase,* by AM-

MANNATI (1559), the grey stone from the quarry of Fossato, is treated with plastic strength.

In the great **Hall,** destined to house the codices, Michelangelo, perhaps not to interrupt che atmosphere of meditation, kept to the most simple lines, though always with solemn majesty. Everything there has been executed after his designs: the *carved ceiling,* by GIOVAN BATTISTA DEL TASSO and ANTONIO CAROTA; the 88 *plutei,* with benches carved by CIAPINO and BATTISTA DEL CINQUE, both famous artisans. The *flooring* itself, designed by Niccolò Pericoli, called the TRIBOLO, follower of Michelangelo, repeats the motives of the ceiling, and was executed by the last craftsman from the Della Robbia workshop, SANTI BUGLIONI. The *glass window-panes* in two colours were designed by GIOVANNI DA UDINE.

The precious things collected in this library are of inestimable value. Among the most famous, a *Virgil* of the 5th century, a *Syriac Book of the Gospels* of 586, the *Pandects of Justinian* of 533, a *Greek Book of the Gospels* of the 10th century, *Dante's Comedy* transcribed by Filippo Villani, the *Codex of the Biadaiolo* (fodder merchant) of the 14th century, a *Decameron* of 1384, a *Horace* with annotations by Petrarch, the *Parchment of the Council of Florence* (1439), *Choir book* with miniatures by ATTAVANTE and LORENZO MONACO, *Psaltery of King Matthew Corvinus* with miniatures by MONTE and GHERARDO DEL FORA, *Prayer-book of Lorenzo the Magnificent* with miniatures by FRANCESCO DEL CHIERICO, *City of Life* by MATTEO PALMIERI, *Notes* of LEONARDO DA VINCI; a valuable collection of autographs, from Petrarch to Napoleon Bonaparte; a collection of port-guides and navigation charts.

In the nineteenth century the architect PASQUALE POCCIANTI added the *Round Room* (1841) for the library bequeathed by Count Angiolo d'Elci, to which was added the stock of Ashburnian manuscripts obtained from the nineteenth century historian Pasquale Villari.

Santa Maria Maggiore. - Going round the side of San Lorenzo around the massive walls of the Chapel of the Princes, we reach *Piazza Madonna degli Aldobrandini,* where is the fine *Riccardi Mannelli Palace,* of the 16th cent., with *bust of the Grand Duke Francesco I* by GIOVANNI BANDINI, called DELL'OPERA, over the entrance doorway. We go down *via dei Conti,* keeping to the right, and come into *via dei Cerretani,* at the side of *Santa Maria Maggiore,* another very ancient church of the old circle of walls, which preserves traces of the first Romanesque construction of the 10th century, and which at the end of the 13th was rebuilt in Gothic style. Over the doorway is a *Madonna* from the Pisan school (14th cent.).

In the **interior** we have the first examples of the Cistercian style with very simple square pillars ending in a notched cornice and ogival arches. On some pillars, fourteenth century frescoes, remains of the decoration of Agnolo Gaddi, Spinello Aretino, Paolo Uccello and Masaccio, which used to cover all the walls. In the main chapel, some very deteriorated frescoes in the manner of Spinello Aretino representing *Episodes referring to King Herod.* In the left-hand chapel is a very important altar-piece from the early 13th century, attributed to COPPO DI MARCOVALDO: a coloured wood-relief showing the *Madonna Enthroned* is surrounded by painted compartments with *Angels, Saints* and the scenes of *the Annunciation* and *the Holy Women at the Sepulchre.* In the same chapel are: a small column of the *Tomb of Brunetto Latini* (d. 1294), buried in this church, Chancellor of the Republic and poet-master of Dante Alighieri; another *tomb* with the figure of *Salvino di Amato degli Armati* (d. 1317), the presumed inventor of spectacles; above, *Roman bust.* On the second altar on the right, a modern painting of *St. Rita* by the contemporary artist PRIMO CONTI.

Here we may end our second expedition, having visited the most important religious nucleus in Florence, with the *Baptistery,* the *Cathedral* and the very ancient *Basilica of San Lorenzo* with the tombs of the Medici.

Chapel of the Princes.

CIVIL ARCHITECTURE
OF THE MEDIEVAL AND RENAISSANCE CITY

*From the tower-house to the palace: Palazzo di
Parte Guelfa - Houses of the Foresi · Palazzo
Davanzati - Palazzo Strozzi - Palaces of · Via
Tornabuoni - Church of Santa Trinita - Palazzo
Rucellai - Church of Santa Maria Novella - Pal-
aces of Via del Proconsolo and Borgo degli Albizi.*

Tower-house in the Piazza Davanzati.

FROM THE TOWER-HOUSE TO THE PALACE

From the nineteenth century *Piazza della Repubblica*, once the centre of the Roman city, now the centre of the modern city, we go under the arcades of the *Palace of the Post Office*. Turning to the left into *via Porta Rossa* we look at the **Loggia di Mercato Nuovo** (of the New Market) of late Renaissance architecture (G. B. DEL TASSO, 1547-'51) and at the small **fountain** on its side, with a bronze boar (called by the Florentines « il porcellino », that is « the little pig ») which is a copy by P. Tacca (c. 1612) of a classical marble piece of sculpture in the Uffizi Gallery. Coming back, at the end of the arcades opens a small square with the **Palazzo di Parte Guelfa** (Palace of the Guelph party) which from this side shows the fourteenth century façade restored in the last century. The rear side, on *via di Capaccio* and visible from Via Por Santa Maria, is from the design of FILIPPO BRUNELLESCHI, completed by GIORGIO VASARI.

This ensemble of architecture can give, synthetically, an idea of the development of the various styles, from the fourteenth to the fifteenth and sixteenth centuries. This development can be followed, in a more apparent way, by going down *Via Porta Rossa* as far as *Piazza Davanzati*, where are the first examples of Florentine civil architecture. On the right we see an example of the old towerhouses of the thirteenth century, developed in height, with small rooms, almost dark on the ground floor on account of the narrow doorways and tiny windows which could easily be reinforced and barred. On the thick wall well built of the hard stone from the quarries of Monte Ceceri, with sturdy development of the lower floor, we note the bridge holes with rough brackets Here were fixed in the rafters which held up the bridges of defence and communication from one tower to another, across the narrow streets, during rebellions, when it was dangerous to come down in the street, and the several towers of a company formed a fortification system, capable of resisting even a long siege. The remains that we see, in fact, are of the **Houses of the Foresi**, that is of one of the strongest Florentine companies, of the type characteristic of the 150 towers which sprang up in thirteenth century Florence, as high as sixty meters, and which were reduced by law in 1250 to not more than twenty-five meters.

Palazzo Davanzati, on the other side offers an example of a private habitation of the fourteenth century. The harder times were passed, and life in the hard-working Guelph Republic was easier and less warlike. The civil architecture, in an atmosphere of more peaceful and fruitful existence, opened to more airy forms and wanted also to satisfy aesthetic exigencies which demonstrated the easier condition of the people grown rich through trade. The local style permitted wide openings, no more with pointed arch or with the architrave, but surmounted by graceful sloping arches. The distribution of the rooms round a central courtyard gave more light and convenience to the interiors, and to the great hall on the first floor, which took on a true and really monumental character. The rooms on the upper floor too were decorated with bright frescoes. High up, in the sunshine and wind, opens the fifteenth century covered terrace, shaded by the sloping roof. On the façade, a varied assortment of irons of typical dimensions and forms, reveals the habits of city life: below,

Palazzo di Parte Guelfa.

Piazza Santa Trinita and Palazzo Feroni.

the hooks to attach the bridles of saddle-horses and beasts
of burden; the staff brackets at the windows which held up
long poles on which hung cloths of gold and draperies; the
flag or torch rings for festive decorations. In the middle of
the façade the great coat of arms proclaims the glory of
that family which in trade had accrued their riches and who
had also begun to cultivate the humanistic studies. From the
DAVANZATI family indeed was a fine historian, BERNARDO,
(d. 1606), wise translator of the tales of Tacitus. Palazzo Davanzati is now the seat of the very interesting **Museum of
the Ancient Florentine House,** where fine furniture, pictures,
objets d'art, etc., from the 14th, 15th, 16th, and 17th centuries,

are so displayed as to revive the aspect of a rich Florentine home.

Stepping back in *Via Sassetti* and turning round to the left into the short *Via Anselmi* we come in sight of a palace which has quite another character. The imposing and most elegant **Palazzo Strozzi** is the purest architectural example of all the Renaissance. We are in the middle of the fifteenth century and Florence is at the height of its splendour. The merchants have become bankers. They have branches in all parts of Europe and in the Levantine ports, and they are ambitious to build splendid palaces in the city, on the ruins of old demolished houses, detached palaces of real masters. The architects responded marvellously to their wishes and so flourished the architecture of the Renaissance, vigourous and at the same time full of grace.

Let us study this palace. All around the base the stone bench invites people to rest in the shade of the rich man's comfortable residence. The rough stone blocks indicate solidity and also a shut-in egoism. But on the first floor the blocks are less rough and the great rooms of

Palazzo Davanzati.

the contented family open to the sun in an airy open space through the fine double arched windows, with graceful ornaments reproducing the family coat-of-arms. The top floor is even lighter still, not shaded by the roof-gutter, but triumphantly surmounted by a very rich, wide cornice which is like a crown of nobility on the forehead of the new-rich man.

We see below, the wrought-iron rings for the horses, with the taper-holders; above, the iron flag-brackets and arras-holders for feast-days, and at the corners, most elegant lanterns, honorary privilege of well deserving families, illuminating the palace on banquet nights.

The palace was begun in 1484, by order of Filippo Strozzi, enriched at Lyons during his exile inflicted on him by the Medici. The design was given by BENEDETTO DA MAIANO who directed the work until his death (1497). He was succeeded by SIMONE DEL POLLAIOLO, called the CRONACA, who added the magnificent courtyard (1507). The family fortunes being changed through city vicissitudes the crowning was interrupted in 1536.

The wrought iron pieces, designed by Benedetto da Maiano and Cronaca, are by a famous artisan, Niccolò Grosso, surnamed the CAPARRA: no finer ones are known. In the interior, the palace unfolds like all those of the time, round a square, columned courtyard, with an airy loggia on the top floor.

Palazzo Strozzi.

Palazzo Rucellai.

On the left of the square we notice another building of the same type, much more modest, the *Palace* of Agnolo and Palla Strozzi, called the *Strozzino*, designed, on the ground floor, by MICHELOZZO (1457) and continued by GIULIANO DA MAIANO (1465). It had a very beautiful courtyard, later altered and destroyed.

By *Via Monalda* we turn into Via Porta Rossa, where we find another typically Florentine palace, now used as an hotel. It is the old **Palazzo Torrigiani** one of the few remaining with an out-thrust façade that is resting on projected corbels. Typical defensive measure, becoming with architectural evolution a protection from bad weather for passers-by and the best way to utilize the space for the owners. The corbel construction was very often subject to decrees which tended to reduce the façade to the normal type and so today few in this style remain. The decoration of bunches of poppies with the motto « So as not to sleep » were adopted as an emblem by a member of the Bartolini Salimbeni family (to which the palace formerly belonged) who being very skilful but having little money, succeeded in being the only merchant present at the arrival of a load of goods by giving his fellow-merchants some opiate wine on the previous night. So he was able to buy goods on credit and having sold them with a high profit, founded the fortune of his family.

Turning to the left, we come into *Piazza Santa Trinita*. On the corner on the left, is the **Palazzo Bartolini Salimbeni** by BACCIO D'AGNOLO who introduced a new kind of architecture in the early sixteenth century (1520-29). The architectural symmetry is now more plastic. To linear design he added sculptural relief of columns and cornices, with effects of light and shade unknown to the fifteenth century architects. The influence of the Roman style, with the heavy cornice and triangular pediments over the windows, introduced almost exotic elements into Florentine architecture, so much so that it became the object of satire and very biting criticism. To these attacks the architect answered with the latin on the architrave of the door: Carpere promptius quam imitari (it is easier to criticise than to imitate).

Thus we have been able to follow the evolution of Florentine architecture, from the severe tower houses of the thirteenth century, to the solemn houses of the fourteenth century, to the splendid and elegant palaces of the fifteenth century, to the plastic chiaroscuro palaces of the sixteenth century. In

Palazzo Bartolini Salimbeni.

our excursion we shall come upon many palaces, and all could be related to these four fundamental styles. The later evolution of local civil architecture, even if taking on foreign elements and forms, always maintained a modesty which showed the continuation of a taste for moderation and harmony.

In *Piazza Santa Trinita* extends the great **Palazzo Spini,** later **Feroni,** austere construction of the end of the thirteenth century, which has still something of the embattled fortification. Once it was also guarded by a corner tower, like that of the Bargello. Opposite, the other thirteenth century **Palazzo Gianfigliazzi,** of smaller proportions but greater elegance. The two palaces used to guard well the old (1252) **Ponte a Santa Trinita.** This bridge, carried away by a flood, was rebuilt by the architects of the church of Santa Maria Novella, Brothers Sisto and Ristoro; swept away again by an exceptional flood in 1333, it was rebuilt by the architects of Santa Reparata (1346); ruined in 1557, it was designed in a new form (1560) under the influence of Michelangelo, by BARTO-LOMEO AMMANNATI, who directed the building of it, finished

Palazzo Larderel.

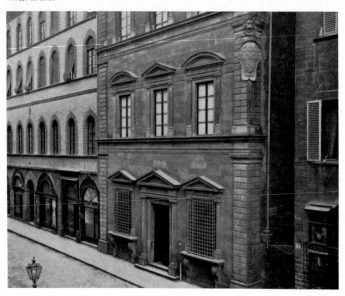

D. Ghirlandaio: A Miracle of St. Francis (Santa Trinita).

in two years (1567-69). The completely new architectural lines, of an elegance without precedent, combined complete beauty with the perfect solution of a problem of necessity, imposed by the violence of the floods, at this, the narrowest part of the river. To avoid the dashing of the waters, rather than opposing a massive weight, as in the Ponte Vecchio, they gave the bridge very sweeping lines, with a most graceful curve. Quite justly, therefore, it has been judged the most beautiful bridge in the world. Without reasonable, necessary practical reasons, it was blown up by the small retreating German rearguard on the 4th of August 1944. It has been now rebuilt, with the salvaged materials in its own original form.

Opposite the Spini palace, and next to the Gianfigliazzi palace, is the **Church of Santa Trinita** (the Florentines pronounce it in the latin way) which gave its name to the square and the bridge. Already existing in the 11th century, outside the « Posterula rossa » (small red city gate) in the walls of the old circle, rebuilt and enlarged in the 13th and 14th centuries, its façade, constructed by the architect BERNARDO BUONTALENTI (1593) is like a fine stone mask. However, in the interior, simple and solemn, are found again the characteristics already seen in Santa Maria Maggiore.

Interior. - Remains, in the interior façade, of the Romanesque church, on which later arose, about 1250, the church in the new ogival style taken from the Cistercians. Remains of the fourteenth century frescoes and also upright tomb-stones on the walls, record the influence which this temple had through the whole history of the Florentine middle-ages.

In the **first chapel on the right,** the 14th cent. *Crucifix of the Compagnia dei Bianchi,* which, in 1399, had thousands of members in Florence, instituted as a spiritual reaction to the laws of private vendetta, with the pardon of injustices and the practice of charity. In the **third,** *Madonna and Saints* by NERI DI BICCI (1491), and in the **fourth,** *Annunciation* by LORENZO MONACO (d. about 1425), by whom are also the frescoes with *Scenes in the Life of the Virgin.* In the **fifth,** *Altar* by BENEDETTO DA ROVEZZANO, reconstructed with various pieces of the great monument to St. Giovanni Gualberto ruined at San Salvi by the Imperial troops in 1530, and *Pietà* of the 14th century.

The first chapel on the right in the transept is a very beautiful example of a patron chapel of the fifteenth century. The great families, ambitious to have a fine palace, also desired, when it was not possible to have an entire church at their disposition, as the Medici in San Lorenzo, to have a chapel dedicated to the cult of their patron saint and destined for the burial of their members. Such was the **Sassetti Chapel,** painted in fresco by DOMENICO DEL GHIRLANDAIO (1483-86), on the outside with the *Sibilla Tiburtina* who announces the birth of Christ to Augustus; in the inside with *Stories of Saint Francis,* some of which plainly show Florence at the time of the painter, in the presence of members of the Sassetti family, and particularly of the Medici family. Thus the scenes of the *Child brought to life* (behind the altar) is a real representation of Piazza Santa Trinita. It is most interesting to see how were in the fifteenth century the Spini palace, on the left, with the sheds and the stone bench, the old, narrow bridge and the façade of the church in Romanesque style. The people represented belong to the Sassetti family and to their consorts. The last figure on the right, with his hand on his hip, is that of the painter. Above this scene, another one full of interest is that of the *Approval of the Order,* which the painter, with intended anachronism, placed in Piazza della Signoria. We see, on the left, the Palace as it used to be, with the « aringhiera » (platform) and the Marzocco. In the background the Loggia of Orcagna without the statues. On the left of the Pope, *Lorenzo the Magnificent,* in sharp profile, between *Francèsco Sassetti* and *Antonio Pucci.* Below, by a stairway, come out the figures of *Poliziano* and *Giulianino* (for whom Michelangelo later made the tomb in San Lorenzo), followed by *Piero* (who was called « the foolish », was thrown out of Florence, and died by drowning), *Giovanni* (who was to be Leo X), and behind everyone, *Matteo Franco,* chaplain of the Medici house, and the poet *Luigi Pulci.* At the foot of the frescoes, the very fine portrait of the patrons, *Francesco Sassetti,* and his wife *Nera dei Corsi.* On the walls, tombs of the Sassetti family attributed to GIULIANO DA SANGALLO, Everything here speaks of a family and its wordly relations in the fifteenth century Florence. On the altar, the *Adoration of the Shepherds,* a very beautiful picture by DOMENICO DEL GHIRLANDAIO.

In the **chapel on the right of the chancel** is preserved the *Crucifix of St. Giovanni Gualberto,* which bowed to him approving the pardon which the Saint bestowed upon his own brother's murderer on Good Friday of the year 1003. In the **Main Chapel,** over a fine 15th century marble altar, is a triptych with the *Holy Trinity and Saints* by MARIOTTO DI NARDO. Over the arches of the two chapels on the left, frescoes by GIOVANNI DA PONTE (about 1434). In the **second chapel on the left,** the wonderful *tomb of Benozzo Federici, Bishop of Fiesole* (d. 1450), a work of LUCA DELLA ROBBIA (1454-56) in which the marble reliefs are framed with a charming frieze of terracotta tiles painted and glazed.

In the **first chapel of the left aisle,** a wood statue of the *Magdalen,* begun by DESIDERIO DA SETTIGNANO (1464) and finished by BENEDETTO DA MAIANO (1468). In the **second,** *Coronation of Mary,* in the manner of Bicci di Lorenzo, and stone tablets to record that Dino Compagni (1250-1324), chronicler of the times of Dante, was buried there, he who in this temple had pleaded with his fellow-citizens to end their fratricidal struggles. In the **third,** *Annunciation* by NERI DI BICCI (1491), and the *tomb of Giuliano Davanzati,* made out of a very fine Roman sarcophagus, on which the figure of the dead man is carved.

In the middle of *Piazza Santa Trinita* stands a *column* of granite from the Island of Elba with the porphyry statue of *Justice.* The column comes from the Roman baths of Caracalla and was given by Pius IV to Cosimo I, who erected it on the spot where he had news of the defeat of his enemies in the battle of Scannagallo, near Marciano (2nd of August 1554). The inscription at the base was renewed in 1570 when Cosimo was given the title of Grand Duke. The statue is by FRANCESCO FERRUCCI called the TADDA (1581). Behind the column is the *Palazzo Buondelmonti,* of the family which caused the terrible factions strife in the 13th and 14th centuries. Here was the first seat (1820) of the *Scientific and Literary Library* of GIOVANNI PIETRO VIEUSSEUX, who created around him a vast and lasting cultural and patriotic movement which influenced the Tuscan Independence movement with important periodicals, such as the *Antologia,* the *Nuova Antologia,* the *Giornale Agrario,* the *Archivio Storico Italiano,* in which the most notable learned Italians collaborated. Very extensive and of the greatest importance were the relations created and maintained with the literary and political fields in France, Belgium, Switzerland, England, and Germany, so that it could be considered a centre of European culture. The influence of Vieusseux was so great that they used to say: in Tuscany there are two Grand Dukes. The Library continues to this day its activity as a circulating library, traditionally frequented by foreigners, on the ground floor of the Strozzi palace. From the column we begin going down **Via Tornabuoni** which has a world-wide fame as one of the most elegant streets, whether for the calm beauty of its slightly curved track, along the fosse of the first circle, or for the buildings which flank it for 400 metres, with the variety of their architecture between the Bridge and Piazza Antinori. In fact it is the traditional meeting-place of foreigners with the elegant Florentine world, and its shops rival each other in exhibiting the most refined and costly things.

At number 3 on the left, the *Minerbetti Palace*, with original elements of the 14th cent.; at number 5, the fine façade, with three floors of the *Strozzi Giaconi Palace*, created by GERARDO SILVANI (d. 1675) for the poet G. B. Strozzi, called the Blind; at no. 7, the *Palace of the Commenda di Castiglione* begun by AMMANNATI and finished by GIAMBOLOGNA, by whom is the *bust of Francesco I*, the extravagant, adventurous prince. Dominating, opposite, is the vast bulk of the Strozzi Palace, which we can here admire from the rear façade, deprived of the big cornice, but still solemn and majestic.

From here we go down the *Via della Vigna Nuova* until we come across another stupendous Renaissance building, the **Palazzo Rucellai**, designed by LEON BATTISTA ALBERTI and built by BERNARDO ROSSELLINO (1446-51) for Giovanni called « della Fabbrica », of this illustrious family which took its name from the « oricella », the plant used in the dyeing of stuffs. All military character has disappeared from the façade, and gracefulness and harmony alone inspire the line of the regular flat blocks, of the light cornice-work and sober horizontal lines, decorated with expressive emblems of the sail full-blown by a favourable wind, and the Medici ring with the diamond that conquers every adverse hardship. Opposite the palace is another type of private civil building, which is the *Loggia*. In sixteenth century Florence there were still twenty-six of them. Every great house had either at the corner or in the immediate neighbourhood, as here, its own Loggia with an unpaved space in front, for dancing or tilting on horseback. Inside the Loggia, on the benches built up in wood or stone, friends and clients of the family met; there they prolonged the evening parties into the summer nights, there were held the great family councils, and there they solemny arranged the betrothals. But, above all, feasts were held there on the occasion of births and marriages and there they solemnly celebrated the first obsequies of members of the family. Thus all the citizens were able to assist at domestic feasts of the nobility, during which gifts of food and drink were distributed to the people. This Loggia, in its noble proportions, was designed by LEON BATTISTA ALBERTI (1468).

Returning we again take Via Tornabuoni. At the corner, on the left, the *Viviani della Robbia Palace*, restored by G. B. FOGGINI (1693), which belonged to the family that was heir to the last descendants of the much celebrated sculptors. Opposite, on the corner of *via Strozzi*, where once stood the Tornabuoni palace, which gave its name to the street, is now the nineteenth century *Corsi Palace* which preserves only in the courtyard the fifteenth-century line of Michelozzo, the first architect of the palace. At the extreme left of this palace, along Via Tornabuoni, is the elegant *Loggia dei Tornaquinci* by LODOVICO CARDI, called the CIGOLI (1613). Opposite, the *Giacomini* later *Larderel Palace*, masterpiece of a great Fiorentine architect, GIOVANNI ANTONIO DOSIO (1580), who left there the interpretation of sixteenth century taste in most composed and sober form, proper to the local tradition. Among the very fine particulars we notice the originality of the cornices brought on to the line of the window-sills, rather than to the height of the floor.

We next come into **Piazza Antinori**, so-called after the family of bankers and silk merchants who in 1490 acquired the palace, then of the Martelli, the design of which is attributed to Giuliano da Sangallo or to Baccio d'Agnolo. It is an expressive example of the persistence of fourteenth century forms at the close of the fifteenth century. Opposite, the *Church of San Gaetano* once dedicated to Saint Michael (1055), called of the Devils, rebuilt in Baroque style in the first half of the seventeenth century on designs by FRA GIOVANNI DE' MEDICI and MATTEO NIGETTI, the architects of the Lawrentian Chapel of the Princes, modified by GHERARDO and PIER FRANCESCO SILVANI (1604-48). It is one of the rare examples of Baroque Florentine style and is distinguished from the buildings of the same period in the rest of Italy by the moderation with which it expresses the ruling taste for exuberance. The interior, refaced with dark « pietra serena » and black marble makes a great contrast with the white of the other marbles and with the plaster-work, giving a sense of cold austerity.

By the short alley at the side of the Palazzo Antinori we come to the *Croce al Trebbio*. A column, erected in 1338, records the strife between Catholics and « Patarini » heretics, who here encountered each other in 1244. In those times the city did not spread to this part, crossed with ditches which fed the industrial establishments which had grown up outside the walls. And outside the walls had stopped the mendicant friars of the two orders of Saint Francis and Saint Dominic who were taking care of the minute populace of the suburbs extending outside the city gates. While the Franciscans had placed their convent by the east gate, here, at the west gate the Dominicans established themselves in 1221, and later built the convent and church of Santa Maria Novella, not far from the Croce al Trebbio.

View of the Church of Santa Maria Novella.

SANTA MARIA NOVELLA

The church, called « novella » because it renewed the very modest pre-existing one, was begun in 1279 by two friar-architects, Sisto da Firenze and Ristoro da Campi, and in general structure was finished in 1348 by another friar, Jacopo Talenti, who also finished the strong and slender *bell-tower*, in Gothic-Romanesque character (1330). It is interesting to note how the Gothic style in Florence engrafted itself upon the severe Romanesque style, assuming an harmonious form and never weakening the wall mass. On the façade, the full plinth and the harmony of the white and black is lightened by the so-called « avelli » (tombs) with pointed arch.

The churches of the mendicant orders gathered in great number the bodies of sinners who wanted, after death, to rest under the broad protection of the two great founder saints. We shall see how the Franciscan one of Santa Croce became in time a city Pantheon. But Santa Maria Novella was favoured no less, where the original « avelli », the graves destined for the defunct, have been preserved on the outside, gathered by families. The façade had this characteristic lower decoration, and when, in 1458, Leon Battista Alberti was called to complete it, he did not bother to take inspiration from the style of the former building, but wisely grafted the Renaissance on to the remains of the Gothic architecture. The grafting has succeeded so well that one scarcely notices the trespass. The very fine main doorway, the great frieze decorated with the device of the Rucellai, (the sail full-blown with a favourable wind), the pilasters in the classical style, frame the façade; the two sloping roofs of the old church would have remained uncovered, had the architect not thought of disguising them with two up-turned scrolls, decorated with inlay work. This new conception of his was an invention which had lasting developments in the architecture of ecclesiastical façades. The tombs, decorated with the cross of the People and the arms of the family to which they belong, also continue along the wall on the right which encloses the old cemetery.

Interior. - Designed like a Greek T cross, with a nave and two aisles, shallow chapels, graceful pillars and sharp pointed arches, which become narrower in width progressively towards the end, it was planned after the scheme introduced into Italy by the Cistercian order, and rendered simpler and clearer by the mendicant orders. The central nave as well as the aisles

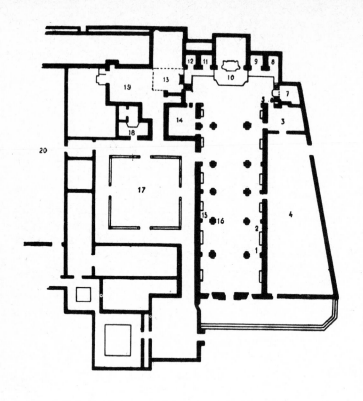

PLAN OF SANTA MARIA NOVELLA AND OF THE CLOISTERS.

1. B. ROSSELLINO: *Monument of the Blessed Villana.* - 2. *Tomb of the Blessed Giovanni da Salerno.* - 3. Chapel of the «Pura». - 4. Old Cemetery. - 5. *Bust of St. Antonino* and, above, *Tomb of T. Aliotti.* - 6. *Cenotaph of the Patriarch of Constantinople* and, above, *Tomb of A. Cavalcanti.* - 7. Rucellai Chapel. - 8. Bardi Chapel. - 9. Chapel of Filippo Strozzi. - 10. Main Chapel of the Tornabuoni. - 11. Gondi Chapel. - 12. Gaddi Chapel. - 13. Chapel of the Strozzi di Mantova. - 14. Sacristy. - 15 MASACCIO: *Christ Crucified.* - 16. Pulpit. - 17. Green Cloister. - 18. Spanish Chapel. - 19. Small Cloister of the Dead. - 20. Large Cloister.

Bernardo Rossellino: Monument to the Blessed Villana.

and the chapels are covered by intersecting vaults. The large windows pierced in the apse lighten the powerful lines of the building. As in all the Tuscan churches of the fourteenth century the walls were once largely frescoed and constituted what was called the « Bible of the Poor », or the pages of a book painted in fresco. The Dominican order was an order of preachers, and so their churches were conceived as vast covered spaces, capable of containing great crowds of people. Let us imagine it as it originally was, with the flooring almost all covered with tomb-slabs, with the pillars adorned with figures of saints and the walls covered with frescoes, which increased in number in the chapels at the end. Well in view, the pulpit in carved marble. In the sixteenth century, when the Gothic style seemed primitive and barbaric, Vasari, superintendant of artistic things in the city, in this, as in the church of Santa Croce, demolished the choir in the centre of the transept, had the floor raised and destroyed the tomb-stones; he white-washed or hid the frescoes covering the walls with large, heavy altars; he raised the windows in the lateral aisles; but his lamentable work could not destroy the general harmony of line of this architecture, which until today, stands up most elegantly in its simple and straight-forward elements.

In this church, as in the others in the city, picturesque and dramatic civil incidents took place. Charles of Valois swore falsely as King's son (1301), preliminary to the persecutions of the white Guelphs and the condemnation of Dante Alighieri; Giovanni Boccaccio placed there the first scene of his « Decameron ».

Interior façade. - In the lunette, *Manger* in mosaic from cartoons of the school of Filippino Lippi.

Right Aisle. - In the second bay, *Monument to the Blessed Villana* (d. 1360) by BERNARDO RCSSELLINO (1451) who gave to the old motif of the pavilion held open by two angels, a new Renaissance grace. We find the same motif in the 14th cent. *tomb of the Blessed Giovanni da Salerno*, on the other side of the altar.

The door on the right leads into the **Cappella della Pura**, a Renaissance building erected in honour of a miraculous Madonna whose image we see in a 14th century fresco in the left-hand corner.

Right wing of the Transept. - Fifteenth century terracotta *bust of St. Antonino*, Archbishop of Florence, of the Dominican order, probably executed from a death mask. Above, *Tomb of Tedice Aliotti*, Bishop of Fiesole (d. 1336) by TINO DI CAMAINO, who was the creator of the last type of these funeral monuments diffused all over Italy from Sicily to Lombardy. On the left, *Tomb of Aldobrando Cavalcanti*, Bishop of Orvieto. Below *Cenotaph of Joseph, Patriarch of Constantinople*, who came to Florence for the Ecumenical council and died here in 1439.

Rucellai Chapel. - We get there by a little staircase. On the altar was the well-known *Rucellai Madonna* by DUCCIO DI BONINSEGNA which is now in the Uffizi Gallery. On the walls remains of 14th cent. frescoes and the *Martyrdom of St. Catherine* by GIULIANO BUGIARDINI. In the centre of the floor has recently been set the *memorial bronze of Lionardo Dati*, a fine work by GHIBERTI (1423) which was formerly at the foot of the steps leading to the high altar and usually concealed by a wood covering.

Transept Chapels. - **Bardi Chapel** with the *Madonna of the Rosary* by VASARI, remains of 14th cent. frescoes and fragments of 13th cent. sculpture.

D. Ghirlandaio: *Birth of St. John the Baptist.*

Chapel of Filippo Strozzi the Elder, with elaborate scenographic frescoes representing *Scenes from the Life of St. Philip,* one of the last works of FILIPPINO LIPPI (1503). On the end wall, *Tomb of Filippo Strozzi,* a late work by BENEDETTO DA MAIANO (1491), lacking the very fine bust of the dead man, which is exhibited in the Louvre. The stained-glass window was executed from a cartoon by FILIPPINO LIPPI.

Main Chapel, of the Tornabuoni. - On the altar, *Crucifix,* in bronze, by GIAMBOLOGNA. In the Choir, inlaid choir-stalls and lectern, attributed to Baccio d'Agnolo, but restored at the end of the sixteenth century. In the vaulting and on the walls, frescoes by DOMENICO GHIRLANDAIO and assistants; on the right, *stories of St. John the Baptist;* on the left, *stories of the Madonna.* It is the finest example of a religious decoration executed not only to embellish a church but also to honour a family and their friends. The portrait of *Giovanni Tornabuoni,* who commissioned this work, can be seen, opposite to that of his wife, *Francesca Pitti,* at the bottom of the end wall. The personages of the frescoes portray relatives and friends of the Tornabuoni family in costumes of their day. So these paintings are not only important for the art of Ghirlandaio but as a city chronicle. The stained-glass window was executed from a cartoon by DOM. GHIRLANDAIO.

Gondi Chapel, architecturally decorated by GIULIANO DA SANGALLO. In the vaulting, remains of frescoes by Greek painters of the 13th cent., who may have been the teachers and inspirers of Cimabue; however, they are among the oldest Florentine wall paintings. On the wall at the end, the celebrated *Crucifix* of BRUNELLESCHI, made in competition with Donatello. That of Donatello is in the Bardi Chapel in Santa Croce.

D. Ghirlandaio: Birth of the Virgin.

Gaddi Chapel, decorated in a sober, austere way by GIOVANNI ANTONIO DOSIO (1575-77) with elements taken from the architecture of the Baths of Diocletian at Rome. On the altar, *Miracle of Jesus*, by BRONZINO. In two low-reliefs, *Stories of the Madonna* by GIOVANNI BANDINI.

Chapel of the Strozzi of Mantua, at the end of the transept, with steps leading up to it. In the niche under the stairs, *Deposition*, of the school of Orcagna. This is one of the fourteenth century chapels integrally preserved as regards the well-known frescoes of NARDO DI CIONE ARCAGNOLO, or ORCAGNA, and his brother ANDREA, in which the success of Dante's poem is attested a few years after the death of the exile (1328-31). *Last Judgement*, on the wall at the end. On the right wall, *Hell*, very rich in Dantean episodes; on the left one, *Paradise*, where we see a worthy *portrait of Dante*. On the altar, large picture by ANDREA ORCAGNA (1357) in its splendid, original frame: *Jesus Christ Triumphant*, who entrusts to St. Peter the keys and to St. Thomas Aquinas the doctrinal government of the church.

Sacristy. - Architecture of JACOPO TALENTI (1350). Over the door, great *Crucifix* attributed to GIOTTO. On the left of the door, marble *washstand* in a shell of glazed terracotta, one of the best works of GIOVANNI DELLA ROBBIA (1498). The majestic *cupboards* were designed by BERNARDO BUONTALENTI.

Left aisle. - Here is to be seen the fresco by MASACCIO, *Christ Crucified with God the Father, Mary, St. John and two donors,* one of the most admirable examples of humanistic painting and of perspective composition. By the second pillar, *Pulpit* designed by BRUNELLESCHI with fine decorative motifs of classical inspiration, and low-reliefs by ANDREA CAVALCANTI, called BUGGIANO, adopted son of the architect.

The Green Cloister.

The Spanish Chapel.

Chiostro Verde (Green Cloister). - By the gate on the left of the façade, we go into the huge convent, now mostly used for civil and military purposes. The first cloister is the oldest, and preserves the Romanesque style (about 1350). On the walls of this cloister were painted scenes from the *Old Testament* in green and reddish colours. So it became called the Green Cloister. Those that we still see, much damaged by the damp, are by one or more painters (about 1430) of the workshop of the genial PAOLO UCCELLO. Painted definitely by the master are the very beautiful scenes representing with great dramatic power the *Deluge* and *Stories of Noah*. These much-damaged frescoes, rich in precious naturalistic details and most original perspective motives were taken down and can now be seen in the adjoining Refectory of the old convent which is now the meeting-room of the Knights of the Holy Sepulchre.

Spanish Chapel. - In honour of St. Thomas Aquinas, the glory of the Order and theologian of the Holy Eucarist, it was constructed in 1359, by JACOPO TALENTI, as a chapel for the meetings of the Chapter of the Order, and was called the Chapel of the Sacrament. The Grand Duchess Eleanor of Toledo, a Spaniard, and wife of Cosimo I, assigned the chapel, about two centuries later, to the gentlemen of her suite, and from then it took its new name. The walls of the Chapel had to be equivalent to a doctrinal tract given by the theologian, Friar Zenobi dei Guasconi, the prior. The actual executor of the paintings was ANDREA DI BONAIUTO (1366-68), during the prevalence of the Sienese Gothic taste in Florentine painting, a style which lent itself more to symbolic than dramatic figuration. On the wall at the end, about the arch, unfold, like a continuous tale, the last stages of the *Passion of Jesus*, from the ascent to Calvary to the descent into Limbo. The scene is crowned by the *Resurrection* represented in the triangular compartment of the vaulting. On the entrance wall, much damaged, *Stories of St. Peter Martyr*, and above, in the vaulting, *Ascension*. But the most important frescoes are those on the side walls, with the representation of two great, extremely condensed allegories. On the left, the *Triumph of Wisdom*, which comes down from high as a gift of grace from the *Holy Spirit* and invests the *Apostles* (scene of the *Pentecost* in the compartment of the vaulting) diffuses itself among the *Prophets* and *Saints*, inspires *St. Thomas enthroned*, with the vanquished heretics at his feet, and finally animates the human activity of the *Seven Liberal Arts* on the right, and of the *Seven Divine Arts* on the left. On the wall on the right is the allegory of the *Church Militant and Triumphant*. At the side of a church are represented the two stars of human society: the *Pope* with all the ecclesiastical hierarchy, and the *Emperor* with all the civil hierarchy. At their feet are the flocks of the faithful symbolized by various sheep, protected from the attacks of the heretic wolves by black and white dogs, representing the Dominican friars, while the three principal saints of the order: *Dominic*, the founder, *Peter Martyr*, the saint of action, *Thomas Aquinas* the saint of doctrine, actively defend the unknowing and helpless faithful from the snares of sin and the assaults of the wicked. The distracted and misled human beings, after the attractions of the three greatest capital vices, *Avarice*, *Lust*, and *Violence*, can purify themselves by *Confession*, and the souls, returned as innocent as children, are gathered into the *Celestial Jerusalem*, by the *Virgin Mother*, by the patron *Saints*, by the *Angels* in the glory of the *Trinity*. In the sweep of the vaulting the corresponding allegory of the Church represented as the *Boat of St. Peter*. The building painted in fresco on the right, and which is the symbol of the Church where the faithful meet, reproduces one of two models which were exhibited in 1367, to decide with a vote of 461 competent men, on the final form of the Cathedral of Florence. It is most interesting to consider how a group of master-artists, among whom was the painter Andrea di Bonaiuto, conceived in Gothic form the solution of the difficult problem of the cupola. This chapel is very important for its decoration as an integral example of the actuation of a concept which they had, in the fourteenth century, for the practical ends of painting to which was attributed the task of making agreable and concrete in the mind of the ignorant the theological and moral truths which they were unable to understand directly from books.

Chiostrino dei morti. (Small Cloister of the Dead). Not far from the Spanish Chapel is a small Romanesque cloister, full of tombs with remains of fourteenth cent. frescoes. In the **Strozzi Chapel,** wall-paintings of the school of Orcagna. In the courtyard we see a lunette with a fifteenth-century *St. Thomas Aquinas*, and a *Meeting of Jesus and Mary Magdalen*, from the Della Robbia workshop.

Chiostro grande. (Large Cloister). There is another large cloister, the largest in the city, in which the arcades are almost an anthology of Florentine painting of the sixteenth and seventeenth centuries, but, like many other old convents, it is occupied by a military school.

Coming out of the church we see one of the most picturesque squares, which for centuries was used for popular spectacles. Opposite is the **Loggia of San Paolo** (1466) repetition of the Loggia degli Innocenti by Filippo Brunelleschi, with medallions by Luca and Andrea Della Robbia (1451-1495), and their portraits on the right and on the left respectively. Under the portico a lunette by Andrea representing the *Meeting of St. Dominic and St. Francis* which is believed to have taken place here, in 1221.

The two *marble obelisks*, resting on *bronze tortoises* by Giambologna and capped by the Florentine lily, served to mark the limits of the « Palio dei Cocchi » (coach races) which from 1563 until the middle of the nineteenth century used to be run on the 23rd of June in this square.

Returning to the Croce al Trebbio, we take the *Via delle Belle Donne*, an old narrow street, with houses of good architecture. From *Via della Spada* we cross Via Tornabuoni, then come again into *Via Strozzi*, turning to the left into *Via dei Vecchietti*, where we find the *Vecchietti Palace* which was altered on the outside by Giambologna (1578), but in the interior preserves the primitive fifteenth century architecture. We notice on the corner of Via Strozzi the reproduction of the *Diavolino* (little devil) with which Giambologna decorated the « Canto del Diavolo » (Devil's corner), already made famous by a miracle of St. Peter Martyr. Going down Via Vecchietti we see on the right a thirteenth century tower-house. A little before, on the right, is *Via del Campidoglio*. The name records how the Capitol arose on this spot in Roman Florence, with the front facing what is now Piazza della Repubblica, from where started our first itinerary.

Andrea di Bonaiuto: The Church Militant (detail of the frescoes in the Spanish Chapel).

To end this excursion, from Piazza della Repubblica we take *Via degli Speziali* and continue along *Via del Corso,* which used to form the principal street of the ancient Roman city, and along which took place the traditional « Barbary horse race ». Just where this road meets *Via del Proconsolo* the Roman camp and the old circle of walls of the city ended. Here used to open the East, later San Piero, Gate.

At the crossing, on the right, stands the very fine **Pazzi Palace** attributed to BRUNELLESCHI, with elegant courtyard by GIULIANO DA MAIANO (1472). On the left, the most original **Strozzi Palace** called the **Palazzo Nonfinito** (unfinished palace) because it was left incomplete by BERNARDO BUONTALENTI and his assistants MATTEO NIGETTI, to whom the courtyard is due, and G. B. CACCINI.

The Corso is continued by the old Borgo di Porta a San Piero, now *Borgo degli Albizi,* on which stand the **Ramirez di Montalvo Palace** (1568) designed by B. AMMANNATI and decorated in blacklead by B. POCCETTI; and the **Altoviti Palace,** later Valori, called **Palazzo dei Visacci** (Palace of the ugly faces) from the strange figures, portraits of illustrious men, on its façade.

So we come to the *Piazza di San Piero Maggiore,* where there remains only the loggia of the church pulled down in the 18th cent. On the square stood a group of the old **tower-houses**, one of which belonged to the **Donati** family, from which came Piccarda, praised by Dante in his poem (Par. IV).

So this journey, begun from the *tower-houses of the Foresi,* ends with the *tower-houses of the Donati,* having gone over, in rapid survey, the development of Florentine civil architecture and visited the ancient churches of *Santa Trinita* and *Santa Maria Novella.*

THE THIRD CIRCLE OF THE WALLS

*Porta al Prato - Porta San Gallo - Porta alla
Croce - Church of Santa Croce - Casa Buonarroti
Horne Museum - Church of Santi Apostoli - Pa-
lazzo Corsini - Church of Ognissanti - Cascine Park.*

THE THIRD CIRCLE OF THE WALLS

From the church of *Santa Maria Novella* it would be well to pass on immediately to the church of *Santa Croce* which is its twin, standing at the far east of the city. Using a car, we can go down *Via della Scala* which opens into *Piazza Santa Maria Novella*, and turning to the left into the tree-lined avenue, we come to **Porta al Prato**. It is one of the piincipal gates which opened in the third circle designed by ARNOLFO DI CAMBIO and finished after 1299. The walls were pulled down after 1865 to give air to the city, and on their perimeter they laid out the *Viali di Circonvallazione*. The principal gates, which since 1526 no longer bore the aspect of high embattled towers, remain in the middle of the squares built especially by the architect GIOVANNI POGGI. We can begin, then, our circuit of the Avenues, starting from Porta al Prato (1299) and following ideally the line of the old walls. After the railway tunnel, we find, on the right, the **Fortezza da Basso** (Lower Fortress), a very fine military construction by ANTONIO DA SANGALLO (1533-35). It grew up naturally outside the old walls, and was built to protect the city when, after the siege, the Medici were made lords of Florence with the title of Dukes.

Following the Avenues, we come to *Piazza San Gallo*, now *Piazza della Libertà*, where another gate of the Arnolfian walls (1283) has remained isolated: **Porta San Gallo**. On the other side of the large fountain, an **Arch of Triumph** erected by JADOD, from Lorraine, (1739), for the entrance into the city of Francesco III who was the first of Lorraine Grand Dukes, succeeding the Medici ones.

Much further on, always along the Avenues, we come upon the **Evangelical** or **English Cemetery** (1828) which was once backing the outside of the old city walls, on the ruins of a convent of the Ingesuati, destroyed during the siege. It has remained isolated like a romantic mound, bordered by cypresses and decorated with rose-beds, and inspired the Swiss painter Arnold Boecklin for his very famous picture called the « Isle of the Dead ». Elizabeth Barrett Browning is buried here.

Going on, we come to *Piazza Beccaria* in the middle of which is the **Porta alla Croce** (1285), and continuing further we arrive at the bank of the Arno where stands the **Torre della Zecca Vecchia** (Tower of the old Mint) erected to guard a « Royal Bridge » projected (1317) but never built. The walls continue on the other side of the Arno on the left bank of which is the fine **Torre di San Niccolò**, the only one which retains its original height and appearance, built on the design of ANDREA ORCAGNA (1324). On the hills appear the old embattled walls which were not pulled down and which encircle the quarter called *Oltrarno*. Going down along the riverside, on the right, we come upon the building of the **National Central Library**, by CESARE BAZZANI (1911-35), of world-wide importance, full of ancient manuscripts, portcharts, illuminated codices, incunabula, bibliographical rarities, rich with about three millions books.

Turning off by the side of it, along *Via Magliabechi*, we come into *Piazza Santa Croce*. This also is a large square, adapted for popular preaching, and we must imagine it, like that of Santa Maria Novella, forming itself gradually in the middle of kitchen-gardens and small workman's suburbs. Only much later grew up the present palaces which we will examine after having visited the church. The latter had remained without the façade, which was only made in 1875, from the design of NICCOLÒ MATAS, with sculptures by GIOVANNI DUPRÈ (*Madonna and central lunette*), EMILIO ZOCCHI (*right-hand lunette*) and TITO SAROCCHI (*left-hand lunette*)

SANTA CROCE

It has the same architectural scheme as Santa Maria Novella: Greek « T » plan, with a nave and two aisles and chapels at the end. Elegant pillars, pointed arches, trestling in the main nave, cross-vaulting over the aisles and chapels. Three doors, a rose-window, large windows letting in plenty of light, vividly coloured in the apse. We must imagine it as it was in the fourteenth century, with the walls cheerful with frescoes, flags, pennons, armour and multi-coloured heraldic shields. After 1560, Vasari also applied to this church his disastrous ideas of renewal, raising the floor, whitewashing and destroying the frescoes, putting large, heavy altars against the walls, and demolishing the choir which used to stand in the transept.

The great popularity of the Franciscan Order owed itself

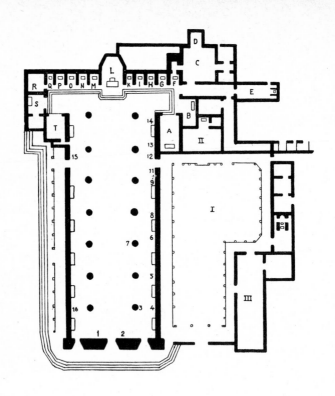

PLAN OF SANTA CROCE.

1. Mon. of Gino Capponi. - 2. Mon. of G. B. Niccolini. - 3. A. ROSSELLINO: *Madonna « of the Milk »*. - 4. Tomb of Michelangelo. - 5. Cenotaph of Dante. - 6. Mon. of V. Alfieri. - 7. Pulpit. - 8. Mon. of N. Machiavelli. - 9. Tomb of L. Lanzi. - 11. DONATELLO: *Annunciation*. - 12. B. ROSSELLINO: *Tomb of L. Bruni*. - 13. Tomb of G. Rossini. - 14. Mon. of Ugo Foscolo. - 15. DESIDERIO DA SETTIGNANO: *Tomb of C. Marsuppini*. - 16. Tomb of Galileo.

A. Castellani or Sacrament Chapel. - B. Baroncelli Chapel. - C. Sacristy. - D. Rinuccini Chapel. - E. Medici or Novitiate Chapel. - F. Velluti Chapel. - G. Bellacci Chapel. - H. Silvestri Chapel. - I. Peruzzi Chapel. - K. Bardi Chapel. - L. Main Chapel. - M. Tolosini Chapel. - N. Benci Chapel. - O. Ricasoli Chapel. - P. Pucci Chapel. - Q. Bardi di Vernio Chapel. - R. Niccolini Chapel. - S. Bardi Chapel. - T. Salviati Chapel. I. First Cloister. - II. Pazzi Chapel. - III. Museum of the Opera di Santa Croce.

not only to the evangelical preaching, full of fervour, but also to the three vows of humility, poverty and chastity, which opposed the fundamental vices of the period: pride, avarice and lust. Even the most confirmed sinners felt the fascination of these three vows, and dying, asked to be received into the Franciscan Third Order, leaving to the Friars large sums to repair their crooked ways with their neighbours (the Franciscan convents were really and truly Institutes of Beneficence), and asked to be buried under the protection of the great Saint. And so, the Franciscan churches became the most ample cemeteries. For more than a century there increased the collective sepulchres of hundreds of families from all parts of the city, and a large number of men, famous in their life-time, had the privilege of a last resting-place here. Side by side with these illustrious tombs were added honorary monuments and the church assumed the task of immortalizing the glory of the most famous people of the whole of Italy. We must make a distinction between the real and true « tombs », the « monuments » of people buried in the church in tombs not far off, the honorary « cenotaphs » of illustrious people not buried in the church, and the commemorating « slabs » which use-

The Annunciation by Donatello and the « Madonna of the Milk » by A. Rossellino.

lessly encumber the walls. Among the many hundreds of memorials, the visitor should avoid wasting his attention on curious observations, and dedicate himself only to the very great number of works of art and to the tombs of the greater men.

Wall of the façade. Stained-glass window from cartoon by LORENZO GHIBERTI, *Deposition fom the Cross;* below, on the right, *Monument to Gino Capponi* (d. 1876), learned historian, by ANTONIO BORTONE; on the left, *Monument to the historian and tragic poet G. B. Niccolini* (d. 1861), by PIO FEDI.

Right aisle. First altar: *Crucifixion* by SANTI DI TITO (about 1579). *First* pillar: *Madonna « of the milk »,* low-relief by ANTONIO ROSSELLINO, on the tomb of Francesco Nori, assassinated in the Cathedral by the Pazzi conspirators (1478) in order to save Lorenzo the Magnificent. On the wall, *Tomb of Michelangelo Buonarroti* (1564) by VASARI, decorated with statues of *Painting, Sculpture* and *Architecture* by various artists, instead of with the Victory group (today in Palazzo Vecchio), or with that of the Deposition (in the Cathedral) by Michelangelo himself, as had been the idea. *Cenotaph to Dante Alighieri* (d. 1321, whose body lies near the church of San Francesco at Ravenna), put up by STEFANO RICCI (1819-30) to record the very great poet, whom Michelangelo, in 1519, had in vain asked if he might be allowed to honour with a sepulchre. *Monument to Vittorio Alfieri* (d. 1803) by ANTONIO CANOVA (1810). Against the opposite pillar, we find the very fine sculptural ensemble in marble, and wood inlay on the little door, of the *Pulpit,* with *Stories of St. Francis* by BENEDETTO DA MAIANO (about 1475). On the wall of the aisle, *Monument*

Taddeo Gaddi: Meeting of St. Anne with St. Joachim.

to *Niccolò Machiavelli* (d. 1527) by INNOCENZO SPINAZZI (1787) with the famous inscription: « Tanto nomini nullum par elogium » (to such a great name no praise is adequate). Further on, *Tomb of P. Luigi Lanzi*, the great art historian (1810). *Tabernacle* in grey stone (pietra serena), gilded in parts, with the *Annunciation* (c. 1430) masterpiece by DONATELLO. *Tomb of Leonardo Bruni*, humanist historian (d. 1444) by BERNARDO ROSELLINO, most beautiful example of a fifteenth century funeral monument. *Tomb of Gioacchino Rossini*, the great musician (d. 1868), a trite nineteenth century imitation of the fifteenth century style, by GIUSEPPE CASSIOLI (1887). *Monument to Ugo Foscolo*, buried here, by ANTONIO BERTI (1939).

Castellani or **Sacrament Chapel,** where the members of the laical Franciscan Third Order used to meet, among which was Dante Alighieri. It preserves the important cycle of frescoes by AGNOLO GADDI and his pupils (c. 1383), with *stories of St. Nicholas of Bari, St. Anthony the Abbot, St. John the Baptist and St. John the Evangelist. Crucifix* by NICCOLÒ GERINI, and against the pilasters, *St. Francis* and *St. Dominic,* statues of the workshop of the Della Robbia. Several tombs among which that of the *Countess of Albany* (the wife of Charles Stuart, « Bonnie Prince Charlie ») from a design by C. Percier.

Bernardo Rossellino: Tomb of Leonardo Bruni (detail).

Baroncelli, now **Giugni Chapel.** On the ouside, *Tomb of the Baroncelli* in Pisan Gothic style (1328). Inside, on the wall to the right, *Madonna of the Girdle,* large fresco by BASTIANO MAINARDI (c. 1490), a pupil of Ghirlandaio. On the other walls, *Scenes from the Life of Mary* (1332-38) painted by TADDEO GADDI, a follower of Giotto, of lively personality though sometimes a little rough. On the altar, the *Coronation of the Virgin,* a panel signed by GIOTTO but lacking the usual powerful style and workmanship of this master. The marble statue of the *Madonna* is a work of VINCENZO DANTI (1568).

Sacristy. From MICHELOZZO's *doorway* we go into the corridor and on the left enter the Sacristy which preserves its fourteenth century architecture, decorated on the right-hand wall with *Stories of the Passion,* fresco rich in laborious allegories, by NICCOLÒ GERINI (c. 1380) assistant to Gaddi. Cupboards by GIOVANNI DI MICHELE (c. 1454) with the back carved by NANNI UNGARO (c. 1530). On the walls, various works of art, among which a Della Robbia *bust of Jesus,* and a *Lavabo* of the school of Desiderio da Settignano. Reliquaries, illuminated missals, and precious sacerdotal ornaments, of Florentine manufacture, of various periods, are gathered in the glass wall-cases. In the central wall opens the

Rinuccini Chapel, closed by a wrought-iron gate (1371), all frescoed with *Stories of St. Mary Magdalen and the Virgin,* by GIOVANNI DA MILANO and his pupils. The altar piece is by GIOVANNI DEL BIONDO (1379). Coming back into the corridor, at the end of which, on the left, is the *Monument to the sculptor Lorenzo Bartolini* (d. 1850), by PASQUALE ROMANELLI, we enter the

Desiderio da Settignano: Tomb of C. Marsuppini (detail).

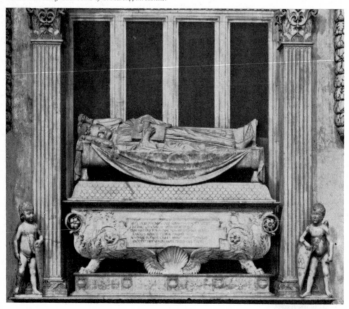

Medici, or **Novitiate Chapel,** built by that celebrated family's architect, MICHELOZZO (1434) by order of Cosimo the Elder. The light and serene architecture is enlivened by a DELLA ROBBIA *altarpiece* while on the right we notice the strange *monument to the jeweler Francesco Lombardi,* composed of various parts, among which a very beautiful low-relief attributed to Donatello.

Returning to the church, we visit in turn the end-chapels, each one founded by the great families of the Quarter and dedicated to a Saint, the patron of the house.

Velluti, later **Morelli and Riccardi Chapel,** which preserves the frescoes of the original *History of St. Michael the Archangel,* very doubtfully attributed to Cimabue.

Bellacci Chapel later **Calderini, Bonsignori, Riccardi** once frescoed by T. Gaddi, now decorated with cold architecture by GHERARDO SILVANI (c. 1640), with vault and lunettes by GIOVANNI DA SAN GIOVANNI, *Stories of St. Andrew the Apostle* (1621).

Silvestri Chapel, later **Giugni,** later **Bonaparte,** once frescoed by Giotto, with Stories of Martyrs. Here is the *Monument of Charlotte Bonaparte* (d. 1839) by LORENZO BARTOLINI and the *tomb of Giulia Bonaparte,* by LUIGI PAMPALONI (1847).

Peruzzi Chapel, with cycle of the celebrated frescoes of GIOTTO representing *Stories of St. John the Evangelist* (c. 1320). These frescoes were covered over with a layer of lime, and were rediscovered and badly restored in 1842. A thorough restoration with modern criteria has now been executed. On solemn occasion a precious relic is exposed on the altar, to which the whole church is dedicated, in a reliquary of rock crystal and gilded silver, by the Venetian goldsmith BERTUCCIO.

Giotto: Banquet of Herodes.

Agnolo Gaddi: Legend of the Holy Cross – The dream of Constantine.

Bardi Chapel, was also decorated with frescoes by GIOTTO with the admirable *Stories of St. Francis* (c. 1318), one of the fundamental works of Italian painting. They were rediscovered from the plasterwork in 1853 and have been recently restored, removing all the 19th cent. restorations and arbitrary repainting. Over the outside arch, the dramatic *Reception of the Stigmata*, and in the vaulting *Allegory of Chastity, Poverty and Obedience*, and *Triumph of the Saint*, also by Giotto. On the altar is a precious painting with *St. Francis and Stories of his life*, by a Florentine painter under the influence of the school of Lucca (end of the 14th century).

Main Chapel, of the **Alberti**, painted in fresco by AGNOLO GADDI, with the *Legend of the Holy Cross* (1380), inspired by the legend by the Blessed James from Voragine. We notice how the Giottesque composition is succeeded by the Gothic quest for effects of movement and exterior dramatic art. On the altar, polyptych with the *Madonna and Saints*, the central panel being the work of PIETRO GERINI while the rest was painted by various Giottesque masters. Over the altar hangs a large *Crucifix*, the work of a worthy follower of Giotto. The beautiful stained-glass windows are a work of the 15th century.

Tolosini Chapel, later **Spinelli** and **Sloane.** On the altar a polyptych, by GIOVANNI DEL BIONDO (1372), with the *Virgin and Saints*. On the walls, frescoes by GASPARE MARTELLINI (1837).

Benci Chapel, later **Capponi**, now of the **Italian Mother.** *The Virgin with her dead Son*, monument by LIBERO ANDREOTTI (1926) in honour of the mothers of the fallen in the 1915-18 war.

Ricasoli Chapel, decorated with *Stories of St. Anthony of Padua* by the nineteenth century painter LUIGI SABATELLI assisted by his sons.

Pulci Chapel, later **Berardi**, later **Bardi della Libertà.** On the altar, glazed terracotta *Altar-piece*, by GIOVANNI DELLA ROBBIA. On the walls, the *Martyrdom of St. Lawrence* and that of *St. Stephen* by BERNARDO DADDI.

Chapel of the Bardi di Vernio. Frescoed by an unknown Giottesque painter whom one calls GIOTTINO, with the *Stories of the Pope St. Silvester.* On the left, two *tombs* from the fourteenth century. On the altar, *St. Giovanni Gualberto and four scenes from his Life*, a panel attributed either to Jacopo di Cione or to Giovanni del Biondo.

At the end of the left wing of the transept, the **Niccolini Chapel** dedicated to the Assumption of the Virgin Mary. Example of a homogeneous ensemble of rich decoration (1571-1664) planned by G.B. DOSIO. Statues by PIETRO FRANCAVILLA; pictures on the altars by ALESSANDRO ALLORI, *Assumption* and *Coronation of the Virgin Mary* (1588), and decoration of the cupola by BALDASSARRE FRANCESCHINI called the VOLTERRANO (1660).

Chapel of the Bardi di Vernio (still in the transept). It was once frescoed by AGNOLO GADDI, of which there remain the *medallions* in the vaulting. Here we find the *Crucifix* (c. 1425) by DONATELLO criticised by Brunelleschi for being excessively true to life. The one which Brunelleschi made, to confront it, we have seen in Santa Maria Novella.

Salviati Chapel. Among the various tombs we notive that of the *Princess Zamoijska* (d. 1837) by LORENZO BARTOLINI, and the *tomb of the archeologist Luigi Canina* (d. 1856) by SANTE VARNI. On the altar, the *Martyrdom of St. Lawrence*, by JACOPO LIGOZZI (c. 1600). In the wall of the transept *Monument to the musician Luigi Cherubini* (d. 1842) by ODOARDO FANTACCHIOTTI (1869).

Giotto: The Death of St. Francis.

Left aisle. Among the various memorials, we notice the fine *Monument to Carlo Marsuppini* (d. 1453), a humanist, by DESIDERIO DA SETTIGNANO, inspired by the one opposite, by Rossellino. There follow other tombs and memorials, and finally, the *Tomb of Galileo Galilei* (d. 1642), mediocre work of G. B. FOGGINI who executed the *Bust* and *Astronomy* (1735), while *Geometry* is by G. TICCIATI.

The tomb-slabs scattered all over the flooring of the church constitute a collection of exceptional artistic and historical interest, which continue from the first years of the 14th century until the end of the 18th. Here we can follow the decorative style of the low-reliefs, in bronze and marble, of inlay and geometric design, of work in hard semi-precious stones, which remains today the boast of the local artists. Very few can be said to be without interest, many are authentic works of art, even if nearly all are anonymous. For this and for the mural monuments the studious visitor is advised to make a more analytical examination which will always prove full of things which he may admire or which may surprise him. Apart from the names of the most illustrious men, like Michelangelo, Vittorio Alfieri, Niccolò Machiavelli, Gioacchino Rossini. Ugo Foscolo, Galileo Galilei, we come upon many memorials of « great spirits » in every field. Apart from the great works of art, like the tombs of Bruni and Marsuppini, we shall discover innumerable marvels, like the fine coats-of-arms and the decoration scattered happily everywhere.

First cloister. - By what is called the *Hammer Door*, on the right of the façade, we come into the picturesque fourteenth century cloister. Many members of well-known families of Dante's time were buried in this cloister; their tombs, as well as some more recent ones, have been gathered in a gallery under the left arcade. On the right as one enters, notice the *memorial to Florence Nightingale*, the precursor of Red Cross nurses, who was born

Lorenzo Bartolini: Tomb of Princess Zamoijska.

Interior of the Pazzi Chapel.

at Florence in 1823. Under the left arcade, near the side door of the church, a *sarcophagus* with the recumbent figure *of Gastone della Torre,* Patriarch of Aquileia, the work of TINO DI CAMAINO (14th cent.).

A magnificent background to the cloister is the **Pazzi Chapel** (1430-45) by FILIPPO BRUNELLESCHI who was here able, as in the Sacristy of San Lorenzo, to put into practice his ideal of sacred architecture, that is a building with central ground-work, surmounted by cupola and lantern.

Outside, a portico in classical style, with frieze decorated with *cherubs' heads,* designed by DONATELLO and executed by DESIDERIO DA SETTIGNANO. A large central arch, corresponding to a half-spherical cupola, decorated with terracottas by LUCA DELLA ROBBIA; in the arms of the portico, barrel vaulting decorated with rosettes. By the wonderful carved door designed by GIULIANO DA MAIANO (1472) we go into the very simple harmonious **interior.** The architectural design is made evident by the simmetry of the grey stone (pietra serena) which stands out on the walls plastered in lime with no painted decoration. Only a terracotta frieze and harmonious medallions with *Evangelists* and *Apostles* by LUCA DELLA ROBBIA, offer a discreet note of colour. The small square apse with round cupola, is soberly decorated by the altar from Donatello's workshop. The *St. Andrew,* in the window, is attributed to ALESSO BALDOVINETTI.

Here also, as in the Sacristy of San Lorenzo, were brought together the most typical artists of Florentine Renaissance art: Filippo Brunelleschi the architect, Donatello the sculptor, Luca della Robbia the decorator, Alesso Baldovinetti the painter.

Second Cloister. - From the right-hand corner of the first cloister, a fine *doorway* by Michelozzo or Benedetto da Maiano, leads into the harmonious **Great Cloister,** designed by BRUNELLESCHI shortly before his death (1453) and probably decorated by BERNARDO ROSSELLINO.

Museum of the Opera di Santa Croce. - From the first cloister on the right, we enter the old Refectory which together with some adjoining rooms was the seat of the Museum of the Opera di Santa Croce. Unfortunately it was terribly damaged by the flood of November 1966 and at the moment of the publication of this guide-book it is still being restored.

The end wall of the Refectory was covered with frescoes from the Giottesque school: in the centre, the *Tree of the Holy Cross*, below the *Last Supper* attributed to TADDEO GADDI. Statues, paintings, detached frescoes which were once in the church, were once exhibited here, among which the bronze statue of *St. Ludovic of Toulouse* by DONATELLO, the detached frescoes of the *Triumph of Death* by ORCAGNA and those representing *St. John the Baptist* and *St. Francis* by DOMENICO VENEZIANO. The magnificent *Crucifix* by CIMABUE has been almost completely destroyed by the flood.

Bell-tower. - Before going out we glance at the Campanile which rises on the right of the church. It is a fine example of stylistic fourteenth century recasting executed by GAETANO BACCANI (1885), and which by some inattentive historian was listed among the most perfect Gothic bell-towers; but the last railing, which breaks the line, betrays the nineteenth century taste of its architect.

Piazza Santa Croce. On the wide square, once a marshy space between humble sheds, there grew up with time palaces

The Great Cloister of Santa Croce designed by Brunelleschi.

of notable importance. On the right as one leaves the church a fifteenth century house with columned terrace. At the end, the most original façade of the *Serristori*, once *Cocchi Palace,* on probable design of BACCIO D'AGNOLO (c. 1470). On the left, a line of palaces with corbel-built façades, which were a local characteristic. In the middle is the *Palazzo dell'Antella*, once of the *Cerchi*, built by GIULIO PARIGI (1619) with the façade completely frescoed in only 27 days, by 12 painters guided by GIOVANNI DA SAN GIOVANNI. On the left side of the façade of the church, the *Monument to Dante Alighieri,* the third of the ugly monuments expianting his injust condemnation, after that in the Church of Santa Croce and the statue in the Uffizi, erected for the sixth centenary of the birth of the poet (1865), work of ENRICO PAZZI.

The evolution of Florentine life can be followed for long periods in this great square. In the fourteenth century great flocks of people came to listen to the voice of the Franciscan preachers, or to take part in the solemn religious and civil ceremonies there. In the fifteenth century, splendid feasts, tournaments, and tilting between the young men of the best families (that in 1469 is famous, won by Lorenzo dei Medici, and another in 1475, when Giuliano dei Medici triumphed, praised by Agnolo Poliziano, the poet). In the sixteenth century, there developed here the *Giuoco del calcio* (Football game), which had such vogue in Florence, even to be held under the fire of enemy artillery (1529), to the sound of resounding music, as a challenge, from the top of the roof of the church. A disc built up in marble on the Palazzo dell'Antella remains still as the centre mark of the playing field. From the democratic life of the Commune, to the parrying of the Signoria, and from these to the games which pleased the people of the Grand Duchy: chariot-races in Piazza Santa Maria Novella, football games in Piazza Santa Croce.

On the right flank of the church is *Via delle Pinzochere*, (once inhabited by the Franciscan Tertiaries, dressed in « binzo » or « bigio », that is brownish, habit) with the *Palazzo da Verrazzano* attributed to BACCIO D'AGNOLO. We come to *Via Ghibellina*, where is the **Casa Buonarroti**, bought by Michelangelo for a nephew, and which the spirited writer, Michelangelo the Younger (d. 1646) and his heirs transformed into a sort of museum in honour of their great ancestor. Several of the rooms are richly decorated with frescoes and canvases relating to episodes in the life of Michelangelo and his family, and there are preserved many portraits, manuscripts and mementoes of the great master. Among his original work are two marble reliefs: a *Madonna and Child* and the *Battle of Centaurs and Lapites*, besides a few interesting models of some of his most famous statues. The collection of designs once preserved here is now kept at the Uffizi. Here are periodically exhibited series of fac-simile reproductions of these designs divided by subject matter.

Coming back into Piazza Santa Croce, at the side of Palazzo Serristori is *Via Torta* whose curved way is due to the fact that the houses stand on the foundations of the old Roman Amphitheatre (end of the Ist cent. A.D.). Following this street, we reach **Piazza Peruzzi**, a typical spot of medieval Florence, where stands the fourteenth century *Peruzzi Palace*, also with foundation on the walls and steps of the amphitheatre, and therefore with a curved façade.

Through an arch we enter *Via dei Benci* where many houses preserve the old fourteenth century architecture, with flat blocks and pointed arches. On the corner of *Borgo Santa Croce* stands a typical tower-house which has below it the four-

Michelangelo: Madonna and Child (Casa Buonarroti).

teenth century *Loggia degli Alberti,* the family from which sprang the great architect Leon Battista Alberti (1494-72), and which owned many houses in this quarter. In one of the palaces once of the Alberti, the architecture of which is attributed to GIULIANO DA SANGALLO, is now the small, but precious

Horne Museum donated by an Englishman, Herbert Percy Horne, in 1916. Here are collected many works of art, paintings, sculpture of all sorts, and collections of objects for household use. Besides several pictures of the Florentine school of the fourteenth century and the Renaissance, exceptionally important is the *St. Stephen* attributed to GIOTTO and a collection of drawings by some of the most famous ancient masters.

Opposite, on the right the fifteenth century *Bardi Palace* attributed to BRUNELLESCHI, where, at the end of the sixteenth century, the famous Camerata dei Bardi met, in which musical drama or melodrama had its origin. Further on, at the corner, the *Alberti Palace,* of the same century, in which Leon Battista died.

Going down *Via de' Neri* and turning to the right into *Via S. Remigio,* we come to the **Church of San Remigio** probably founded in the time of Charlemagne and dedicated to Saint Remy, Bishop of Reims. It was rebuilt in the 14th century and the interior is a harmonious example of Gothic architecture. The panel with the *Madonna Enthroned* is the work of a painter contemporary of Cimabue.

Following *Via de' Neri* we reach the *Loggia del Grano,* which we have already seen in our first itinerary; turning to the left we come to *Piazza de' Giudici.* Here on the right the fourteenth century *Palazzo dei Castellani* now houses the **Accademia della Crusca** (Bran Academy, with a sieve as its emblem, meaning that its object was to « sift » the Italian language in order to purity it) and the **Museum of Science,** two glorious institutions founded in the 17th cent., which demonstrate the prodigious literary and scientific activity of what is arbitrarily called a decadent period. Here we find several of Galileo's optical instruments (1609), the first barometer of Evangelista Torricelli (1644), the microscopes of G.B. Amici, on the Galilean prototypes, and many precious old scientific curiosities.

We cross the end of the *Loggia degli Uffizi* and go down the arcades of the *Lungarno degli Archibugieri,* finally coming to the *Ponte Vecchio.* To the right stretches what was the old

Church of Santi Apostoli.

Roman camp, on which the mediaeval city was born, with the tower-houses, some of which still stand out of the war's destruction, with the old Romanesque churches, among which that of **Santo Stefano al Ponte**, which tradition says was founded in the time of Charlemagne. The unfinished façade, of the most typical Romanesque-Florentine style, goes back to the first years of the thirteenth century. The interior, altered in the seventeenth century by TACCA, has been restored after the last war's damages. Taking *Borgo Santi Apostoli* we enter the picturesque *Piazzetta del Limbo*, in which is one of the most ancient Florentine churches of the Romanesque period.

Church of Santi Apostoli. - Legend says it was founded by Charlemagne, but the first written mention of it goes back to 1075. It was founded on a wall of the nearby Roman Baths, over a child-cemetery called the « Limbo », outside the first circle of the walls. Its simple lines of Roman inspiration were a prototype of many other Florentine churches: Filippo Brunelleschi himself brought them into the conception of San Lorenzo and Santo Spirito. Its lines and the tone of the materials make it a most solemn building, despite its modest proportions.

Interior. Of particular interest is the raftered roof with painted beams, perhaps the only one preserved, with a recent repainting, of those typical of the 13th and 14th cent.

In the capitals of the first two columns, which came from the nearby Baths building, we see the model for the others, which originated this element of local architecture, brought to the most exquisite perfection by Brunelleschi and by his followers.

On the third altar on the right, one of the best paintings by VASARI, *The Immaculate Conception*, painted in 1541, five years before the Council of Trent. In the apse, *Funeral Monument of Archbishop Antonio Altoviti* (1574) from a design by G. B. DOSIO.

On the end wall of the left aisle, the exquisite *Tabernacle* by ANDREA DELLA ROBBIA. On the left wall, *Tomb of Donato Acciaioli* (1339), a work of the Pisan School, and *Monument of Oddo Altoviti* by BENEDETTO DA ROVEZZANO (1507) anticipating the bizarre decorations of the seventeenth century. In this church are preserved, in a fine brazier of enamelled copper of the 15th cent., stone splinters which legend says were brought from the Holy Land by the crusader Pazzino dei Pazzi. On Holy Saturday they are solemnly taken to Piazza del Duomo and between them make the spark to set light to the popular Florentine device called the « Scoppio del carro ».

Returning to the Lungarno, after the Ponte Santa Trinita, we notice the *Masetti Palace* where the poet Vittorio Alfieri died in 1803, and the *Gerini Palace*, where Alessandro Manzoni lived in 1827, when he came to Florence to « risciacquare i suoi cenci in Arno », that is to refreshen and clean up his language. Then we pass under the grandiose **Palazzo Corsini**, by PIER FRANCESCO SILVANI (1648-56) crowned with statues. On the first floor is the *Corsini Gallery*, the greatest private collection of works of art in Florence, arranged with masterly taste,

Palazzo Corsini.

D. Ghirlandaio: St. Jerome (Ognissanti).

untouched by the historical-didactic preoccupations which nowadays dominate nearly all the public collections.

The decorations of the rooms, the choice of the furniture, of the stuffs is precious in itself, but not a few works of art displayed are of great interest, especially for the knowledge of the local pictorial school of the 16th and 17th cent.

We should notice: a fine collection of *Medici portraits* by JUSTUS SUSTERMANS and the *portrait of Geri della Rena* by the same artist; the cartoon for the *portrait of Pope Julius II*, by RAPHAEL or at least from his school; *a portrait of a Man* by RIDOLFO DEL GHIRLANDAIO, of robust construction. Very interesting are also: two round panels, one with the *Madonna and Saints* by LUCA SIGNORELLI and the other with the *Madonna and Angels* by FILIPPINO LIPPI; the front of a chest with allegorical figures of *Philosophy and four Liberal Arts* probably also by FILIPPINO; a small panel with *Christ Crucified* by a follower of Giovanni Bellini; a series of 8 small panels with *Apollo and seven Muses* by GIOVANNI SANTI, the father of Raphael; a *Madonna with Child and St. John the Baptist* by PONTORMO; four dramatic *Scenes of the Passion* by DOMENICO FETI (17th century), the *Allegory of Poetry* by CARLO DOLCI.

Out on the Lungarno, we follow the line of the river,

until *Piazza Goldoni*, with the marble *statue* of the Venetian playwright by Ulisse Cambi (1873). From this square run several streets. We take *Borgo Ognissanti*. The name of Borgo records that also this part of the city was once outside the walls (we have, in fact, come back to the vicinity of Santa Maria Novella). Here spread out what we call the industrial quarter, because of the many ditches of water which ran towards the Arno and which used to provide motive power and water for the working and washing of the wool. One of the roads which lead into Piazza Goldoni, from Piazza Santa Maria Novella, is in fact called *Via dei Fossi* (ditches). The wool industry, which became later the boast and fortune of the city, existing already since its foundation, was developed and made perfect in the convents of the Benedictines (11th cent.) and later by the Umiliati friars, who « with the work of their own hands » founded on this spot, in 1251, their convent and workshops. From these grew up the fulling-mills, the spinning-mills, the dye-houses in which was formed the fortune of nearly all the great Florentine families, and which gave life to all the other arts, more or less complementary to the wool trade, which remained for many centuries the most important. On the area bought by the Umiliati friars, there grew up in 1256 the

S. Botticelli: St. Augustine (Ognissanti).

Church of Ognissanti, altered in the seventeenth century, and from which the original line has gone. The *façade* by MATTEO NIGETTI (1638), is one of the first examples of Baroque architecture, and, if it seems today rather moderate, it was judged then as « the most incorrect, and beyond all the rules that could have been conceived », so violent in its design and details, seemed the break from tradition.

The **interior** of the church was also altered in the seventeenth century but still preserves some fine Renaissance altars. On the second altar on the right, of the Vespucci family who had their house in the neighbourhood, we can admire a fresco by DOMENICO GHIRLANDAIO (1470) representing the *Vespucci family under the mantle of the Madonna.* Among the various people, it is believed one can recognize, in the kneeling young man, Amerigo who gave his name to the new continent, and in the young lady on the right, the famous Simonetta Cattaneo, married to a Vespucci, loved by Giuliano dei Medici and sung by Poliziano. Below, *Deposition* by DOMENICO GHIRLANDAIO or by his brother DAVID. About half-way down the church, still on the right, *St. Augustine,* fresco (1480) by SANDRO BOTTICELLI (the painter's family also lived in this quarter), and opposite, on the left-hand wall, *St. Jerome* by DOMENICO GHIRLANDAIO (1480). In the transept chapel, on the right, in the flooring, the round *tomb-stone of Mariano Filipepi and children,* among whom is the celebrated painter called Sandro di Botticello or Botticelli (d. 1510). The *cupola* of the church is painted in fresco by the seventeenth century colourist GIOVANNI DA SAN GIOVANNI. In the **Sacristy,** a *Crucifix* of the school of Giotto and a fresco of the *Crucifixion* attributed to TADDEO GADDI.

Raphael: Cartoon for the portrait of Pope Julius II (Palazzo Corsini).

D. Ghirlandaio: The Madonna of Mercy and the Vespucci Family.

Next to the church is the **Cloister** in the fifteenth century style of Michelozzo, with *Stories of St. Francis* by JACOPO LIGOZZI (1625) and GIOVANNI DA SAN GIOVANNI (1616-19). A doorway leads into the large **Refectory,** where we admire the *Last Supper* of DOMENICO GHIRLANDAIO, composed two years before Leonardo da Vinci left Florence (1480), and which certainly inspired him for his very famous painting in Milan.

Back in *Piazza Ognissanti*, we see the *Busiri-Quaratesi-Pisani Palace*, of the early fifteenth century, with corbels and « grafito » decorations used here for the first time in Florence.

The Via Borgognissanti continues with the *Via del Prato*, as far as the gate from which we started. From this, turning to the left into the avenue, in a short while we come to the beginning of the Cascine Park.

CASCINE

In the past the tongue of ground which lay between the Arno and the Mugnone was called the *Island*, and was abandoned and almost wild. At the beginning of the sixteenth century this piece of land was bought by the first Duke of Florence. His successors made a wide avenue of pines there, and formed an oasis of grass and trees which took the name of *Cascine*, because there were the cowsheds which provided milk for the Grand Ducal Court. Open to the public in the second half of the eighteenth century, it became the favourite park of the Florentines, especially in the nineteenth century, when the avenues were filled with an uninterrupted file of lordly carriages. From the square where is the big *equestrian statue of Victor Emmanuel II*, by EMILIO ZOCCHI (1890), by two avenues which cross picturesque, varied gardens, woods, meadows, fields for games and races, with buildings and little monuments in romantic and nineteenth century style, after three and a half km., we come to the end of the park, where is the surprising, picturesque *Monument to the Indian*. A Maharajah of Kalepoor, returning from England, died at twenty years of age in Florence (1870). The Brahman rite called for him to be cremated at the meeting place of two rivers. They chose the spot where the Mugnone joins the Arno, and put up this characteristic and exotic coloured monument.

We have gone round the perimeter of the old walls, visited the famous *Church of Santa Croce*, followed the sunniest *Lungarni*, and from the part where once stood the industrial suburb of Florence, we have come out towards the *Cascine Park*, which lies between the Arno and the Mugnone, at the extreme West of the city.

THE MEDICI QUARTER

*Palazzo Medici-Riccardi - Church and Convent of
San Marco - Cloister of the Scalzo - Coenaculum
of Sant' Apollonia · Gallery of the Accademia
Church of Santissima Annunziata - Archeological
Museum - Convent and Church of Santa Mad-
dalena dei Pazzi - Church of Sant' Ambrogio
Theatre of the Pergola.*

THE MEDICI QUARTER

From the north side of Piazza del Duomo runs *Via de'
Martelli,* where, at the end, on the left, is the **Church of San
Giovannino** (St. John the Evangelist), work of AMMANNATI
(1578), who spent all his gains there and was buried there
(1592) near his wife Laura Battiferri, the celebrated poetess
(d. 1589).

Since 1775 the church has belonged to the glorious convent of the Scolopi, or Fathers of the Order of Pious Schools,
who looked after the education of youth. The convent was
the large building at the side of the church, today occupied
by a government high school.

This area has many memories connecting it with the history of aerial navigation. In the house of the Martelli, in
1507, lived LEONARDO DA VINCI, the first man to study, with
scientific criteria, the problem of the mechanics of flight and
the use of the parachute. In the courtyard of the convent, then
belonging to the Jesuits, FATHER FRANCESCO LANA-TERZI, from
Brescia, made, at the end of the 17th cent., an experiment with
his « flying boat », a machine which should have raised itself
by the force of the pneumatic vacuum. In the basement of
the convent is buried FATHER EUGENIO BARSANTI, from Pietra-
santa, (1821-1864), inventor of the internal combustion engine
(1853) which found wide use in aeronautics.

On the top floor of the old convent the *Astronomical Observatory* is still in activity founded by FATHER LEONARDO XIMENES
(1716-86), and from his name called Ximenian, the meteoro-
logical and sismological observations of which have continued
without interruption since 1813.

Palazzo Medici, later **Riccardi**. The continuation of Via
Martelli is the old *Via Larga* (now *C. Cavour*) so called in the
fifteenth century because it was unusually wide. The streets
in the mediaeval city were all narrow and winding, but when
Cosimo the Elder thought of building his great palace, the
new, wide, straight street was laid out, the expression of new
times.

The city centre now moved from Piazza della Signoria
towards the new street where the lord of Florence resided.
And so Via Larga marked the new meridian which passed

Palazzo Medici-Riccardi: The Courtyard.

from the established political centre in Palazzo Medici, to the established religious centre in the convent of San Marco.

Cosimo entrusted the construction of the palace to his trustworthy architect MICHELOZZO DI BARTOLOMEO (1396-1472), who gave the building the typical line of the fifteenth century Florentine palace. Square plan with columned courtyard in the middle; loggia at the side; stone bench at the base. The ground-floor is embossed, retaining something of the fortress, but on the first floor the wall is made smoother, scarcely marked by blocks, between which are elegant double-arched windows. On the third floor the wall is even lighter and so are the windows. A large, powerful, sedate cornice crowns the palace. It now has a horizontal addition, but in the fifteenth century it was a perfect cube, like Palazzo Strozzi. There were only 10 windows by Michelozzo. The other 7 were added in 1670. In fact, while in the former we see the emblem of the Medici family, that is, seven « balls » (repeated also in the shield on the southern corner) and the personal emblem of Piero, son of Cosimo, the ring with a diamond and three feathers; in the adjoining windows we see the « key » of the Riccardi family

Benozzo Gozzoli: Detail of the frescoes in the Medici Chapel.

who enlarged the Palace (repeated also on the shield on the northern corner). Also the corner loggia was closed in 1517 and in its wall were opened the « kneeling » windows, on designs by Michelangelo, the first to be seen in Florence in that style.

In this palace, which Cosimo « Pater Patriae » (1389-1464) wanted to build for his family, his son Piero lived (1416-1469), who carried on the embellishments, and the Magnificent Lorenzo (1448-1492) held his court there in regal luxury. Reigning princes were guests here, such as the Sforza, the Malatesta, and here, as in a royal palace, Charles VIII of France, took up residence in 1494. The popular government saved the palace from being sacked, after the flight of Piero, son of Lorenzo, from Florence, but the works of art collected there were dispersed, and sold by auction. After eighteen years the Medici came back into the palace and, in 1536, Emperor Charles V was given hospitality there, from whom Alessandro dei Medici had received his investiture as Duke of Florence.

In 1540, as definite affirmation of his seigniory the second Duke of the city Cosimo I, transferred the official seat of the

Benozzo Gozzoli: Detail of the frescoes in the Medici Chapel.

family and court from the private palace in Via Larga to the Palazzo della Signoria, which had been for almost two and a half centuries the seat of city government. The palace still remained the property of the family, but with the transfer of Cosimo I, the magnificent furnishings and works of art still existing were taken to the new palace and later to the Uffizi building.

The Roman sarcophagi, which we have seen in the visit to the Baptistery, were once in the courtyard of this palace. The magnificent bronze horse's head, which we can admire in the Archeological Museum, was in the garden at the back of the palace and had been adapted as a fountain. The two statues of Marsyas flayed alive, now in the Uffizi, Roman works restored by Verrocchio and Donatello, decorated the doorway to the garden; the David by Donatello, sequestrated by the Signoria and taken to their palazzo, and the other David by Verrocchio which Lorenzo gave to the Signoria, were in this courtyard: today they are in the Bargello Museum. Of the garden, reduced to a few square meters by the new buildings of the Riccardi, there remains almost nothing. On a large granite bowl was the statue of Judith by Donatello now in Piazza della Signoria; but the inscription put there after the flight of Piero, the unworthy son of Lorenzo the Magnificent, in 1495, was supposed to be an allegory against tyrants and not even the Medici dukes thought it opportune to take away the record of such a vivid interpretation. Also the copy of the Laocoon made by Bandinelli at Rome, which we have seen in the Uffizi, was in this courtyard. Of the original decoration of the building there remain only eight medallions attributed to BERTOLDO (d. 1491) pupil of Donatello, and to MASO DI BARTOLOMEO, called MASACCIO (not to be confused with the painter), reproducing Roman gems belonging to Lorenzo the Magnificent.

The **interior** of the Palace, completely altered by the Riccardi, only preserves a few rooms of the original Medici quarters on the ground-floor, deprived of all mural decoration; but on the first floor remains, although damaged by the construction of the main stairway, the splendid Chapel, a real gem of fifteenth century art.

The **Chapel**, the idea of Cosimo the Elder, but commissioned by Piero, perhaps inspired by his wife Lucrezia, was build by MICHELOZZO, who designed the box-ceiling, and placed there the stalls in intarsia. On the altar was placed a very' fine painting of Filippo Lippi, representing the *Virgin in Adoration of the Child*, assisted by St. John the Baptist and St. Bernard, two of the Medici patrons. The reproductions of God the Father and of the Holy Spirit show that the Most Holy Trinity is present on earth as the inspirer of wisdom and love to men of good will. The painting, later sent to Berlin and substituted by a copy with variations by NERI DI BICCI (1418-93) is the centre and the key of the conception of the scenes which continue on all the walls. The painter BENOZZO DI LESE GOZZOLI (1459-60) was called to paint in fresco the walls, representing there the participation of the creatures of the sky to the *Adoration of the Child*, with the *Adoring Angels*, and of the wise men, in the *Procession of the Wise Kings*.

He imagined the most fantastic and delightful pictorial decoration, of Angels who people an enchanting earthly landscape, and of persons on foot and horseback who congregate from great distances, in a procession which spreads itself over the Tuscan countryside, like a flowing, many-coloured river, on all the walls of the chapel.

The significant religious fresco contains also a political interpretation because, among the personages in the procession, who were to be the most learned, the most wise, the most magnificent, Benozzo portrayed men of the Medici world of those years, and so the adoration of the Divinity can remain as a secret exaltation of the family of the Commissioner. The first wise king, on the white horse, is the young Lorenzo (b. 1448). He is followed, also on horseback, by his father, Piero di Cosimo, the Gouty (b. 1416), with the high red cap, and his uncle Giovanni (b. 1421), with a scarf knotted on his hair. Among the other horsemen, the one in front is Prince Galeazzo Maria Sforza (1444-76), and, the last, in profile, Prince Sigismondo Pandolfo Malatesta (1417-1468), whose visit in the palace they wanted to record. In the crowd, above, the painter also portrayed himself, writing on his conical cap « Opus Benotii ». On the wall at the end, the second king is the portrait of the Emperor of Byzantium John VII Paleologus (1390-1448). On the other side of the windows, the three pages on horseback represent the sisters of Lorenzo, Maria, Bianca and Nannina. Finally, on the right hand wall, cut in half and moved on account of the works on the staircase, the third king is the portrait of Joseph, Patriarch of Constantinople, who died twenty years earlier during the Council, at Florence. In the first personages on the right, it is believed that we can recognize Filippo Strozzi, Vittorino da Feltre, and Niccolò da Uzzano.

While Benozzo was painting, the Turks appeared in the Mediterranean, and all western Christendom trembled. The vision of the procession of the Wise Kings recorded the Crusade against the infidels, also started in Florence in the Spring of '59, and which Pope Pius II wanted all the Italian princes to join, also the Medici, bankers of Christianity. The care taken by the painter in the execution of the details of the costumes, of the decorations, ornaments, animals, landscape, make his work extremely interesting for us who can never again assist at a similar parade of fifteenth century magnificence.

The rest of the palace, magnificently enlarged by the Riccardi, present rooms decorated with superb and princely taste. Of particular interest is the **Gallery** with the vault frescoed by Luca Giordano (1632-1705) with marvellous pictorial bravura. The frescoes represent the *Apotheosis of the Medici family*, with a complex series of allegories which is a catalogue of mythology current in seventeenth century literature. The bold foreshortening, the almost impressionistically fresh colouring, the astonishingly graceful composition, go to show that at the end of the 17th cent. painting still had marvellous manifestations.

Coming down again into the courtyard we glance at the *stairway* in the left-hand corner, planned, one thinks, by Michelangelo. Under the arch which gives access to the garden, is a fine statue of *Orpheus*, by Baccio Bandinelli (1493-1560). On the walls a part of the collection of Riccardian marbles, coming from excavation in the territory of Florence and Rome. In the ground floor rooms to the left, is the **Medici Museum,** arranged since 1929 to house there works of art and documents of particular iconographic interest, among which the *Funeral mask of Lorenzo the Magnificent*, the *portraits of the children of Cosimo I* painted by Bronzino, the *portrait of Cosimo I as a child* by Ridolfo del Ghirlandaio, a splendid *Madonna and Child*, by Filippo Lippi (c. 1450), the presumed *portrait of Bianca Cappello* by Alessandro Allori.

Those who have time should also visit the **Riccardiana Library,** founded in 1600 by Riccardo Riccardi, and transported to this its specially built seat which is a singular example of exquisite taste and noble culture. The ceiling with the allegory of *Human talent liberated from the servitude of ignorance,* is another exuberant work by Luca Giordano (1683).

Along the old Via Larga there grew up at various times palaces in diverse styles. Near the Medici palace grew up the house in which Lorenzino killed Alessandro dei Medici, the first Duke of Florence, in the night of Epiphany 1537.

Opposite is *Palazzo Covoni* built by Gherardo Silvani (1623) for Piero Capponi, whose striking devices decorate the terrace and the windows.

At the corner of *Via Guelfa*, on the left, is the fine fifteenth century *palace* of the *Rosselli*, later of *Bernardetto dei Medici*.

Further on, at number 39, the *Palazzo Dardinelli*, later *Fenzi*, built, as far as the second floor, by SANTI DI TITO, about 1580, and at number 45, the **Marucelliana Library**, founded by the learned Florentine Francesco Marucelli (1625-1703), author of the first vast, systematic, biographical collection, called by him « Mare magnum ». Besides a large collection of autographs and incunabula, there is preserved a precious collection of more than 30000 old engravings.

At the corner of *Via degli Arazzieri* on the site of a large Dominican Convent, still called of St. Catherine, was once the seat of the Library and Archive of the Academy of Fine Arts, and in 1830 the works of art discovered in Egypt in the expedition of Ipposito Rossellini, now passed to the Archeological Museum in Via della Colonna, were exhibited there. In the period when Florence was the capital, the large but unembellished seat of the Ministry of War in the first kingdom of Italy was built there (1867).

SAN MARCO

As we have already said, Via Larga, which began with Palazzo Medici, ended with the Convent of St. Mark. Here, in the middle of the fields, there existed since the 12th century, a convent of Vallombrosan friars, and later of the Salvestrines, where the Dominican friars of San Domenico of Fiesole were transferred, reformed by the Blessed Giovanni Dominici. In 1437, Cosimo, in order to lessen his remorse for some money which he thought not very honestly acquired, on the suggestion of Pope Eugene IV, gave orders to his architect MICHELOZZO to rebuild the Convent, building there with ten thousand florins; but the sinner thought the penitence too mild and willingly quadrupled the burden laid upon him, assuming in addition the expense of the furnishing, missals, choir-books, apart from the library and the restoring of the church. So this construction preceded the building even of the private house of Cosimo, at the other end of Via Larga, the work of the same architect. The old Romanesque-Gothic church of 1299 was enlarged only; but the convent was rebuilt almost from the

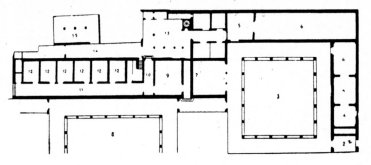

PLAN OF THE GROUND FLOOR.

1. Entrance from Piazza San Marco. - 2. Vestibule. - 3. Cloister of St. Antonino. - 4. Pilgrims' Hospice. - 5. Room of the Font. - 6. Large refectory. - 7. Chapter Hall. - 8. Cloister of St. Dominic. - 9. Small Refectory. - 10. Vestibule of the Guests' Quarter. - 11. Corridor of the Guests' Quarter. - 12. Cells. - 13. Small Cloister. - 14. Courtyard of the Granary. - 15 Cloister of the Salvestrines.

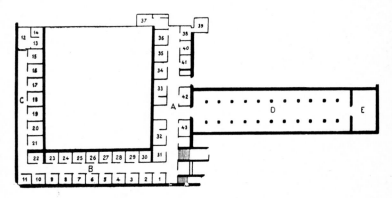

PLAN OF THE FIRST FLOOR.

A. First Corridor. - B. Second Corridor. - C. Third Corridor. - D. Library. - E. Greek Room.

12, 13 e 14. Cells of Savonarola. - 31. Cell of St. Antonino. - 33. Cell of Beato Angelico. - 38 and 39. Cells of Cosimo the Elder.

197

Convent of San Marco: First Cloister.

foundations and so had a united character which imprudent additions and alterations have not been able to destroy.

This was the first monastery which took on elegant and serene Renaissance forms, adapted to conciliate the spiritual exigencies of the monastic life with the grandiose intentions of the atoning donator. The severe rule of the reformed Dominicans was certainly present in every phase of the construction, in the mind of the genial architect and in that of the intelligent patron.

To understand what a fifteenth century convent was, we immediately visit the part which is today the Museum, and which includes the building restored by Michelozzo. Around the harmonious **cloister** Michelozzo's architecture is less severe than that of Brunelleschi, but more inviting. The luminosity of the plaster surfaces is enclosed by simple stone elements and by plain brick mouldings. While on the ground floor the arches gently surround the cloister, on the first floor there open discreetly the little windows of the conventual cells. Large Medici coats-of-arms repeat that for a good seven years everything was ordered, provided and paid by Cosimo's bank. « He had ordered the Bank that all the money that should be drawn on the account of a senior monk of the convent should be paid to maintain this account up to such a sum as should be desired ». It is extraordinarily evident that the fundamental criterion of mural painting was not a purely decorative task, as we today think through lack of education, but was solely a stimulus to ascetic meditation on the part of the mystical onlookers. And it could not be otherwise inasmuch as all the works lay under the vigilance of an exceptional prior: Antonio Pierozzi (1389-1459) who was later Archbishop of Florence, and was canonized with the name of S. ANTONINO DA FIRENZE. In that convent everything was under his inspiration and his love.

His claustral companion was a friar-painter called, although born in Mugello, Fra Giovanni da Fiesole, and later called because of his spiritual art, BEATO ANGELICO, (1387-1455). Sant'Antonino, in agreement with Michelozzo entrusted Fra Giovanni with the pictorial decoration of the convent, according to his plan of spiritual wisdom. He did not therefore commission him to cover the walls with narrative pictorial cycles, but to put in the most suitable places, arguments for paintings adapted to a more profound meditation and more ascetic contemplation. And so, today, entering the cloister, the stories later painted in the lunettes should be neglected. These lunettes are all most interesting as Florentine iconography, and quite rich in pictorial merit. They are by BERNARDINO POCCETTI (1548-1612) and other worthy painters of the end of the sixteenth and beginning of the seventeenth century: Rosselli, Cinganelli, Vanni, Cerrini, Tiarini, Coccopani, who, after the canonization of Antonino, here narrated his life and miracles, contravening however his desire to leave the cloister completely in plaster, with a few paintings by Angelico of unagiographic character, but most ascetic. The first which we see upon entering is the very fine *Crucifix with St. Dominic*. It used to suggest to the friars the fundamental rule of their life: to be always near the cross of Jesus, suffering with the Saviour. In the lunette above the door which gave access to the church, the figure of St. *Peter Martyr*, with his finger to his lips, hinting silence and meditation. In the lunette above the door to the Chapter Room, St. *Dominic* shows the book of the Rule and the penance strap. In fact in the **Chapter Room** the friars accused themselves of their sins, and were punished. The room is therefore dominated by the grand fresco of the *Crucifixion*. It is an allegoric, not a narrative fresco. Christ is redemption. Beside him the good thief who is saved, the wicked one who is lost. Saints of every period and order are mystically present at the sacrifice of Jesus, together with the Holy Women who form a powerful group in their hieratic composition. At the foot of the fresco runs a frieze formed by two branches which divide from St. Dominic and surround the figures of the Dominican Saints.

Over the **Refectory** door a *Pietà* reminds the friars of the sufferings of Christ. Today in the entrance there are gathered various works of art by another great painter of the Dominican Order, FRA BARTOLOMEO DELLA PORTA (1475-1517), a fervent follower of Savonarola, whom he upheld by arms, taking the Dominican habit after his death.

In the Refectory the large fresco at the end, representing the *Supper of St. Dominic*, is by the « mannerist » follower of Fra Bartolomeo, GIOVANNI SOGLIANI (1492-1542). On the walls, paintings and frescoes by FRA BARTOLOMEO and by his pupils and followers. The fresco of the *Last Judgement* by FRA BARTOLOMEO and MARIOTTO ALBERTINELLI (1474-1515) is said to have suggested to Raphael the grouping of the personages in his famous fresco in the Vatican, the « Dispute of the Sacrament ».

Back in the cloister, we see how Beato Angelico has painted over the door of the Hospice, *Jesus dressed as a Pilgrim met by two friars*: it is the admonition to harbour the poor as Christ himself. In the old **Hospice** have been collected the framed works of ANGELICO the painter. Here the talents

B. Angelico: The Marriage of the Virgin.

ECCE VIRGO CONCIPIET ⁊ PARIET FILIVM ⁊ VOCABIT NOMEN EIVS EMANVL. YSA. VI. C

ECCE CONCIPIES IN VTERO ⁊ PARIES FILIVM ⁊ VOCABIS NOMEN EI' IHESVM. LVCE . I . C .

REGES TARSIS ⁊ INSVLE MVNERA OFFERĒT REGES ARABV ⁊ SABBA DONA ADVCĒT. PS. LXXI. C

B. Angelico: Annunciation.

B. Angelico: Annunciation.

of this miraculous artist are evident: stylistic moderation, pictorial serenity, classical composure, mystical beauty. Among the many paintings coming from various places, we must not miss admiring at least the *Madonna dell'Arte dei linaioli* (Madonna of the Guild of Flax workers) (1433) which has a frame with the famous twelve *musical angels*; the *Last Judgement*, with the saved men who express celestial joy, and the damned ones whom the friar abandoned to the brushes of assistants; the admirable squares of the *Stories of Jesus* which used to form the doors of a great tabernacle guarding a crucifix (in many of them is the hand of assistants, and particularly of Alesso Baldovinetti); finally the grand *Deposition* where the extreme colours are harmonized with the most delicate art.

A quick, steep staircase leads to the **floor of the cells.** At the head of the stairway there is the welcoming *Annunciation* in an architectural, almost claustral cornice, with a most beautiful adolescent angel and the Virgin almost consumed by an intense prayer-watching. Under the fresco is the *Cell of Antonino,* with various relics of the Saint. So as not to repeat ourselves, we will immediately say that the friar painter has painted in every cell a mystery of the Christian faith, either joyous, or sorrowful, or glorious. Not all the frescoes in the cells are of equal artistic value, because Angelico was assisted in the work by various disciples, among whom the young BENOZZO GOZZOLI (c. 1420-1497). However in all these paintings there is the spiritual and artistic influence of the friar painter. Along the corridor on the right is the very elegant **Library,** designed by the Convent's architect MICHELOZZO (1441), by order of Cosimo and with the consent of Antonino, to house the eight hundred precious volumes which the humanist Niccolò Niccoli had left to remain in the service of the studious, for whom, more than for himself, he had collected them from all parts, consuming all his substance. The one of San Marco can be considered the first public library of the Renaissance.

At the end of the corridor is the *Cell of Cosimo*, the munificent lord of the city wanting to have the place of his spiritual retreat in San Marco. In the cell's vestibule Angelico painted a *Crucifix* between two Dominican Saints, Mary and St. Cosmas, protector of the Medici. In the cell is the fresco of the *Adoration of the Magi*, with evident allusion to the wealthy lord who gave honour to the Divine Saviour in San Marco.

Going back again, we enter the left-hand corridor, dominated by the celestial vision of the *Madonna enthroned between Saints*. In the cells of this corridor are Angelico's best frescoes: the *Annunciation*, the *Transfiguration*, *Jesus in the Praetorium*, the *Marys at the Sepulchre*, the *Coronation of the Virgin*. In the corridor at the end open the seven *cells of the Novitiate*. For the novice, that is for the young men who had to form themselves for a life of renunciation, conquering the first temptations, Angelico could only propose one argument of meditation: that of the *Crucifix*. Every cell has, in fact a crucified Christ and a friar at the feet of the gibbet in a position of prayer and penitence, each one varied according to the attitudes which Saint Dominic assumed, as one could read in the biography of the Patriarch reported also by Saint Antonino in his « Chronicle ».

At the end of the corridor we come to the cell occupied at the end of the fifteenth century by FRA GIROLAMO SAVONAROLA, celebrated and venerated for his spirited work of public and moral reform of the republican government of the city and for his fiery preaching in defence of liberty, against the Medicean hegemony which brought him to a tragic end in the flames (23 May 1498; in Piazza della Signoria).

In one of the first rooms are gathered iconographical documents of the martyr, among which a powerful *portrait* executed by Fra Bartolomeo. A second room is the reformer's study with note-books and manuscripts of his sermons; the third is his real cell, with relics, among which a *banner with Crucifix* which was attributed to Beato Angelico.

Again descending the stairway, we enter on the right the **Small Refectory** with fresco by DOMENICO DEL GHIRLANDAIO representing the *Last Supper*, rich in pleasing details (after 1480).

Entering again the cloister we should notice, in front of the Chapter Room, a large bell which summoned the people to the sermons of Savonarola; it was named « the mourner » because the reformer mourned and wanted people to mourn on the state of Christians and the condition of Florence. Taken down from the campanile by the « palleschi » (the partisans of the Medici) after the execution of the friar, it was horsewhipped through the streets of the city like a condemned man and later exiled outside the walls, in the Campanile of San Salvatore al Monte.

The **Church of San Marco** attached to the convent, restored in 1437 by MICHELOZZO was internally altered by GIAMBOLOGNA (1580), then by PIER FRANCESCO SILVANI (1678) and the simple and austere façade was rebuilt (1777-80) by the Carmelite friar GIOACCHINO PRONTI. The lowrelief with the *Entry of Saint Antonino into Florence* (1446) and the statue of *St. Dominic* are by AGOSTINO NOBILI; the statue of *Saint Vincent Ferrer* and the *Lion of St. Mark* by GIOVAN BATTISTA CAPEZZUOLI: very modest work and of a not very happy, yet measured, style.

In the **interior** the carved and gilded ceiling gives to the building a tone of richness without pomp, in which we again mourn the loss of every Michelozzan character. Over the door, large *Crucifix* of Giotto's school. The *altars* were designed by GIAMBOLOGNA (1590). On the altars various paintings, among which, on the right, *St. Thomas Aquinas who offers his Summa to Christ*, by SANTI DI TITO (c. 1568); *Madonna Enthroned* by FRA BARTOLOMEO; *Praying Madonna*, Byzantine mosaic (c. 705), surrounded by *Angels* of a much later style (c. 1650). In the **corridor** which leads to the Sacristy, various slabs, among which the round bronze one which marked until 1901 the place in Piazza della Signoria where Savonarola had been burnt. In the **Sacristy** by MICHELOZZO, *sarcophagus with lying statue of Saint Antonino*, bronze by FRA DOMENICO PORTIGIANI (d. 1602) on the model of Giambologna. But the uncorrupt body of the Saint, which for more than a century laid in this tomb, is in the left transept of the church and exactly under the altar of the **Chapel of Sant'Antonino**, finished after designs of GIAMBOLOGNA between 1580-89 at the expense of Averardo and Antonio Salviati. On the architrave of the altar is the very lovely *Flying Angel* which is little noted, but is a companion to the Mercury in the National Museum. The two frescoes in the vestibule represent two scenes of the solemn ceremony of the *Translation of the Saint*. They are by DOMENICO CRESPI, called the PASSIGNANO (c. 1558-1638) who filled them with lively portraits of people, from the Grand Duke Ferdinand I, to the nobles of his court and the high prelates of his time. The chapel, rich in *marble and bronze decoration* by GIAMBOLOGNA and PIETRO FRANCAVILLA, has *paintings* by ALESSANDRO ALLORI, BATTISTA NALDINI and FRANCESCO MORANDINI called the POPPI. The frescoes in the *cupola* are by BERNARDINO POCCETTI. This is an ensemble particularly interesting for appreciating the taste of Florentine artists at the end of the sixteenth century, as also for a record of the costumes of the time. Another interesting ensemble of the same period is the **Chapel of the Holy Sacrament,** on the left of the chancel (generally closed), which is completely decorated with frescoes by POCCETTI and paintings by SANTI DI TITO, PASSIGNANO, EMPOLI and FRANCESCO CURRADI.

On the left wall of the church two inscriptions record that there were buried in San Marco the most famous Giovanni Pico Conte della Mirandola (d. 1494), called the « phoenix of geniuses », together with his friend, the poet Girolamo Benivieni (d. 1542), and the other great poet Agnolo Ambrogini, called the Poliziano, (1454-84).

Cosimo de' Medici, Sant'Antonino, Michelozzo, Beato Angelico, Niccolò Niccoli, Pico della Mirandola, Girolamo Beni-

B. Angelico: Last Judgement (detail of Paradise).

vieni, Agnolo Poliziano, Girolamo Savonarola, Domenico Ghirlandaio, Fra Bartolomeo, these names stand to show what we have already said, namely that San Marco had become the spiritual centre of fifteenth century Florence.

The *square*, diminished by a paltry garden surrounding the irrelevant *statue of general Manfredo Fanti*, by PIO FEDI (1873), was for many centuries one of the centres of city life.

At the corner of *Via degli Arazzieri*, is the fine **Palazzina della Livia** built by BERNARDO FALLANI (1775) at the order of the Grand Duke Pietro Leopoldo, for the dancer Livia Raimondi. Nearby once used to spread the great *St. Mark's garden* bought by Clarice Orsini, wife of Lorenzo the Magnificent, and which had capital importance in the artistic events of the Renaissance. Lorenzo the Magnificent, who here collected ancient statues and bas-reliefs brought largely from Rome, gathered around these models many young Florentines who showed an interest in the arts, so that they might be encouraged to practice the art of drawing. The old sculptor Bertoldo who was the most zealous custodian of this first nucleus of the Academy and of the Florentine artistic collections, taught there among others, the great Michelangelo (1488-92). When in 1494 the Medici collections in the Via Larga palace and in this garden were dispersed, there had been added, to the original collection of sculpture, paintings and designs by Donatello, Filippo Brunelleschi, Masaccio, Paolo Uccello, Lorenzo di Credi, Angelico, fra Filippo Lippi, which were models for Leonardo da Vinci, Michelangelo, Raphael and for nearly all their contemporaries.

In the next *street*, therefore called *of the Arazzieri*, was founded the first Medici tapestry manufactory (1545), created by Cosimo I.

Coming back to Via Cavour, at N. 57 we find a most original building. BERNARDO BUONTALENTI (1536-1608) built for the Grand Duke Francesco this palace of harmonious architecture, of placid, solemn horizontal rhythm, with great spaces between the windows, decorated with bizarre sculptural pieces distributed with shrewd measure. It came to be called the **Casino Mediceo**, not because it was small, but because it stood almost in the country. In this seat Antonio de' Medici, presumed son of the Grand Duke Francesco I and Bianca Cappello, set up his workshops of artistic industry, among which the first porcelain manufactory in Europe. Now it is the seat of the Court of Appeal. From the quiet, airy courtyard, in the centre of which is a fountain with *Diana bathing* from the workshop of Giambologna, we go, to the right, to the first-floor rooms decorated with frescoes, with the achievements of the Grand Dukes Cosimo I, Francesco I, and Cosimo II, most vivid and interesting for portraits and costume. But essentially interesting is the grand stairway with the series *of 12 lunettes* painted by MATTEO ROSSELLI (1622) recording the most glorious exploits of the two last Grand dukes who were Grand masters of the Order of the Knights of St. Stephen, and where are reproduced places and people copied from nature with great fidelity and therefore of great documentary value.

Next to the Casino is the little **Chiostro dello Scalzo**, seat of a Florentine Confraternity called of the Scalzo (1376) because the cross-bearer went in procession bare-footed. Here are very fine chiaroscuro frescoes with *16 stories of St. John the Baptist*, begun by ANDREA DEL SARTO in 1514, finished in 1526, with the exception of two, which are by FRANCIABIGIO (1518-9).

Continuing down Via Cavour, we turn to the left into *Via Salvestrina*. At the corner of *Via San Gallo* is the **Palazzo Pandolfini**, built by GIOVANNI FRANCESCO and ARISTOTILE DA SANGALLO (1520) on designs by Raphael, an excellent example of civil architecture of the sixteenth century of the type of the Palazzo Uguccioni in Piazza della Signoria and other noble buildings of the second half of the century. The original asymmetrical construction leaves it uncertain whether the right side was left accidentally unfinished, or deliberately left so as not to cut off air and light from the left part. The first-floor windows and the large, crowning cornice are models of harmony, resulting from the fusion of Florentine architecture with the modern style originated from the study of the buildings of ancient Rome.

Almost opposite is the façade which GIUSEPPE SALVETTI made in 1787 for the great **Hospital of Bonifacio,** founded in 1377, with the name of St. John the Baptist, but which Florentines have always called by the name of the good Podestà Bonifacio Lupi, Marquess of Soragna, who undertook its enormous expenses for his soul's redress. It was first destined for the incurables and later housed (1788) the madmen which Pietro Leopoldo of Lorraine wished to be treated as sick people and no longer as dangerous ones. The geniality of Vincenzo Chiarugi from Empoli (1759-1820), creator of a now inconfutable theory, but which was in his day considered extravagant and daring, here created the first centre of psychiatry later spreading through the world the principles of a new science of human healing.

Continuing along Via San Gallo we come to the **Church of San Giovannino,** called **of the Knights,** from the sisters of St. John of Jerusalem or of Malta, who lived in the convent nearby at the end of the 14th century.

In the **interior** the architecture of the two altars at the beginning of the two aisles are attributed to PIER DI GIOVANNI TEDESCO and are examples of the taste of the late Gothic style. At the end of the right aisle, *Annunciation* attributed to JACOPO DEL SELLAIO and *Coronation of the Virgin* by NERI DI BICCI; at the end of the left aisle, *Manger* by BICCI DI LORENZO. In the Choir the very beautiful painting with *Christ Crucified between the Virgin and St. John* on a cut-out panel is by LORENZO MONACO.

Further on, the elegant **Loggia dei Tessitori** (weavers) which an architect close to Cronaca built during the last years of the fifteenth century for the guild of those artisans.

At the corner of Via degli Arazzieri, the **Church of Jesus the Pilgrim** called **of the Pretoni,** rebuilt and painted in fresco at the end of the sixteenth century, where is the *tomb-stone of the parish-priest Arlotto* (1484) celebrated and always popular for his bantering and jesting, the last of which is in the epigraph here paraphrased: « This tomb the parish-priest Arlotto made for himself and for anyone wishing to get into it ».

Turning into *Via XXVII Aprile,* we come to the **Coenaculum of the Convent of Sant'Apollonia.**

Here are to be seen the finest works of ANDREA DEL CASTAGNO, one of the most robust and sculpturesque Florentine painters of the early Renaissance. The end wall is filled by the scene of the *Last Supper* with its vigorous and dramatic figures. The three episodes of the *Crucifixion, Deposition* and *Resurrection* which were frescoed above the Last Supper, have been detached for restoration and can be seen on the left wall; in spite of their bad state of preservation they show that grandeur and pathos characteristic of the master at his best. Here have also been brought the series of historical personages which decorated the villa of the Gonfaloniere Filippo Carducci at Legnaia:

three men of letters, *Dante, Petrarch, Boccaccio*, glorifiers of Florentine poetry; three ladies of virile spirit, *Queen Tomiri*, fighter for her country, *Queen Esther*, who dedicated the cunning of feminine policy to her fatherland, and the *Sibyl of Cumae*, who announced the advent of the Messiah; three outstanding Florentine political and military men, *Niccolò Acciaioli, Farinata degli Uberti* and *Pippo Spano*. Two lunettes representing a *Pietà* and a *Crucifixion* are also the work of Andrea del Castagno.

By Via degli Arazzieri we turn into Piazza San Marco. Opposite, on the left, is the unadorned building of the **University**, in its seat originally assigned (1429) by Niccolò da Uzzano, on the edge of the town, to receive and enlarge the old Florentine « Sapienza » or « Studio », and which subsequently housed a cannon-foundry (during the siege of 1529-30), a lion enclosure, the Grand ducal riding school. Next to the university in *Via Lamarmora*, are two museums of great importance.

The **Museum of the Institute of Geology, Paleontology and Physical Geography** which has its remote origin in the first scientific collections begun by the Medici Grand dukes, and which houses collections of paleontological material of exceptional interest.

The **Museum of the Botanical Institute** also originated from the learned curiosity of the Medici lords, with a collection of more than half a million rare plants.

Andrea del Castagno: Last Supper.

The nearby **Giardino dei Semplici,** which Cosimo I founded (1545) to house and experimentally cultivate exotic plants, to study their properties and usefulness, justifies the famous attribute of «City of flowers», given to Florence at the end of the 14th century, and in a much more practical than aesthetic way. Here was a wide and lasting field for studies for the distillation of perfumes, for the growing of mulberry-trees, for the extraction of essential oils for curative use, for the research of vegetal antidotes, for the refinement of aromatic specialities used in sweetmeats and ice-creams. On this land the first experiments were made in the cultivation of tropical plants in hot-houses and here was tried the adaptation of the potato, of cocoa and coffee, imported by Florentine travellers and studied by scientific experimenters.

In the garden which was the first botanical orchard in the world, designed by TRIBOLO (1543), is a statuary group by BARTOLOMEO AMMANNATI, with a graceful *Victory triumphant over fallen Violence*, which seems to allude to these pacific triumphs which the new Medici seigniory promoted in Florence.

We return to Piazza San Marco: at the beginning of *Via Ricasoli* is the fine **Loggia di San Matteo**; it was built in the 13th century when Guglielmo Balducci founded the adjoining

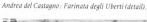
Andrea del Castagno: Farinata degli Uberti (detail).

hospital, known as the *Ospedale di Lelmo*. In 1784 the Grand Duke Pietro Leopoldo assigned this building as the seat of the Academy of Fine Arts. Under the airy loggia are three *terracotta pieces* from the workshop of the Della Robbia and a *lunette* frescoed by MARIOTTO DI NARDO (1413).

Along Via Ricasoli is the **Gallery of the Accademia,** in which is one of the most fascinating collections of Michelangelesque sculpture. The tormented spirit and the almost superhuman power of the great sculptor are here synthetized in the youthful symbolic statue of *David* and in the so-called *Prisoners*. The tragic *Pietà* from Palestrina, near Rome, has also been brought here, since 1940. The *Prisoners* are some of the decorative figures which were to find a place on the tomb of Pope Julius II (c. 1519) and which, unfinished, preserve the signs of the first creative passion of genius. It seems that these figures awoken from their stony sleep try to come out of the marble by their own power and almost convulsively liberate themselves from their dull material. Before these sculptured blocks there comes into one's mind, more than the painful hesitation of the artist, the words of comfort which Luca Signorelli addressed to him, in the quarry of Macel dei Corvi: « Do not doubt that the Angels will come from heaven to take you by the arms and help you ».

Of equal power is the rough draft of *St. Matthew*, one of the twelve Apostles, which were commissioned of him by the patrons of Santa Maria del Fiore (1504). Also the figure of the most dramatic of the Evangelists, like the Prisoners, expresses the battle which the artist had to keep up against the force of nature. Michelangelo himself announced this in one of his most potent quatrains:

Non ha l'ottimo artista alcun concetto	*The good artist has no idea in his mind*
Ch'un marmo, solo in sè non circonciva	*That the marble alone in itself may (not enclose*
Col (suo) soverchio, e solo a quello (arriva	*In its mass, but to expression only (can attain*
La man che ubbidisce all'intelletto.	*The hand, that is obedient to the mind.*

In the « Tribuna » is the statue of **David,** sculptured (1505-04) to substitute the Judith of Donatello on the front of the Palazzo Vecchio, as a virile allegory to exhort the people to defend liberty in the name of the Lord. This is truly the concrete symbol of the spirit which animated the last Florentine Republic. They had to put their confidence in courage and strength and in their own faith, to oppose and resist, like the young man of Bethlehem, a coalition of enemy troops much stronger than the Philistine Goliath. The sculptor, who in the years immediately following conceived and began the task of frescoing the vaulting of the Sistine Chapel and the design for the tomb of Pope Julius II, expressed in this work the boldness of his twenty-six years, which in another sixty years of sculptural, pictorial, architectural and poetical activity, was not exhausted, even in the undertaking of the Cupola of St. Peter's (1560).

Although the exceptional interest of this gallery resides in the unparelleled works of Michelangelo, one should not overlook the collection of paintings which is quite important. Owing to the damages which this gallery suffered from the flood of 1966, the rooms — except the Michelangelo Hall — are being now restored and it is not yet known which will be the location of the paintings. Anyhow there are various groups of pictures which will be exhibited: one comprises some fine examples of the Tuscan School of the 13th and 14th century, among which the panel of the so-called MAGDALENE MASTER with the figure of this Saint and scenes from her life; several tabernacles and panels on gold ground by BERNARDO DADDI, TADDEO GADDI, ORCAGNA, PACINO DI BUONAGUIDA and a beautiful *Pietà* by GIOVANNI DA MILANO. Another group gathers the works of masters belonging to the 15th century but still under the influence of the Gothic style, among which LORENZO MONACO is outstanding. In the collection of 15th century painting we should notice the delightful « *Madonna of the Sea* » and another *Madonna with Angels* by BOTTICELLI and a very interesting front of a chest depicting a *Wedding Procession* in fifteenth century Florence. Finally in the group of 16th century painting are works by FILIPPINO LIPPI, FRA BARTOLOMEO, RIDOLFO DEL GHIRLANDAIO, PONTORMO, ALESSANDRO ALLORI and a beautiful picture of *St. John the Baptist in the desert* which was once attributed to Raphael and now to his school.

The **Academy of Fine Arts** is an institution which has become emblematic through the centuries and which for polemical reasons came even to be considered with diffidence. But it here has a glorious history, rich with splendours. The arrangement of the figurative, artistic activity, had in fact in Florence its origin with the foundation of the company (1339) called of St. Luke's the Evangelist whom legend calls a painter. In this company « good, equitable and loyal painters » already matriculated in the art of the Doctors, together with the Apothecaries who sold the ingredients for the colours, lent reciprocal assistance, both spiritual and material, creating a type of religious solidarity between the workshops in which alone teaching was practised, with personal criteria of artisan character.

Through the initiative of the sculptor FRA GIOVANNANGELO DA MONTORSOLI, collaborator of Michelangelo and Servite friar, the *Company of St. Luke* assumed (1562) the official task of teaching the three arts of design in public form, and took the name of *Academy*, which had its origin in Florentine Neoplatonism.

The religious spirit of the circle of the Servites of Mary, in which grew up the tradition of local art flowering in the warmth of the faith, suggested its first device: three crowns (architecture, painting, sculpture), with the motto of Dantean inspiration: « A Dio quasi nepote » (Almost a grandchild of God), a reference to art as daughter of human talent and man as child of God. The first academicians were Giorgio Vasari, Francesco da Sangallo, Bartolomeo Ammannati, Agnolo Bronzino, Vincenzo de' Rossi, Michele di Ridolfo del Ghirlandaio, besides Fra Giovannangelo da Montorsoli, around whom was gathered in the first « chapter » a superb company of the most noble and excellent artists of the art of design. The Grand Duke Cosimo I was respectfully elected official chief, but the effective head as father and master of these three arts was Michelangelo Buonarroti, now in the last years of his glorious life (he died on November 18th, 1564).

The evolution of the Academy is necessarily that of the history of

Michelangelo: David.

art, and the teaching followed the steps of the masters, who could hardly keep pace with Michelangelo.

Through the Grand Duke Pietro Leopoldo's enlightenment all forms of religious tone were repudiated, and the old Academy of Design assumed (1786) the actual name and the task of a government school. To the investiture of the academicians, which was once upon a time done before the altar, there was substituted the method of democratic election for the masters, and of the selection by examination for the pupils.

All the better works done by local art in the early nineteenth century had its origin in this Academy, with PIETRO BENVENUTI, painter, (1769-1844), LORENZO BARTOLINI, sculptor (1777-1850), GIUSEPPE BEZZUOLI, painter (1784-1855), CESARE BACCANI, architect (1792-1867), through the works of whom were put into effect and practice the exclusively theoretical criteria of teaching. And about this institute, as a reaction and contrast, grew up the lively, glorious movement of the so-called « Macchiaioli » painters, promoted by the sculptor ADRIANO CECIONI (1838-86). GIOVANNI FATTORI (1825-1908) taught

Michelangelo: Pietà from Palestrina.

Botticelli: « Madonna of the Sea ».

and died here, after twenty-eight years of teaching, and his method of employing colours is to this day recognizable in the works of the best Florentine masters.

Turning to the left by *Via degli Alfani*, just after crossing *Via dei Servi*, we see on the right a strange construction in the road where was once a fulling-mill of the wool guild, called by the Florentines the *Castellaccio*.

At the corner of this road stands the **Rotunda of Brunelleschi**; it is one of the most interesting specimens of Florentine architecture. We have mentioned elsewhere that the architectural ideal of the Renaissance was a building with central plan, very regular, almost a polyhedrom, the expression of a perfect spirit of equilibrium. Brunelleschi was only able to actuate this ideal of art of his in small works, as in the old Sacristy of San Lorenzo and in the Pazzi Chapel of Santa Croce.

In 1434, the guild of the Calimala merchants and the monks of the nearby convent of S. Maria degli Angeli, built together an oratory, using for it the bequests of Bishop Andrea and Cavaliere Matteo Scolari. The task was given to Filippo Brunelleschi. His design, which may have been derived from the Chapel of Charlemagne at Aachen, has the characteristics of an internal octagonal-polygonal plan, the outside walls being double in number. According to Vasari, « most bizarre » in design, it is certainly unique in Italy. Its construction being interrupted as the money was used in the war against Lucca, the oratory disappeared under the wall-works, and after five centuries it was brought to light in deplorable conditions. The original part being restored and renewed, it was covered by Rodolfo Sabatini (1937) with a small cupola after the original design, so preserving the scheme of the early edifice, with Renaissance central plan.

A few steps from the Rotunda is the most harmonious of Florentine squares. If Piazza Signoria is the most beautiful fourteenth century Florentine square, and in its irregularity marks the agitated years of communal strifes, the **Piazza della Santissima Annunziata** is the most lovely square of modern times, and in its regularity follows the tracks of humanistic laws, for which the search after harmony was equal to the search for pleasure. Perfectly square, the piazza is developed on the architectural motif, offered by the original porticoed

Andrea della Robbia: Medallion on the façade of the Hospital of the Innocenti.

façade of the **Hospital of the Innocenti**, marvellously designed by BRUNELLESCHI (1421-34). The decoration in polychrome terracotta blended in the white of the lime-stone and the blue-grey of the « pietra serena », presents itself as one of the most charming finds of Renaissance style. The *medallions* by ANDREA DELLA ROBBIA (c. 1463) represent only swathed children, that is, those abandoned children, sons of shame and misery, which the Republic took in and brought up in the hospital, and whom the people called « Innocenti », in memory of the new-born babes massacred by order of Herodes, as blameless victims.

The work of beneficence and assistance to children which

the Florentines had begun in the Hospital of San Gallo. since the 12th cent., served as a model to all the others of that type, and had here in 1419 its full development, through the initiative of the Silk-weavers Guild. Entirely preserved, for the perpetual continuation of this pious institution, the building is an example to us of the indissolubility of the concept of beauty and practice, of aesthetic pleasure and piety, of civil decorum and religious spirit.

The generosity of the Florentine silk-weavers made this Hospital a work of art and almost a museum. And a museum is in fact gathered in five rooms in the interior, where are preserved, among other things, the splendid painting of the *Adoration of the Child Jesus* (1488) by DOMENICO GHIRLANDAIO, the *Madonna with Child* (c. (1448) by LUCA DELLA ROBBIA and the painting of the *Madonna with Child and St. John the Evangelist* (c. 1460), which is almost certainly one of the first works of SANDRO BOTTICELLI. Of the fresco decoration with which the charming BERNARDINO POCCETTI embellished the hospital, we notice the composition of the *Story of the Innocents,* in the 4th room, which is an anachronistic allegory of the refuge which the innocents find in the infanticide persecution. Among the pleasing details of the life of the recovered children and of the city costumes of 1610 are the life-like portraits of the very young Grand duke Cosimo II and of the dignitaries of the court.

Symmetrical with Brunelleschi's portico, to complete the square, ANTONIO DA SANGALLO THE ELDER and BACCIO D'AGNOLO designed, in 1516, the portico of the *Confraternity of the Servites of Mary.* On the third side, in front of the façade of the once Gothic church, which had been restored and rebuilt about the middle of the fifteenth century by MICHELOZZO MICHELOZZI, by ANTONIO MANETTI and by PAGNO PORTIGIANI, about 1600 GIOVANNI CACCINI designed the portico in harmony with the pre-existing ones. In the fine **Palazzo dei Grifoni,** on the fourth side of the square opposite the Church, BARTOLOMEO AMMANNATI for the first time (1563) showed to the Florentines the colouristic possibilities of an architecture in which stone appeared only as an accessory element to brick. So the enclosure was completed, the square taking on an almost uniform aspect which makes it quiet and harmonious. In the centre, the equestrian statue carried out by GIAMBOLOGNA (1608) before his death, of the beneficent **Grand duke Ferdinand I**, symbolized in the queen bee who commands her well-ordered people without arms, as the device on the shield on the base shows.

The two grotesque **fountains** by PIETRO TACCA (1629) were originally made for the port of Leghorn and only at the wish of the Grand duke Ferdinand II were they destined to become part of the square.

The Church of the Santissima Annunziata, the most venerated and the richest of the Florentine sanctuaries, grew up without the walls of the second circle as a little oratory called of the « cafaggio » as it was founded between fields and pastures, in 1250, by the Seven founder Saints of the Order of the Servites of Mary, Who were they? They were seven young men of most noble Florentine families, who, following an apparition of the Madonna, called themselves her Servites and founded (1233) a hermitage on the woody summit of Monte Asinario or Senario, ten miles from the city, towards the Mugello.

Andrea del Sarto: « Madonna del Sacco ».

The scope of their religious order was to appease the quarrelsome and vindictive spirit of the Florentines by means of devotion to the Madonna. An image which they had painted in the oratory (1252) represents the *Annunciation* and has become famous for its miracle. The legend tells how one Bartolomeo, a painter, reached the point of frescoing the face of the Virgin and frightened by the task of portraying the lines of God's favourite creature, he went to sleep, and in his sleep an angel miraculously finished the work of art. This holy legend engrafted itself increasingly in the hearts of the faithful, and Michelangelo himself, looking at the head of the Madonna, thought it not the work of a human hand. So great was the devotion for the Annunziata, that among the principal arguments for enlarging the circle of the city walls, in 1321, was decidedly that of including in it the wonderful image of Mary, protectress of Florence.

One of the first enlargements of the oratory was made by the elder brother of one of the seven founders, Chiarissimo Falconieri, who intended to return to the Florentines, as a justly pious work, as much as he had wickedly taken from them in the exercise of usury, in the course of his life as a cloth merchant. And with other oblations, made by Florentine merchants to atone for similar sins, the church was further enlarged by the masters wo were building the new walls, among

Pontormo: Visitation.

whom was NERI DI FIORAVANTE, architect of Santa Maria del Fiore.

It is opportune to remember that not only was the religious life of Florence attached to this Sanctuary, but also the civil one. Even the Florentine calendar was made to begin the year with the date of the Incarnation, that is the Annunciation, celebrated on the 25th of March. This use lasted, not without practical complications until 1750, in contradiction to all the rest of the world. In this Sanctuary the cult of the Virgin assumed the most spontaneous and popular form, opposed to the official and liturgical one of the other churches. For public calamities and for individual graces, there come and go to this day crowds of faithful people, to ask for succour and comfort. Every day one can see here the offerings of white flowers which newly-wed brides offer to the Queen of Virgins, in a rite which has been carried on for perhaps seven hundred years.

In a new phase of the enlargement of the Sanctuary, it became necessary, on account of the great number of votive gifts offered by the Florentines, to add the cloister which stands between the portico and the Church itself, and which came to be called the *Chiostrino dei voti*. It was built by ANTONIO MANETTI, on the design of MICHELOZZO (1447). For several centuries, here were exposed votive wax statues, life-size, of Popes, Sovereigns, Prelates, Warriors, Dignitaries, dressed and armed, with precious ornaments, painted shields, objects of personal use, which through natural decay have been lost, without leaving any other trace except the records in the chronicles.

Also the nearby *Chiostro Grande* was filled with them until the 18th cent. In 1630, there were 600 wax statues, 2000 votive-offerings in papier-maché, and 3600 small votive pictures.

Altered in the 17th cent., in the 18th cent., and also in the 19th cent., the church is the most pompous in the city. Especially during the Grand duchy, the Medici and Lorraine Court uniting themselves to the cult of the citizenship, the original fifteenth century architecture became almost overwhelmed by the pomp of the 17th and 18th century taste, and the church acquired a character of magnificent grandeur and exuberant decorative enthusiasm. Today among the sober and unadorned Florentine churches it is the one which most astonishes us with its splendid, warm richness.

In the **Chiostrino dei Voti,** the life of the Madonna is narrated on the right side in frescoes of great value, executed by the greater painters of the sixteenth century. ROSSO FORENTINO when 17 years old painted here (1513) the *Assumption* (in the figure of San Rocco, pilgrim, on the left, is the portrait of the celebrated satiric poet Francesco Berni, he too little over twenty and thankful to the Madonna that he had been saved from the pest). PONTORMO, twenty, painted here (1513) the *Visitation;* and FRANCIABIGIO, twenty-two, painted here the *Marriage of the Virgin* (1513), spoiled by him with blows of the hammer, in anger at seeing it had been uncovered before he had finished it; ANDREA DEL SARTO, twenty-five, the eldest, painted here the *Nativity* (1511) and the *Adoration of the Magi* (1511-14) with most life-like portraits among which, on the right, his own.

To the left of the entrance door is the lovely *Manger* by a painter of a preceding generation; ALFSSO BALDOVINETTI (1460) who, following the usage of his time, wanted to make new experiments in pictorial tecnique, with bad results, as we see in parts where the colour has faded. And of the same generation is the first of the stories of San Filippo Benizzi, propagator of the order of Servites, painted by COSIMO ROSSELLI: the *Vocation and Clothing of the Saint* (1476). All the other stories of the Saint were painted by ANDREA DEL SARTO, who, at twenty-four years of age (1510) showed in this work the first measure of his power. They are: *Alms to a leper, Punishment of blasphemers, Healing of one obsessed, Resurrection of a child, Healing of another child*, in which scene the old sculptor Andrea della Robbia is portrayed on the right. The singular exhibition of this series of works, in which four very young painters began their vast activity, was to have the greatest importance in the artistic life of Florence. Around the black-robed Servites of Mary was gathered a crowd of great painters and it was through a Servite friar, the sculptor Giovannangelo da Montorsoli, that, as we have seen, the great movement of the Academy was constituted, to which we have already referred.

The small monument on the wall of this cloister, with a *bust of Andrea del Sarto* sculptured by GIOVANNI CACCINI, does not mark the place of the tomb of the great « faultless » painter, who was buried instead in front of the high altar, in the year of the plague and of the fall of the Republic (1530). The fine wooden *Crucifix* was carved by ANTONIO DA SANGALLO.

The **interior** of the church, very grand and rich, with arches and pillars covered with rare marbles, with the magnificent *ceiling* designed by BALDASSARRE FRANCESCHINI, called the VOLTERRANO (1664), and the large choir, covered by the original semispherical *cupola* planned by LEON BATTISTA ALBERTI (1444), has an undeniable charm.

To the left is the **Tempietto della Santissima Annunziata** built before the miraculous fresco. Conceived by MICHELOZZO, it was carried out (1548) by PAGNO DI LAPO PORTIGIANI with 4 Corinthian columns and very fine entablatures. The little *cupola* was designed by BALDASSARRE FRANCESCHINI (1674). The bronze corded *grill* is the work of MASO DI BARTOLOMEO (1447). The silver *altar* by EGIDIO LEGGI (1600) is a precious example of Florentine silversmith-work, copiously represented here in its artisan skill, by the grille, the chandeliers, ornaments and votive lamps. The nearby **Oratory,** is a charming example of the local art of the working of semi-precious stones in the decorative incrustation of the plinth, with symbols taken from the ancient Lawrentian litanies in praising the Virgin. Here may be seen the very fine small painting with the *Head of Jesus* by ANDREA DEL SARTO.

The detailed inspection of the church, with its excessive mass of works of art would take a long time and leave nothing but confusion in the mind of the visitor. But on the works of two exceptional artists, very different one from the other, it is worth while to pause. They are two painters of the same name and of opposite temperament, who worked at different times in the Sanctuary. About ten years before the « most sweet and delicate » ANDREA DEL SARTO expressed himself in painting, the « most terrible » ANDREA DEL CASTAGNO had been working in this church. Of his work, owing to various alterations of the church, there only remain two frescoes, in the **two first chapels on the left:** *God the Father with St. Julian*, the comforting patron of sinners rehabilitated through expiation, and *The Trinity with St. Jerome between Albina and Marcella*, in which the foreshortening effect of the crucified Son overcomes in power every other representation of the sort. In those two examples of strongly realistic painting, the ascetic intention of the author, whom common talk unjustly charged with murder, exercices the most profound effect upon the onlooker.

In the **fifth chapel on the right,** *Funeral monument of Orlando de' Medici* by BERNARDO ROSSELLINO. In the chapel on the left of the **right transept** is the tomb of the fruitful but not always happy sculptor BACCIO BANDINELLI (d. 1559), with a large group of the *Pietà* sculpted by the artist himself.

At the end of the **Choir** is the chapel which GIAMBOLOGNA (1598), another prolific sculptor, built as a place of interment for himself and any Flemish artists who might die in Florence. The bronze *Crucifix* and the six bronze reliefs with *Scenes of the Passion* are works of this master. On the altar is a small fourteenth century panel with the « *Madonna del Soccorso* ».

In the **left transept,** statue of the *Baptist* by MICHELOZZO. Here, a door on the left leads into the **Cloister of the Dead,** designed perhaps by Michelozzo (1473) and decorated with a series of *frescoes* celebrating the history of the order of the Servites of Mary, 14 of which are by the most prolific BERNARDINO POCCETTI. They are all of a great interest for the iconography of the city and the costumes of the 17th cent. but only one, which interrupts the series in the arch over the door of the church, is really worth contemplation. It is the celebrated *Madonna del Sacco* (1525), which marks the highest point in the art of ANDREA DEL SARTO. The originality of the composition and its great simplicity give the utmost relief to the characteristics of the « faultless » painter, who expresses here more than anywhere else, and perhaps for the first time, that comprehension of beauty of forms and colours from which originates what we call realistic art. Below, to the left, the *tomb of Chiarissimo Falconieri,* father of Blessed Giuliana, nun of the Servites of Mary and founder of the Mantellate convent.

At the extremity of the same side is the **Chapel of St. Luke,** where since 1562 was the seat of the *Confraternity of Painters,* of which we have already spoken. Here young painters received the comfort of religion and the protection of the Academic college. Here a crowd of painters, sculptors, architects had their tombs, from Pontormo (1567), to Benvenuto Cellini, Franciabigio, down to Lorenzo Bartolini (1850); and under the arcades of this cloister was started the custom of exhibiting the works which the artists offered for public sale.

Before going out we notice on the wall of the cloister which flanks the church, the funeral *monument of Guglielmo Beraldi*, who fell in the battle of Campaldino, in which Dante Alighieri also partecipated (June 11th, 1289). The portrayal of the equipment of a knight in battle is the only one which remains of that time.

On the side of the church starts *Via Gino Capponi*, at the beginning of which, to the right, is the **Cloister and Oratory of St. Pietro Martire** with frescoes of the late 16th cent. by various artists, among which Poccetti, Passignano and Allori. Further on is the superb **Palazzo Capponi** a beautiful example of Florentine Baroque style, with a large garden. Coming back towards the square, at the corner of *Via della Colonna* is the entrance to the **Archeological Museum,** which is one of the most important museums of its kind for its collections of Egyptian, Etruscan and Greco-Roman material.

Detail of an Egyptian bust (1500-1450 B.C.)

The **Egyptian section,** begun by the Grand Duke Leopold II, in 1824, was enriched with the material collected by the Tuscan expedition directed by Ippolito Rossellini which explored Egypt and Nubia together with a French expedition directed by Champollion, in 1828-29. This was the first Egyptian museum to be created in Italy and it comes second only to that of Turin for the richness of its collections and the beauty of its works, through ich one can follow the development of the art of the Nile valley for man centuries, so systematic was the choice of the early collectors.

More important still, above all for local interest, is the **Etruscan section,** rich in an immense archeological material collected since the days of Cosimo I and enlarged by continual discoveries. Besides some outstanding and very famous pieces of sculpture, like the *Minerva,* the « *Arringatore* » (haranguer), the « *Chimera* », we see sarcophagi, urns, small bronze sculptures, jewellery and all those precious furnishings which were found in the numerous tombs of the Etruscan territory. Several interesting reconstructions — mostly done with authentic material — of such *Etruscan tombs* have been made in the garden of the museum.

The **Greco-Roman section** is more modest in proportions but contains important works of art, like the bronze statue of the « *Idolino* », one of the very rare original Greek sculptures of the 5th century. This section has also the merit of preserving the scarce traces of the Roman foundation of Florence.

A collection of vases and terracottas includes pieces of Etruscan and Greek manufacture, among which the famous *François vase,* a Greek work of the 6th century which was found in an Etruscan tomb.

A visit to the Archeological Museum is warmly recommended not only to get acquainted with the Etruscan civilization, but also to realize how Tuscan art has preserved the realistic and humanistic characteristics of that ancient art and how the plastic and pictorial quality of the Tuscans has a most remote and unending root.

Continuing down Via della Colonna, on the right, in the old seat of the **Convent of Maria di Cestello,** later of **Santa Maria Maddalena dei Pazzi,** and precisely in the Chapter room is visible the great triptych frescoed by PERUGINO (1493-95), representing *Christ on the Cross with the Magdalen between St. Bernard and the Virgin Mary* on one side, and *St. John the Evangelist and St. Benedict* on the other. In the background we see a tranquil and most charming Umbrian landscape, giving the accompanying tone to the melancholy resignation depicted in this painted meditation, with a spirit of peace expressed by each detail, which had a particular significance in the days in which it was painted: the days of the violent tragedy which came upon the city, from the death of the Magnificent Lorenzo until the punishment of Savonarola. In the figure of the Crucified One there appears no blood and in the sorrow of the Saints there is no sign of despair.

Basrelief of the Goddess Maat (1300-1200 B.C.) in the Archaeological Museum

The « Arringatore » (Etruscan statue in the Archaeological Museum).

The **church** of the convent later dedicated to **Santa Maria Maddalena dei Pazzi** is in the nearby *Borgo Pinti*. To the right is the **Cappella del Giglio,** graceful sixteenth century construction, with a brilliant pictorial decoration by the prolific BERNARDINO POCCETTI (1599) with *Stories of the Saints Nereo and Achilleo, Bernard and Filippo Neri*. On the altar, *Martyrdom of Saints Nereo and Achilleo* by PASSIGNANO.

A **courtyard** precedes the church, of the basilican atrium type, by GIULIANO DA SANGALLO (1492-1505); the columns have strange Ionic capitals which they say were copied from an ancient original found at Fiesole. The **interior** of the church too belongs, in its main lines, to the end of the fifteenth century, and tradition has it that it was designed by GIULIANO DA SANGALLO, whose style is shown in the beautiful decorations in « pietra serena ». The list of the works of art taken from this church and transported elsewhere in the galleries of Florence or Paris, includes authentic masterpieces of Botticelli, Lorenzo di Credi, Ghirlandaio. (A little beyond the church, in the same street, in the *Palazzo Ximenes,* used to be the seat of the diplomatic representative of the French Republic and Napoleon took up residence there in 1796; Napoleon, who was chiefly responsible for the removal of so many works of art). Some of the very fine Renaissance frames which once contained these paintings are still to be seen in the lateral chapels and contain now some pictures of less important masters of the 16th and 17th centuries, among which we may note: *Madonna and Saints* by DOMENICO PULIGO (1475-1527), *Prayer in the Garden of Gethsemane* by SANTI DI TITO (1591), *Coronation of the Virgin* by COSIMO ROSSELLI (1505).

Triptych by Perugino in the Convent of Santa Maria Maddalena dei Pazzi.

The **Chancel** was rebuilt in 1685 to welcome the body of the Florentine Maria Maddalena de' Pazzi, canonized in 1669 and who later became the patron Saint of this church. The building was carried out by PIER FRANCESCO SILVANI on designs by CIRO FERRI who is also the author of the altarpiece (*The Virgin and St. Maria Maddalena de' Pazzi*). At the sides, canvases by LUCA GIORDANO with *Scenes from the Life of St. Maria Maddalena de' Pazzi*. The statues of *Penitence* and *Faith*, on the right, are by INNOCENZO SPINAZZI, those of *Religion* and *Innocence*, on the left, by ANTONIO MONTAUTI. The frescoes in the cupola are by PIETRO DANDINI. This homogeneous ensemble displays once more the sense of measure of the Florentine artists in the expression of the Baroque style.

Continuing along Borgo Pinti we turn to the left, and by *Via dei Pilastri*, come to the ancient **Church of Sant'Ambrogio,** which, from the chapel of a Benedictine monastery, before 1000 A. D., and certainly founded in memory of the visit of the great Bishop of Milan (393), later became one of the most distinguished eucharistic sanctuaries. In fact it was here, in 1230, thirty-three years before that at Bolsena, that the miracle of priest Uguccione happened when this priest, not having dried the Chalice well, found the day after, that the wine left in the same had become clots of blood.

The church, in Romanesque-Gothic style, was changed several times by restorations: fine Renaissance altars stand along the side walls and the chancel shows a very harmonious architecture of the 18th century.

In the **Cappella del Miracolo,** on the left of the chancel, we may see the exquisite tabernacle by MINO DA FIESOLE representing *God the Father*, above, the *Child Jesus between Saints Benedict and Ambrose*, and the scene of the *Mass of Priest Uguccione*, below. At the sides, the two glazed terracotta *Angels* are among the finest of the DELLA ROBBIA (1513). The fresco with the *Translation of the Relic* is one of the best works of COSIMO ROSSELLI (1486) and is also interesting because it shows the costumes of that time and the selfportrait af the artist.

Among the other valuable works of art in the church we should notice: the frescoes of the late 14th century and of the early 15th century on the altars on the right, and the *Triptych* by BICCI DI LORENZO; on the left the panel with the *Madonna, Angels and four Saints adoring the Child Jesus* by ALESSO BALDOVINETTI, the *Madonna in Glory and two Saints* by COSIMO ROSSELLI, and a wooden statue of *St. Sebastian* by LEONARDO DEL TASSO (1500) who is buried here together with many members of his very active family of carvers and sculptors. Before the Confraternity of Painters in the Santissima Annunziata came into being, many artists were buried in this church: Mino da Fiesole, Andrea del Verrocchio, Francesco Granacci.

We retrace Via dei Pilastri and Via degli Alfani, to the corner, on the left, of *Via della Pergola*. Along this street, so-called from an ancient fulling-mill of the Wool Staplers Guild, grew up the famous theatre which took the name of the street, the **Theatre of the Pergola** which was built in wood by the architect FERDINANDO TACCA, in 1652, and, differing from the Palladian theatres which imitated the Roman theatres, had an oval form, with several rows of boxes; stage with movable scenes and large painted curtain.

It was the new type of Italian theatre, in which the development of the entirely Florentine art of scenery became easier, and from which gloriously originated theatrical scenography and mechanics, founded upon the use of changing architecture, the invention of fantastic buildings, the effect of contrasting lights, colours and machinery of all sorts. The construction came to be imitated all over the world, and

Detail of the tabernacle by Mino da Fiesole in the Church of Sant'Ambrogio.

became the expression of a new musical taste in spectacular style, dear to the refined society of the age and also to the people of the greater cities. The first representation (1657) of the melodrama « The podestà of Colognole » by Giovanni Andrea Moniglia, with music by Jacopo Melani, marked the birth of comic opera, which had an immediate and vast success. The theatre was rebuilt in masonry by the architect GIULIO MANNAIONI (1738), who maintained its original form. Successive restorations in the early nineteenth century did not alter the light, harmonious character of the building which still stands a perfect example of theatrical architecture. Here were performed for the first time the *Ifigenia*, by Gluck (1667), the *Gran Cid*, by Paisiello (1775), the *Idelda*, by Cherubini (1784), *Macbeth*, by Verdi (1848), and the *Trittico*, by Puccini (1919).

At the end of Via della Pergola, we turn to the right into *Via Sant'Egidio*, which joins *Piazza di Santa Maria Nuova*, so called from the **Hospital** which has a very glorious history. It was founded in 1286 by Folco Portinari, father of Beatrice, loved by Dante, following the charitable tradition which Florentine monks had kept alive for nearly three centuries (1031) with the incomes of the monasteries, and still more, with charitable contributions. The orders, or Statutes, of this hospital, which the Portinari family enlarged and enriched, are among the most ancient which we know, and served as a model for the other institutions of the sort, as distant as Paris and London. Almost all the Hospital services have recently been transferred to the foot of the hills near Careggi and offer great advantages by their modernity, and by the importance of the centre of studies which is centred there.

The building, monumentally enclosing the square, was designed by BERNARDO BUONTALENTI and executed by GIULIO PARIGI (1611).

In the **Church of Sant'Egidio** altered on designs by LORENZO DI BICCI (1418), on the right is the *tomb of Folco Portinari*, founder of the hospital. In the apse, *Madonna with Child* by ANDREA DELLA ROBBIA.

In front of the Hospital, in the former convent of the Oblate Nuns is the seat of the **Museum of « Florence as it was »** where paintings, drawings and etchings — also of remarkable artistic value — reproduce the aspects of the town and its environs through the past centuries.

By *Via Maurizio Bufalini*, called after the founder of experimental pathology, and by *Via de' Pucci*, passing in front of the fine **Tabernacle of the Five Lamps** with a *Madonna* frescoed by an unknown painter of the forteenth century and another by Cosimo Rosselli, we turn opposite Palazzo Medici, so ending the excursion around the Medici quarter of the old Florentine centre, where the fifteenth century Renaissance art was allowed to affirm itself.

We have seen, in fact, besides the fifteenth century *Medici Palace*, the *Convent of St. Mark*, the *Cloister of the Scalzo*, the *Rotunda of Brunelleschi*, the *Square and Church of the Santissima Annunziata, Santa Maria Maddalena dei Pazzi, Sant'Ambrogio* and the *Hospital of Santa Maria Nuova*, all monuments, which, even if they had more remote origins, only received in the Medici and Renaissance period the artistic impress which makes them so famous today.

FLORENCE BEYOND THE ARNO

*Ponte Vecchio - Church of Santa Felicita - Palazzo
Pitti - Boboli Garden - Museum of the Specola
Church of San Felice - Church of Santo Spirito
Church of Santa Maria del Carmine.*

The statue of Summer by Giovanni Caccini on the Bridge of Santa Trinita.

FLORENCE BEYOND THE ARNO

The quadrilateral perimeter of the old Roman city was wholly on the right bank of the Arno and it might be said that that Roman camp was the defence of a bridge: the bridge which straddled the Arno at its narrowest part — a key-point in a network of roads, at the foot of Fiesole — and connected Northern with Southern Etruria. Thus for a very good reason the Florentines called that bridge the *Old Bridge* since it must have been there from the time of the Etruscans, where previously there had been a ford. Beyond this very old ford, on the slopes of the hill, on the site of the small Etruscan and, later, Roman necropolis, was established one of the cemeteries of the first Christian colony in the Roman township. A number of traces of it have recently been found in the substructures of the church of *Santa Felicita*. Thus we see that, in Florence as in Rome, until barbaric custom had suppressed the ancient form of ritual and hygiene, the dead were always buried outside the city walls.

In this area, beyond the bridge, at the head of the road to Siena and Volterra, numerous remains have been brought to light to reveal to us something of that obscure period of the origins of the three civilizations, Etruscan, Roman and Christian.

There is a record, as far back as 972, of a bridge, with a timber structure on pillars of masonry, but that does not disprove that the construction was already long established. The mediaeval city was all still on the right side of the river, and for this reason the bridge remained outside it, beyond the *Porta Santa Maria*, the high, fortified towers of which guarded and closed its access. Reconstructed in stone throughout, it was destroyed by the flood of 1333, one of the most violent of many, which are indicated by numerous tablets scattered throughout the city. In 1345, after measures had been taken to direct the course of the waters between high walls, the bridge was again built across the river by NERI DI FIORAVANTE, who made it a part in a system of fortifications, reinforced by towers. It is this bridge which exists today, the only one of the six bridges spared by German mines in 1944 because of its fame; and which even now, though considerably weakened, reigns over the river. By the second half of the thirteenth century many houses had sprung up beyond the bridge and a number of crowded «borghi» (suburbs) had formed there: the *Borgo a San Jacopo*, the *Borgo di Piazza* (now Via Guicciardini), the *Borgo Pitiglioso* (now Via dei Bardi). When in 1260 the walls had to be extended, this group of houses which had spread beyond the river and become known as the *Oltrarno*, was included within the boundaries of the city. These new walls, which have since completely disappeared, started from the river-bank, near what is today the *Ponte alle Grazie*, where the old Porta Romana stood; they wound round the small hill of *San Giorgio* and behind the *church of Santa Felicita*, passed before the other church of *San Félice in Piazza*, where the Porta di San Piero in Gattolino stood, and from here, enclosing the flat stretch of the Cuculia, regained the Arno at the point where the *Ponte alla Carraia* was later built and near which was the first Porta San Frediano. The last city wall, which can still partly be seen from the Ponte Vecchio, was begun in 1285. From *Porta a San Niccolò*, the only gate which has kept its original height and appearance, the walls ran to the present *Porta Romana* and *Porta San Frediano*, completely surrounding the hills of San Giorgio and Boboli, rich in water supplies and stone quarries. This wall which we have already followed, on the opposite side of the Arno, along the avenues of the outskirts of the old town, protected the city during the siege of 1529-30 and its construction, which was completed in about half a century, was directed by the same architects who built the Duomo, among them ARNOLFO DI CAMBIO, ANDREA PISANO and ANDREA ORCAGNA.

To visit this part of the city, let us now cross the **Ponte Vecchio** (1345) with its picturesque little houses perched over the arches. Soon after its completion its two lateral arcades were occupied by shops let by the Comune to the Butchers and Meat vendors of the town. In the sixteenth century Grand duke Cosimo I authorized their sale, ordering the « vile arts » to be expelled from them and stating that they should be occupied only by goldsmiths, silversmiths and jewellers. Subsequently their owners sought to enlarge them with additions at the back of the shops, which projected beyond the width

of the bridge, and had to be supported by brackets, producing a picturesque and somewhat strange disorder.

At the beginning of the bridge, from the early years of
the fourteenth century, there was a stone statue representing
a warrior on horseback and a legend tells that it was a statue
of Mars, the god of war, to whom the Roman city of Florence
was dedicated. At the feet of this figure where there is today
a tablet with quotations from Dante, on Easter morning 1265,
the supporters of the Amidei killed Buondelmonte dei Buondelmonti, thus starting the long and bloody conflict of the
factions which came to be called, first the Guelphs and the
Ghibellines, and then the Blacks and the Whites. The Florentines blame all their misfortunes on the malificent influence
of the god of war who was superseded as a guardian of the
city by St. John the Baptist.

Half way across the bridge the shops give place to a kind
of belvedere from which we enjoy to view of the river and
its bridges. A fountain with a bronze *bust* by the sculptor
RAFFAELLO ROMANELLI (1900) records the work of the great Florentine goldsmith *Benvenuto Cellini*. Along the whole length cf
the bridge on the left, abose the shops, runs the covered
gallery which GIORGIO VASARI built in five months, in 1565, to
permit Duke Cosimo I to pass under cover from Palazzo Vecchio to Palazzo Pitti.

In the Summer of 1944 to hinder the advance of the Allied
Troops, the German blew up five of the six bridges over the
Arno; their conscience prevented them from destroying the
Ponte Vecchio but what they did was much worse. To block
the approaches to the bridge they resorted to the dastardly
expedient of virtually destroying all the buildings for a radius
of 650 ft. at both ends of the bridge. In this way the ancient
« borghi » which had sprung from the bridge-head itself, were
demolished. The first and oldest part of Borgo Pitiglioso, later
Via dei Bardi, of the Borgo di Piazza, later Via Guicciardini
and of Borgo San Jacopo, three streets which formed an extremely beautiful « wedge » running to the bridge, were blown
up, and very ancient towers and palaces of great beauty were
reduced to mountains of rubble. Grief for this irreparable loss
will always remain in the hearts of the Florentines, the more

bitter in view of the utter uselessness, even from the military point of view, of this wanton destruction.

Crossing the bridge, on the right we find *Borgo San Jacopo*, the first part of which has been destroyed, but which still holds in the second part, on the left, the typical *tower-house of the Marsili*, with Della Robbia terracotta decorations which were placed on its façade in the 19th cent. On the right is the **Church of San Jacopo sopr'Arno,** a Romanesque building of the 12th cent., later restored and decorated with a *portico* of the 13th cent. taken from San Donato a Scopeto. According to Vasari the *cupola* of this church was built by BRUNELLESCHI, without scaffolding, a preliminary experiment before beginning to build the large cupola of Santa Maria del Fiore.

Going back, a few steps from the bridge, on the left, is **Santa Felicita,** which we have already mentioned, built on the site of an oratory and cemetery of the early Christians of the fifth century. The church was dedicated to the mother of the seven Maccabei brothers, Roman martyrs for the faith of Christ and remained through the ages an important centre of religious life. Many times rebuilt, its present form is due to the architect FEDERICO RUGGERI (1736). Under the portico stand various tombs: the *tombstone of the merchant Barduccio Chierichini* (1416), the 16th cent. *monument* executed by RAFFAELE DA MONTELUPO (1518) for *Cardinal Luigi de' Rossi* and finally that for the painter and court-singer *Arcangela Palladini* (1622) by AGOSTINO BUGIARDINI. This church, which can be reached through the covered passage between Palazzo Pitti and Palazzo Vecchio, which runs above its portico, became the church of the court of the Grand Dukes who were much attached to it and enriched it with numerous works of art.

The **interior,** is influenced by the restrained architectonic style of Ruggeri, which already (1736) points to Neo-classicism. We note, above, the choir gallery and the tribunes from which the Grand Dukes' family watched religious ceremonies. The **first chapel on the right,** now the **Capponi Chapel,** was designed by FILIPPO BRUNELLESCHI for the Barbadori (c. 1425) and is one of the most admirable of his constructions with square ground-plan, « which was the new vogue at that time and very beautiful ». On the altar stands a luminous *Deposition* by PONTORMO (1528) who also painted the fresco of the *Annunciation* and three *Evangelists* in the splays of the dome; the fourth is a work of the first period of AGNOLO BRONZINO. On the **fourth altar** is the cold but grandiose and realistic composition of ANTONIO CISERI representing the *Martyrdom of the Maccabei Brothers* (1863). On the right of the crossing opens the **Sacristy** (1470) of Brunelleschian inspiration, attributed to Michelozzo and by some to Leon Battista Alberti. On the walls, *Adoration of the Magi* by a Florentine follower of Gentile da Fabriano, a polyptych with the *Madonna and Saints*, one of the best works of TADDEO GADDI, *St. Felicita and her seven Sons* in picturesque fifteenth century costumes, by NERI DI BICCI. In the apse, a *Crucifix* attributed to PACINO DI BUONAGUIDA, a fifteenth century *Pietà* and a *Madonna and Child* by GIOVANNI DEL BIONDO.

In front of the high altar of the church is the *tomb of the Guicciardini family*, where the great historian and politician Francesco, one of the most important prose writers of the 16th century in Italy, was buried in 1540.

The chapel in front of the Capponi Chapel is a copy of the latter, built at the end of the 16th century for the Canigiani family; on the altar, *Assumption* by BERNARDINO POCCETTI.

Coming out of the church, in the small passage on the side, we stop to look at an interesting collection of fragments of funeral inscriptions of the early Christians of the city (4th and 5th cent.) found in the sub-structures of the church which are still waiting for serious examination.

In the short stretch of the *via Guicciardini* once stood the house where the great historian and man of letters NICCOLÒ MACHIAVELLI lived and died (1469-1527); in the same street, on the left, stands the palazzo where FRANCESCO GUICCIARDINI (1483-1540) and SAINT FILIPPO BENIZZI, one of the Servites of Mary (1233-1285), were born; finally via Guicciardini runs into the large Piazza Pitti, dominated by the massive strcture of *Palazzo Pitti*.

Palazzo Pitti.

PALAZZO PITTI

The central nucleus of this palace was one of the numerous buildings which the rich merchants and bankers of Florence had built for themselves by the architects of the Renaissance. The Pitti, merchants who boasted royal titles and unlimited riches, were among the most dangerous rivals of the Medici. Around them gathered the most intriguing and circumspect of the opponents of the Medici family, spurred above all by interests in the banking world. Matters went to such a length that there gradually arose in Florence a « Partito del monte » (Party of the Mountain) (Palazzo Pitti stands on a slight elevation) in contradistinction to the « Partito del piano » (Party of the Plain) (Palazzo Medici rises besides the flat Via Larga). To give proof of his economic power, when the palace of Cosimo the Elder was as yet unfounded, Luca Pitti commissioned BRUNELLESCHI (c. 1440) to design for him a palace which would surpass all the other palaces of Florence in size and majesty. Although extremely grand, the project of Brunelleschi did not go beyond the usual Renaissance proportions, that is to say it was of square plan, its vertical and horizontal expanses being equal. When we look at the palace today we should keep in mind that the original part designed by Brunelleschi is that in

Boboli Garden: The Amphitheatre.

the centre and takes in no more than seven windows. The master's design was executed only after his death, by LUCA FANCELLI, from 1458 onwards, and it is said that Luca Pitti, whom Cosimo had by now preceded in the building of his palace, ordered that the windows of his abode should be as big as the door of the palace in the Via Larga. Eight years later when the Pitti family had fallen into disgrace, overwhelmed by the wealth of the Medici, financially exhausted by the political and mercantile omnipotence of their rivals, the building was suspended and the courtyard remained open on the side facing the hill. In 1549 Buonaccorso Pitti sold it to Eleonora of Toledo, the wife of Cosimo I, and thus the palace of their rivals became the court of the Medicean dynasty. The new residence was connected to the old one, the Palazzo della Signoria, by the gallery already mentioned. But if the palace in the form conceived by Brunelleschi was imposing for a family of merchants, it was not considered particularly imposing for a family of Princes. And so in 1560 AMMANNATI added to the building the vast courtyard, and in the seventeenth century GIULIO and ALFONSO PARIGI further enlarged the palace by lengthening the façade. Then in the eighteenth century GIUSEPPE RUGGERI added the side wings at right angles to the main block so that finally the palace completely crowned the small hill on which it had stood isolated three centuries before. This progressive development has given the building, which now occupies three sides of the extremely large, sloping square, an effect of calm and solemn serenity. The problem of reconciling beauty with immensity of proportions, which presents no small difficulty, is here resolved more successfully, than in any other palace in the world. At first glance, when the eye runs over the whole extent of the building, we do not realise its exceptional size (the façade is 272 ft. long and 118 ft. high and the whole occupies an area of more than 104.000 sq.ft.). But as we ascend the slope of the square, the front of the palace appears progressively higher, we see the mighty rough-hewn blocks of the rustication, some of them several metres long and we appreciate the really gigantic proportions of the building. The sole decorative element allowed are the crowned heads of lions, between the brackets of the windows on the ground floor. Noteworthy is the fact that in this building were no longer used the double-arched windows which were an element of lightness and grace. The interior of the palace, which, from the outside, we should expect to be severe and forbidding, is however, in complete contrast with it in its endless succession of gay, magnificent halls. The decoration was executed without interruption throughout more than three centuries of the princely existence of the various Grand dukes. The uninterrupted continuation of the enterprise begun by Grand duke Cosimo, almost up to our own day, has produced a variety of styles passing from the manner of the sixteenth century artists, through the gradual process of evolution until it almost merges into the forms of the late nineteenth century. The collection of furniture, household furnishings and works of art of every kind constitute together an exhibition of incalculable wealth, which the predominating understanding of magnificence alone renders homogeneous. An entire week would be insufficient to acquaint oneself with every detail of this immense complex, conceived and modelled with the express purpose of impressing the extent of the wealth and taste of six generations of the Medicean dynasty on guests and visitors, who were meant to leave it overwhelmed and full of wonder. This should be kept in mind throughout the visit, by necessity hurried and superficial. Here again, as for the Uffizi Gallery, we shall make only a rapid and schematic sketch of the contents of this amazing monument. It is impossible to record even summarily, the infinite series of festivities for which the courtyard, the gardens and halls of the palace provided the decor, and which, taken up again in our own day have kept alive a part of its glorious reputation, having originated and provided a magnificent model and development for the art of melodrama, decor, concertgiving, fêtes-champêtres, dramatic performances in the open air, ballets and gala receptions imitated thereafter in courts and theatres throughout Europe.

Interior. - Having stated that the dominant note of the decoration of the palace is grandeur, we shall not continue to repeat this, but give only rapid, compressed indications of the chief features of interest. The Doric *Atrium* by PASQUALE POCCIANTI (1850) is a worthy precedent to the superb *Courtyard* by AMMANNATI. In this his first important architectural undertaking in Florence (1558-70), the architect developed Brunelleschi's conception of how rustication should be used as an expression of the building material from being simply a natural phenomenon to its becoming an agent and an integral part of humanistic construction. It is almost true, as the Florentine tradition has it, citing it as a boast of old Luca Pitti, that the whole of Palazzo Strozzi could be put into this courtyard.

Below the terrace is *Moses' Grotto*, with the statue of the patriarch sculpted in porphyry by Raffaele Curradi and other allegorical figures of various hands. Under the arcade are antique Roman statues and a bas-relief dedicated to a mule which was used to transport building material for the construction of the courtyard (on the end wall of the portico on the left). The decorative details of doors, windows and cornice deserve careful examination for they provided a veritable pattern-book from which architects throughout the sixteenth and seventeenth centuries reproduced and developed their ornamental motifs.

From the portico on the right we enter the **Chapel** with Neo-classical frescoes by ADEMOLLO, a rich altar in marble inlay and an ivory *Crucifix* attributed to GIAMBOLOGNA.

From the right corner of the courtyard starts the state staircase with classical and Renaissance busts on the landings; on the third landing we find the *Genius of the Medici* by GIAMBOLOGNA. The *Vestibule* on the first floor, leading to the former Royal Apartments and to the Palatine Gallery, is now only used as an exit while the entrance is from the Bacchus Gate, on the left of the Palace.

Going on to the second floor, we find the **Gallery of Modern Art**, where works of sculpture and painting of artists who worked between the beginning of the nineteenth century and our own day have been collected and exhibited. Particularly noteworthy is the part dedicated to the « Macchiaioli », that group of artists who were the most vital in nineteenth century Tuscan painting, contemporaries of the French Impressionists and no less interesting than they are.

It is not possible to give a definite and detailed description of this gallery as it is undergoing a new arrangement, with new rooms eventually

Giovanni Fattori: Ladies at the Seaside (Modern Art Gallery).

to be added to it. We shall therefore only give a very brief account of the works of art exhibited at the present moment.

In the first rooms we see paintings of the 19th century: large historical pictures, landscapes, portraits, genre paintings. We should note the works by FRANCESCO HAYEZ, STEFANO USSI, ANTONIO CISERI, ANTONIO FONTANESI, FILIPPO PALIZZI, GIUSEPPE DE NITTIS, PAOLO MICHETTI, ARISTIDE SARTORIO, ANTONIO PUCCINELLI, MICHELE GORDIGIANI.

Another group of rooms is reserved to the « Macchiaioli »: SILVESTRO LEGA, TELEMACO SIGNORINI, GIUSEPPE ABBATI, RAFFAELLO SERNESI, VINCENZO CABIANCA, CRISTIANO BANTI, EUGENIO CECCONI, EGISTO FERRONI, ODOARDO BORRANI, CESARE CIANI. The most outstanding personality among them is GIOVANNI FATTORI; besides his large paintings of soldiers and horses, we should devote our attention to the small landscapes, real pictorial jewels in which the colour spots have a wondeful firmness and tonal exactitude.

There follows a smaller collection of artists of the beginning of the 20th century, more or less under the influence of the « Macchiaioli », and finally a large collection of contemporary Italian artists, among which many who have won a prize in the « Premio del Fiorino », a national exhibition which is held at Florence every Spring.

Going downstairs and out of the palace, we turn on the right and crossing the portico of the right wing we enter the *Couryard of Bacchus* where we find the entrance to the Palatine Gallery or Pitti Gallery and to the **Museum of Silverware.** The latter occupies several rooms on the ground floor, the first three of which are decorated with allegorical and perspective frescoes by MICHELANGELO COLONNA and AGOSTINO MITELLI and the fourth with very fine allegories glorifying the enterprises of Lorenzo the Magnificent frescoed by GIOVANNI DA SAN GIOVANNI and some of his followers. In these rooms and the following is displayed a large part of the incalculable wealth of the Grand Dukes: silver and gold pieces for table and chapel use, very precious vases and bowls in rock-crystal and semiprecious stones, cameos and jewellery. In the rooms at the back are exhibited ivory and tortoiseshell works, painted glass, rugs, embroideries. On the upper floor is a large collection of porcelain.

Coming back to the vestibule, we go up the great staircase which leads to the **Palatine Gallery** or **Pitti Gallery** so called not because it was assembled by the Pitti family but because it is housed in that family's palace. Credit for this extraordinarily fine collection is wholly due to the Medici family. It was Ferdinand II who had the idea of establishing this superb gallery, when, in 1640, he had five large rooms decorated by Pietro da Cortona, to receive the works of art brought by his wife, Vittoria della Rovere, from Urbino.

The collection was subsequently increased and enriched by Cardinal Leopoldo dei Medici, and all the subsequent Grand Dukes of the Medici and Lorraine dynasties alike, added to its wealth. The original Pitti Gallery consists of 500 pictures, all masterpieces of the greatest artists. It is an extremely carefully chosen collection as is sufficiently indicated by the names of Raphael, Titian, Tintoretto, Rubens, Van Dyck, Velasquez and Murillo. A collection of character, exquisitely selected and arranged, not with any scientific or didactic criterion, but as a display of richness in the dwelling place of the Court, dictated by the aristocratic taste of the seventeenth century. It was opened to the public as a Gallery only in 1833.

Detail of a cameo with portraits of Cosimo I and his family (Museum of Silverware).

The staircase, built in the last years of the 19th cent., takes us to the *Vestibule* from where we pass, to the left, into the main body of the great gallery.

Iliad Room. - Decoration by Luigi Sabatelli (1819). RAPHAEL: *The Pregnant Woman*, painted at the time of his residence in Florence (1508); RIDOLFO DEL GHIRLANDAIO: *Portrait of a Woman;* ANDREA DEL SARTO: *The Assumption of the Virgin* (1519), and opposite it the other *Assumption* (1526); TITIAN: *Portrait of a Gentleman* and *Philip II of Spain;* SUSTERMANS: *Prince Waldemar, son of the King of Denmark*, and *Prince Mattias dei Medici;* VELASQUEZ: *Philip IV of Spain*, which served as model for the equestrian statue by Pietro Tacca.

Room of Saturn. - Ceiling by Ciro Ferri, after a design by Pietro da Cortona (1663-65). In this room are collected various works by RAPHAEL: the two *Portraits of Angelo and Maddalena Doni*, of the time of Raphael's second Florentine period (1506), that of Angelo, solemn and powerful, and that of Maddalena which shows the influence of the « Gioconda » which Leonardo had begun two years previously; the *portraits* of *Cardinal Dovizi da Bibbiena* and of *Tommaso Inghirami;* the *Madonna of the Granduca*, so-called because Ferdinand III of Lorraine was so attached to it that he had it always with him, in his palace, country-villa or on his travels alike; the extremely famous *Madonna of the Chair* was painted at the height of Raphael's power as a fully matured personality (1516); the *Madonna of the Baldaquin* was left unfinished by

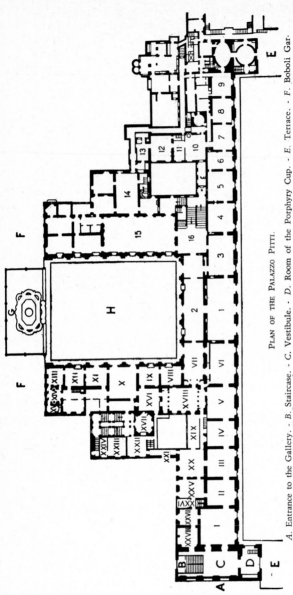

PLAN OF THE PALAZZO PITTI.

A. Entrance to the Gallery. - *B.* Staircase. - *C.* Vestibule. - *D.* Room of the Porphyry Cup. - *E.* Terrace. - *F.* Boboli Gardens. - *G.* Artichoke Fountain. - *H.* Courtyard.

I. Iliad Room. - II. Room of Saturn. - III. Room of Jupiter. - IV. Room of Mars. - V. Room of Apollo. - VI. Room of Venus. - VII. Castagnoli Room. - VIII. Room of the Allegories. - IX. Room of the Fine Arts. - X. Room of Hercules. - XI. Room of Aurora. - XII. Room of Berenice. - XIII. Room of Psyche. - XIV. Small round room. - XV. Bathroom of Maria Luisa. - XVI. Room of the Ark. - XVII. Chapel of the Relics. - XVIII. Room of Music. - XIX. Poccetti Room. - XX. Room of Prometheus. - XXI. Corridor of the Columns - XXII. Room of Justice. - XXIII. Room of Flora. - XXIV. Room of the Putti. - XXV. Room of Ulysses. - XXVI. Bathroom. - XXVII. Room of the Education of Jupiter. - XXVIII. Room of the Stove.

1. Room of Niches. - 2. Room of Statues. - 3. Green Room. - 4. Throne Room. - 5. Blue Room. - 6. Chapel. - 7. Room of the Parrots. - 8. Yellow Room. - 9. Queen's Bedroom. - 10. King's Bedroom. - 11. Study. - 12. Red Room. - 13. Antechamber. - 14. Room of Bona. - 15. Ball Room, also called White or Stucco Room. - 16. Vestibule.

246

Lapislazuli flask of the 16th cent. (Museum of Silverware).

the painter when he was called to Rome (1508) and completed by another hand. By one of Raphael's pupils, probably GIULIO ROMANO, is the *Vision of Ezechiel*, on the design of the master (c. 1510) and of « pagan » inspiration.

Room of Jupiter. - Ceiling by Pietro da Cortona (1643-45). PERUGINO: *Madonna adoring the Child*; ANDREA DEL SARTO: *St. John the Baptist*, a superb portrait, and the *Annunciation*; FRA BARTOLOMEO: *Deposition*; PIERO DEL POLLAIOLO: *St. Jerome*; RAPHAEL: the *Veiled Lady*, a splendid portrait of the famous Fornarina « whom Raphael loved until he died » (recognisable as the model of the Madonna of San Sisto); RUBENS: *Holy Family*

Room of Mars. - Ceiling by Pietro da Cortona (1646) and Ciro Ferri. MURILLO: *Madonna with Child*, a group of extreme grace and refinement; RUBENS: *The Philosophers*, painted to record the meeting of the painter and his brother with the philosophers Justus Lipsius and Jan Van der Wouwere, at Verona; PAOLO VERONESE: *Portrait of Daniele Barbaro*, another of the outstanding portraits which gave rise to many subsequent essays and interpretations of character; RUBENS: *War*, a somewhat facile allegory, powerfully executed; TITIAN: *Cardinal Ippolito de' Medici in Hungarian costume*; VAN DYCK: *Cardinal Luigi Bentivoglio*, a portrait of striking perfection which has the added merit of presenting to us the intelligent features of the author of a great work, the « History of the War of Flanders »; TINTORETTO: *portrait of Luigi Cornaro*.

Room of Apollo. - Ceiling begun by Pietro da Cortona (1647) and completed by Ciro Ferri (1660). TITIAN: *Mary Magdalen*, the most satisfactory of various replicas of the subject, and *Gentleman*, known as the

Velasquez: Philip IV of Spain (detail).

Raphael: « Madonna del Granduca » (detail).

« *Man with green eyes* », of mysterious and moving depth; ANDREA DEL SARTO: *Deposition*, a fine *Self-portrait* and two paintings representing the *Holy Family*; DOSSO DOSSI: *Nymph pursued by a Satyr*, formerly attributed to Giorgione on the strength of its fantastic subject; TINTORETTO: *Portrait of Vincenzo Zeno;* ROSSO FIORENTINO: *Madonna and Saints*, with vivid colouring; VAN DYCK: *double portrait of Charles I of England and Henriette of France.*

Room of Venus. - Ceiling by Pietro da Cortona (1641-42) assisted by Ciro Ferri. TITIAN: *La Bella*, probably the Duchess Eleonora Gonzaga of Urbino; SALVATOR ROSA: two large *Seascapes*, prototypes of a genre which had a great vogue, and which developed the landscape, from being merely an accessory element into a pictorial subject in itself; TITIAN: *Pietro Aretino*, portrait presented to Cosimo I in 1545 by the man of letters who had himself depicted in all his glory as a master of pen, terrible and redoubted; RUBENS: *The Return from the Fields* and *Ulysses on the enchanted Island of the Feaci*, compositions of genius and grandeur in which earth and sky are loaded with fabulously dramatic action; TITIAN; *The Concert*, a most evocative work which after laboured polemics and much perplexity was denied to Giorgione and attributed to his great contemporary.

Ridolfo del Ghirlandaio: Portrait of a Woman.

Raphael: Portrait of Maddalena Doni.

From the Room of Venus we pass into the **Castagnoli Hall,** so-called on account of the decoration by this painter (1754-1832), and where we can see the *St. Sebastian* by SODOMA, painted for the Company of St. Sebastian in Siena, the anomalous languor in the Saint's expression being derived from the influence of Leonardo; further the pleasing *Young Bacchus* by GUIDO RENI.

From the Castagnoli Hall we pass into the **Apartments of Volterrano** (Baldassarre Franceschini called Volterrano, 1611-89), who executed the frescoes of the *five Allegories* in the first room therefore called **Room of the Allegories.** There follow the **Room of the Fine Arts** with ceiling by Domenico Podestà (1814) and the **Room of Hercules** with frescoes by Pietro Benvenuti (1828) in neo-classical style, and the **Room of Aurora.** In these first rooms of the Apartments of Volterrano have been gathered some paintings of the Florentine School of the 17th cent.: VOLTERRANO, GIOVANNI DA SAN GIOVANNI, SUSTERMANS, EMPOLI, CIGOLI. Notice the magnificent vase of Sèvres in the Room of Hercules. The following **Room of Titus and Berenice** (with ceiling by Giuseppe Bezzuoli, 1784-1855) contains a collection of very fine paintings by SALVATOR ROSA.

Going back to the Castagnoli Hall, we enter the **Room of Music** and then the **Poccetti Gallery** with frescoes by this artist and some interesting paintings by RUBENS, DOMENICO FETI, SALVATOR ROSA and SPAGNOLETTO.

Room of Prometheus. - Ceiling by Giuseppe Collignon (1842). FILIPPO LIPPI: *Madonna,* one of the most beautiful works of the master derived from the « tondi da parto » (confinement salvers) and the inspiration of a crowd of Florentine works of the fifteenth century of which the most important examples in this room are the *Madonna adoring the Child* by FRANCESCO BOTTICINI and the *Holy Family* by LUCA SIGNORELLI. Besides these we find a *Portrait of a Woman* und a *Portrait of a Youth* by BOTTICELLI and *St. Francis* by SPAGNOLETTO.

Gallery of the Columns. - Here is assembled a quantity of small paintings mostly by Flemish artists, among which many pleasant *landscapes* by CORNELIUS POELENBURG, and the fantastic *Orpheus in Hell* by PETER BREUGHEL called « degli inferni » (of hells).

Room of Justice. - Ceiling decorated by Antonio Fedi (1830). PAOLO VERONESE: *Baptism of Christ;* TITIAN: *portrait of Tommaso Mosti* and *The Saviour;* TINTORETTO: three *portraits of Men* and *Venus, Volcano and Cupid.*

Room of Flora. - *Italic Venus* by CANOVA, which Ludovic, King of Etruria, had commissioned in 1805 to substitute the Medici Venus which had been seized by the French, in Palermo, where it had been unwisely taken for supposed safe-keeping; ANDREA DEL SARTO: two paintings with *Stories of Joseph;* BRONZINO: two *portraits;* PONTORMO: *Adoration of the Magi.*

Room of the Putti. - Ceiling by Antonio Marini (c. 1830). Here is assembled a small collection of most precious works of the Flemish school, among them the small RUBENS: *The Three Graces,* considered a masterpiece. The two paintings of *still-life* by RACHEL RUYSCH (1716) are very famous and admired for the precision and the liveliness of the very small details. Coming back into the Room of Prometheus, we pass into the

Room of Ulysses. - Ceiling by Gaspare Martellini (1815). RAPHAEL: *The Madonna dell'Impannata* (so-called from the window closed by a panel of linen, as was customary before the use of glass window-panes), a work said to have been executed by a pupil on designs of the master; ANDREA DEL SARTO: *Madonna with Child and Saints;* FILIPPINO LIPPI: *Death of Lucretia;* TINTO-

RETTO: *portrait of Andrea Frizier*; DOLCI: *Mary Magdalen*, a typical example of the works which satisfied the taste of the official society in the second half of the seventeenth century.

Bathroom in Empire style by Giuseppe Cacialli.

Room of the Education of Jupiter. - CRISTOFANO ALLORI: *Judith*, a superb group of three portraits of allegorical intention (depicting the model Mazzafirra, her mother and the truncated head of the artist); CARAVAGGIO: *Sleeping Cupid;* various very finicky works by DOLCI.

Room of the Stove. - The *lunettes* of the ceiling are decorated by MATTEO ROSSELLI 1622) and the walls by PIETRO DA CORTONA (1640), with the *Four Ages of the Earth*. From this room we go back to the Room of Venus and we enter the former Royal Apartments.

Dining-room or **room of the Niches.** - Series of *portraits of the Medici family* by SUSTERMANS. Left is the **Gallery of Antique Statues** with a beatiful view on the Amphitheatre of the Boboli Garden. Going back into the Dining-room we pass into the **Green Room** with ceiling by Luca Giordano and Gobelins tapestries; the **Throne Room** with tapestries of the same series of that in the Green Room and magnificent vases; the **Blue Room** and the **Chapel.**

The three following rooms, the first of which is called **Room of the Parrots,** formed the apartment of Queen Margherita of Savoy while the three rooms on the left of the Room of the Parrots formed the apartment of King Umberto I.

Raphael: « Madonna of the Chair » (detail).

Andrea del Sarto: St. John the Baptist.

Raphael: The Veiled Lady (detail).

From the ante-chamber of the King's apartment we enter the **Room of Bona** in which the frescoes depicting the *Conquest of Bona* (1605) *and Prevesa* (1607) were executed by POCCETTI with original iconographical elements and are thus valuable as historical documents of the most glorious feats of the Tuscan military sea forces. From this room we reach the **Ballroom** or **White Room** decorated with 18th cent. stuccoes and the **Vestibule** from which we go down to the ground floor by the state staircase.

The visit to Palazzo Pitti is finished, but we shall not have a complete vision of this old, spacious royal palace unless we visit what makes a necessary addition to the palace, and

Rubens: The four Philosophers.

what we can call « a royal palace in the open air », which is the very famous **Boboli garden**. The Pitti palace has a hill behind it, the fields of which were formerly cultivated and were called « Bogoli » or « Borgoli ». In 1459, Cosimo I commissioned the architect Niccolò Pericoli, surnamed the TRIBOLO for his restlessness, to design a great garden on the slopes of the hill, behind the recently acquired palace. Ten years before Tribolo had also designed the garden of the Villa at Castello, but this one, much larger, was to be a worthy background for a royal palace. The artist designed the plan, which is substantially what we see today, but he died (1550) before beginning the great task. His work was continued (1560) and decorated with details first by AMMANNATI, then by BUONTALENTI (1583), and finally, in the seventeenth century the part called the « Isolotto », was enlarged with scenographic ideas, by ALFONSO PARIGI the younger (1628-56). The Boboli garden is therefore the result of the genius of four great architects, trained in the school of fantasy of the creators of pageants and court festivals: the architecture, combined with the sculptures of a crowd of less important artists, and above all with the superb ornamentation of the carefully placed trees, have created an unsurpassed, though much imitated, example.

We enter the garden by the *Bacchus Gateway*, at the left end corner of the façade, and after a few paces we come to the **Grotto of Buontalenti** (1583), an artificial grotto, composed of three areas covered with false incrustations. In the *first grotto* the idea of its decoration was suggested by the provisional arrangement, however arbitrary and fantastic, of the four *Prisoners* which Michelangelo had sculpted for the tomb of Julius II and which, remaining unfinished in Florence, should have been carried to France (now the originals are in the Gallery of the Fine Arts Academy, and are substituted here by copies). Here, instead, in their apparent roughness, they became enclosed between false stalactites, in a theatrical scenery of literary rusticity, with idyllic *frescoes* by BERNARDINO POCCETTI. The other *statues* by BACCIO BANDINELLI complete the decoration between the grass and maiden hair plants. The fanciful Buontalenti had closed the lantern with a crystal basin, full of running water, with different coloured fishes, and the light once used to fall through this odd ceiling.

Murillo: Madonna and Child.

Titian: The Concert (detail).

The *secondo grotto*, called *Ninfeo*, covered with shells and decorated with mythological pictures, has in the centre the group of *Teseus and Helen* (1560) by VINCENZO DE' ROSSI, and a *basin* by BATTISTA LORENZI.

In the *third*, with *decorations* by POCCETTI, there is another fountain with little satyrs looking at the most lovely Venus called the *Venus of the little grotto* (1573), one of the happiest

Botticelli: Portrait of a Lady.

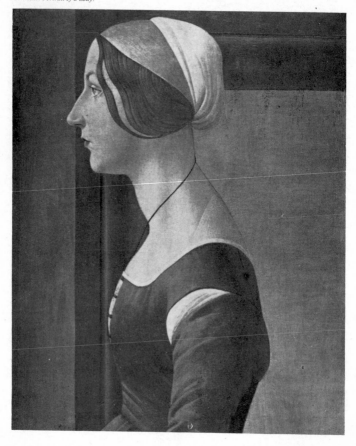

Cristofano Allori: Judith (detail).

works of **GIAMBOLOGNA**. Today the grotto is dry and silent, but one must imagine it, fresh, mysteriously lit, with murmuring water-spouts and all its fountains in action, the dripping rocks and vegetation on the dark background of the shining walls, the white marbles vibrating with continually changing reflections, to take account of the exquisite refinement of the place, which was inspired by the allegories of men of letters, in a style between the rustic and the courtesan, between the fantastic and the idyllic, for the foreign guests of the Medici Court who, between magnificent banquets and theatrical spectacles, could find here motives of no smaller wonder and excitement to the already tired fancy.

The avenue which curves up between rows of ilexes, with Roman statues in porphyry and marble, leads to the **Amphitheatre** designed by **TRIBOLO**, as rustic architecture, later built in masonry, in the Roman circle style, but made more gra-

Jan Frans Douven: The Elector and the Electress Palatine.

cious by its green setting against which stand out the tabernacles with antique statues, both originals and copies. In the middle, a large *Roman basin* and an *Egyptian obelisk*, brought from Thebes in the 2nd. cent. B. C.

From the amphitheatre we can enjoy a distant view of the city and, nearer, the architecture of the great **Courtyard** of the palace, the work of AMMANNATI (1560-63), with the *Fountain of the Artichoke* (1641) by FRANCESCO DEL TADDA. The terrace which closes the courtyard was used for the building of the stage for the great open-air spectacles, to which the palace was the background and the amphitheatre the pit. From the spectacles for the marriage of Francesco I and Bianca Cappello (1579), to the series of festivities prepared by Emilio del Cavaliere, super-intendant of spectacles (1588-1598), to the games, balls, masques, hunts, tournaments, comic, mimic and tragic representations, held there for over a century, the Boboli Garden is even today used as an immense scenery, bright under the spring and autumn skies. After a long period of inactivity, this is today happily renewed, and in this wonderful frame, comedies are represented and musical works performed with marvellous effects.

At the end of the amphitheatre, Roman statues of *Septimus Severus*, and a *Magistrate*, at the sides of a Phidiac *Ceres*, a copy perhaps by Alcamenes, pupil of the great sculptor. Higher up, a large round basin, called the *Fountain of Neptune*, from a bronze statue of that god, work of STOLDO LORENZI (1565). On the last level, the statue of *Abundance* begun by GIAMBOLOGNA and finished by TACCA (1636).

Above a rampart of the old walls built by Michelangelo for the defence of Florence (1529), in front of a small villa is the **Garden of the Cavaliere** with the *Monkey's Fountain* by PIETRO TACCA. From here the panorama on the other side of the hill opens out, with the view of Monte Oliveto and the Certosa. The Garden is dominated by the most elegant lines of the **Palazzetto di Belvedere**, work of the architect GIOVANNI DEI MEDICI guided by Buontalenti and which, now useless as a fortress, has been fitted up as a cultural and tourists' centre, offering a splendid view of the city from its ramparts (see page 288).

Going down the side of the hill, we come to a green bower in front of a sort of outbuilding of the Palace, which is the

Boboli Garden: Fountain « of the Isolotto ».

Apartment of the Meridiana, a construction in Neo-classical style by Gaspare Paoletti and Pasquale Poccianti (1832) which takes its name from a meridian drawn on the floor of the atrium. The ceilings of the rooms are an interesting display of Florentine art of the Academic period. Here King Victor Emmanuel II had his favourite and modest residence, during the time Florence was the capital of Italy.

There still remains to be seen the part of the garden planned by Alfonso Parigi (1618). Not far from the Fountain of Neptune, a straight avenue, called the *Viottolone* (large lane), which descends steeply between two majestic rows of cypress trees, leads to the **Piazzale dell'Isolotto** (Square of the small island), surrounded by black ilexes, in the middle of which is a delightful water-garden, with lemon and orange trees and statues, which together make one of the most charming ensembles of garden architecture. In the centre of the island rises a very fine *Ocean Fountain* by Alfonso Parigi (1618), upon which was adapted with some changes the replica of the figure of the Bolognese *Neptune* by Giambologna (1571), surrounded by statues of the young *Nile*, the grown *Ganges* and the old *Euphrates*. Around it, other white figures rise from the water, among which *Perseus and Andromeda*, also attributed to Giambologna.

In the adjacent groves are scattered, a little everywhere in the shrubbery, bizarre statues and grotesque, pastoral, rustic groups, such as those representing the *Game of « Saccomazzone »* by Orazio Mochi and Romolo del Tadda and the *Game of the « Pentolaccia »* by Giovan Battista Capezzuoli, after the florid taste of the time when the fine rustic literary works of Michelangelo Buonarroti the younger, Lorenzo Lippi and their innumerable followers, were appreciated and enjoyed. Coming back, still between most lovely vegetation, statues, life-like groups and fountains, we finally come to the exit, in *Via Romana*, with our eyes full of wonder and our souls at peace.

But the Boboli garden is not only a marvellous scenario in which it is easy to perceive the enchantments of the rural feasts and of the open air theatricals, which were the passion of the Medici Court in the seventeenth and eighteenth century. The garden was also an experimental site of the Grand ducal family and Court, where the study of botany was held in great honour. In the Boboli garden were in fact started experiments on the cultivation of the « Papata », that is the potato, of the mulberry-tree, of the dwarf pear, and other exquisite varieties of fruit and exotic plants, which the Grand dukes had brought to Florence, at great expense, from every part of the world, that they might be known and used.

Boboli Garden: The Amphitheatre and the Palazzetto di Belvedere.

Superb testimony of the continuation through the centuries of the scientific progress promoted by the Medici Grand dukes, since the end of the sixteenth century, and marvellously carried on until the revelations of Galileo and his pupils, later united in the foundation of the *Accademia del Cimento*, the first scientific academy in the world, is the celebrated **Museum of Physical and Natural History**, more briefly called the **Specola** (Observatory), on the *Via Romana* (no. 17).

The Grand duke Pietro Leopoldo of Lorraine bought this palace, where Malatesta Baglioni had lived when he was entrusted with the command of the defence of besieged Florence (1529-30), and he destined it to gather the scientific material left by the Medici, so rich and indiscutably important for the history of progress. Open to the students in 1807, the zoological, botanical and minerological collections (put together since the days of Francesco Redi) were made public, as well as collections of scientific instruments which had even a more remote origin, and which GALILEO GALILEI, EVANGELISTA TORRICELLI, VINCENZO VIVIANI, and the Academicians of the Cimento had enlarged and enriched with new inventions (they have today been taken to the Science Museum in Piazza dei Giudici). The zoological material was first arranged by NICOLA STENONE and by the naturalist GIOVANNI TARGIONI TOZZETTI. Of great interest is the collection of figures in coloured wax, which has its origin in the industry of votive offerings which were made to be put in the churches. The first models of Cigoli indicated that since early in the seventeenth century scientific use could be made from faithful reproductions of the human body, so that the odd art was developed in the work of the Syracusan GAETANO and MICHELE ZUMBO through encouragement of the Grand duke Cosimo III. But the maximum fidelity in the reproduction of the forms and colours was attained by FRANCESCO SUSINI, LUIGI CALAMAI, FRANCESCO and CARLO CALENZUOLI to whom we owe most of this collection unique in its type.

In **Galileo's Tribune,** built by GIUSEPPE MARTELLI, we have an interesting ensemble of frescoes, with stories from the life of the great scientist, and of Tuscan scientific glories, painted by Giuseppe Bezzuoli, Nicola Cianfanelli, Gaspare Martellini, Luigi Sabatelli and his son Luigi. The statue of Galileo is by Aristodemo Costoli, busts and medallions by Emilio Demi, Gaetano Grazzini, Lorenzo Nencini, Luigi Magi. The Tribune, ordered by Leopoldo II, was quickly finished for the third Congress of Scientists, in 1841. A visit to the Specola will be instructive for everybody, but particularly profitable for followers of the positive sciences.

Coming out of the Museum, on the left the road leads to **Porta Romana** (1326), where, high up on the inner side of the gate, one will notice a Giottesque *Madonna enthroned with Saints.*

Returning to the Specola and going on a few paces, on the left we find the **Church of San Felice,** with a side still in Gothic style but with a Renaissance façade, by a follower of Brunelleschi, perhaps Antonio Manetti (1474). Also the carved wood door is of the fifteenth century.

The **interior** has one single nave, with a large sixteenth century choir over the first half of the church, for the use of the nuns who occupied the nearby convent. The three chapels of the chancel are of the fifteenth century. **First altar on the right**: fresco attributed to NICOLA GERINI (1368-1416), *Pietà;* **Fifth altar on the right**: coloured terracotta group *Pietà*, by the CIECO DA GAMBASSI (the Blind man from Gambassi) (1603-42); **Sixth altar on the right**: RIDOLFO DEL GHIRLANDAIO, *Madonna and Saints* (c. 1520); in the place of the seventh altar is a large lunette with a fourteenth century fresco, *Assumption of the Virgin Mary.* **Seventh altar on the left**: GIOVANNI DA SAN GIOVANNI, *St. Maximus helped by St. Felix* (1635) (the angels are by VOL-TERRANO). **Sixth altar on the left**: NERI DI BICCI, *Tryptych* (1467); **Fifth altar on the left**: JACOPO DA EMPOLI, *Madonna and Saints* (1595). Notice the Giottesque *Crucifix* high up, on the wall of the choir. **First altar on the left**: *Tryptych* by a pupil of Botticelli.

In the church square is the **Casa Guidi,** where an epigraph by Niccolò Tommaseo records the English poetess ELIZABETH BARRETT BROWNING, who lived here a long time, and died here (1861).

We take the spacious **Via Maggio,** or Via Maggiore (greater), so called for its unusual width. In ancient Florence, there were two wide and straight arteries: Via Larga (broad), on the right of the Arno; Via Maggio « di là d'Arno », that is on the left bank. This street, which the Ponte Santa Trinita joins to Via Tornabuoni, was the official itinerary of the processions, of the carnival masquerades, of the crowds celebrating Spring time, of the rows of decorated carts, of the military parades, receptions, obsequies, and was one of the favourite meeting-grounds for stone fights and for the «challenge» of the foot ball players. The exceptional beauty and variety of the way from the Piazza del Duomo to the Canto del Centauro (the cross roads at the beginning of Via Rondinelli, where originally was the group of the Centaur by Giambologna, now under the Loggia della Signoria), to the Column of Justice on Piazza Santa Trinita, and over the bridge to the Piazza San Felice, until the unexpected view of the Pitti Palace, on top of the hill, were made more wonderful by the magnificence of the decoration. It is not possible that our fancy, used to the shabby taste of the last bourgeois century can effectively imagine this almost continual exhibition, on the façades of the palaces and churches, of tapestries, brocades, festoons of leaves and fruit, of torches and lanterns, of engravings, pictures and statues. At the cross roads rose temporary triumphal arches, and improvised monuments and buildings. A real crowd of architects, sculptors, painters, especially from the sixteenth century onwards, gave a great part of their activity to these exuberant manifestations, invented and guided by literary courtesans. And in this public, free gaiety, in this activity of ambitious work, the people of Florence and the neighbourhood, found, for at least three centuries, a fresh source of happiness which satisfied their fanciful needs and which helped them to overcome much suffering.

For foreign visitors, for illustrious guests, these streets were one of the many spectacles of Florentine splendour. And also now, although reduced to the bare architectural scheme of the places, happily not damaged by tasteless alterations, we pass down Via Maggio with a sense of lightheartedness, scarcely feeling tired from the walk.

Among the fine sixteenth century palaces of Via Maggio, at no. 26, the most popular is the **House of Bianca Cappello** (with the coat-of-arms of the travelling hat) which Francesco I had renewed by BERNARDO BUONTALENTI (1567) for the famous Venetian who gave much, and not all false, material to the stories and gossip of the people and of the men-of-letters.

Turning to the left in *Via dei Michelozzi,* we come out into *Piazza Santo Spirito* where stands the

CHURCH OF SANTO SPIRITO

belonging to the Augustinian convent of the same name, which built up the most important religious centre in the city on the other side of the Arno, one of those important centres not only spiritual but intellectual and social. We must think that next to the church there stood an enormous convent, which has lately unfortunately been taken as headquarters for the military District. The convent with libraries and schools, used to have hostels for pilgrims, refectories for the poor, and also a hospital for the sick, because in the Middle Ages, convents carried on hospital work in every sense, according to the commandments of the Seven Works of Corporal Mercy, apart from those of Spiritual Mercy.

Its foundation goes back to 1250 and the first church, built twelve years later, was enlarged and grew more and more important, as in the plain of the Oltrarno the suburbs extended and the number of houses increased between the old and the new city walls. The old church now was embellished with great works of art by Cimabue, Giotto, Stefano, Lippo Memmi. But the convent's greatest splendour was about the end of the fourteenth century and the beginning of the fifteenth, when there gathered around it the first humanist followers of Francesco Petrarca, who had proclaimed Saint Augustine his spiritual master.

It was really in the fifteenth century that the church received its final architectural line, in a model by FILIPPO BRUNELLESCHI, who had imagined it as the twin church of San Lorenzo, with the façade facing towards the Arno. But his first project underwent notable changes, and was executed, with little fidelity, after his death, by ANTONIO MANETTI, and by SALVI D'ANDREA.

The *façade* has never been made, and appears like a wall, plastered and badly shaped at the top. The *cupola* was also designed by Brunelleschi, but executed after his death by Salvi d'Andrea (1481). The fine *campanile* was designed by BACCIO D'AGNOLO (1503).

The exterior does not give an idea of what is within: many of Brunelleschi's windows have been filled in, and the look is that of a neglected building awaiting an intelligent restoration.

The bell-tower and the cupola of the Church of Santo Spirito.

But the **interior,** also by contrast, appears as one of the most superb examples of Renaissance architecture. Even though accepting the traditional scheme of the Latin cross plan, which was not, as we have seen, Filippo Brunelleschi's ideal, he gave this church the stamp of his genius. The arcading, instead of stopping at the beginning of the transept, also develops as a Latin cross, parallel to the walls in a succession of very light arches carried by 35 elegant Corinthian columns in grey stone, so forming an internal portico, sublimely harmonious, with original, almost sylvestrian effects, especially in the intersection of the transept. The impression of airyness and majestic width aroused by this unexpected sight, is quite unforgettable.

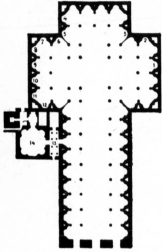

PLAN OF S. SPIRITO

1. FIL.NO LIPPI: *Madonna.* - 2. B. ROSSELLINO: *Sarcophagus of Neri Capponi.* - 3. L. DI CREDI: *Madonna.* - 4. Flor. School of the 15th cent.: *Annunciation.* - 5. School of D. Ghirlandaio: *Manger.* - 6. RAFF DEL GARBO: *Madonna.* - 7. F. BOTTICINI: *St. Monica* - 8 C. ROSSELLI: *Madonna.* - 9. A. SANSOVINO: *Marble Altar.* - 10. RAF. DEL GARBO: *Holy Trinity.* - 11. RAF. DEL GARBO: *Madonna and two Saints.* - 12. RAF. DEL GARBO: *Madonna and four Saints.* - 13. Vestibule. - 14. Sacristy.

The forty round-backed chapels, with the original low altars, repeat in the plan the semicircular rhythm of the arches, so that the whole building assumes a marvellous stylistic unity, which not even the inconsiderate decorative additions have succeeded to upset.

The illumination diffused with perfect uniformity and the form of the chapels with their niches bring into singular prominence each of the works of art on the altars. In this marvellous gallery it would be good to see again the works of art which were inconsiderately taken away. The **internal façade,** with the great harmonious doors, was executed by SALVI D'ANDREA (1483) on obvious designs by Brunelleschi.

The ensemble of the **Chancel** is a work of the early 17th century (GIOV. CACCINI and GHER. SILVANI), very rich and picturesque but little in harmony with the pure lines of the building. Behind the high altar, there is a wooden *Crucifix,* attributed to MICHELANGELO when he was twenty years old.

In the **right transept:** in the fifth chapel, the *Madonna with Child, St. John the Baptist, St. Martin and St. Catherine the Martyr who present the donors Tanai and Nanna dei Nerli,* by FILIPPINO LIPPI (in the background the view of the suburb with the gate of San Frediano). In the seventh chapel, behind a bronze grating, the *Sarcophagus of Neri Capponi,* work of BERNARDO ROSSELLINO.

In the **apse**: first chapel, *Madonna and Saints* by LORENZO DI CREDI. Seventh chapel, *Annunciation*, work of Florentine school of the fifteenth cent. Eighth chapel, *Manger*, work of school of Domenico Ghirlandaio.

In the **left transept**: first chapel, *Madonna with Child, Angels and Saints*, attributed to RAFFAELLINO DEL GARBO. Second chapel, *St. Monica who founds the Order of the Augustinians* by FRANCESCO BOTTICINI. Third chapel, *Madonna with Child and Saints* by COSIMO ROSSELLI. Fourth chapel, *marble altar* by ANDREA SANSOVINO. The paintings in the fifth, sixth and seventh chapels are attributed to RAFFAELLINO DEL GARBO: they represent: *St. Catherine and St. Mary Magdalen adoring the Trinity; Madonna with Angels, St. Bartholomew, St. Nicholas of Bari and two donors; Madonna with Child and four Saints.*

Under the organ we enter the fine *Vestibule* of ANDREA SANSOVINO and then the large octagonal **Sacristy** by GIULIANO DA SAN GALLO and CRONACA (1456). The grand construction is framed by couples of Corinthian columns of grey stone which are transformed into the ribs of the cupola and meet in the lantern.

From the Vestibule we go down to the **First Cloister,** of the seventeenth century, by GIULIO and ALFONSO PARIGI (c. 1600) with frescoes by seventeenth cent. Florentine painters. The **Second Cloister,** an original architecture by AMMANNATI (1564-69), with *frescoes* by BERNARDINO POCCETTI, is occupied by the military District. From here we go to the *Corsini Chapel*, with tombs of the family in Gothic style and fourteenth century frescoes.

Since a few years the **Great Refectory** has been open, which is the only remaining part of the fourteenth century convent and where is a small

Church of Santo Spirito: Interior.

art Museum given to the monks by Romano the antiquarian. One enters it from the square on the left of the church façade, and besides a grandiose fresco representing the *Last Supper* and the *Crucifixion*, attributed to NARDO DI CIONE, we may admire various fine piece of fourteenth century sculpture.

Coming out on the square, we see at the left corner the **Guadagni Palace** (1503) attributed to Simone del Pollaiolo called CRONACA, with a beautiful « grafito » decoration and an airy terrace under the great overhanging roof. On the opposite side of the square is *Via Sant'Agostino* which joins *Via dei Serragli*, important artery which starts from Ponte alla Carraia.

Crossing Via dei Serragli, from *Via Santa Monica* we enter *Piazza del Carmine*. Here was once another large convent, that of

Filippino Lippi: Madonna and Child (Santo Spirito).

SANTA MARIA DEL CARMINE

with a church in Romanesque-Gothic style going back to 1268. A fire almost completely destroyed it in 1771; the fire left only two chapels and the sacristy.

In one of these chapels, that of the **Brancacci** family, the last on the right, the highest and most fruitful testimony of Italian painting was saved. Between the Scrovegni Chapel at Padua, frescoed by Giotto, and the Roman Sistine Chapel frescoed by Michelangelo, this Florentine Brancacci Chapel, frescoed by MASACCIO (Tommaso Guidi, called Masaccio, 1401-28) represents an arrival and a departure point in the history of painting, marked by these great Tuscans. The dramatic force, the expressive power, the pictorial relief of Giotto here join the fullness of profond humanism, of restrained plastic power and of marvellous perspective colouring. Giotto's lesson is conveyed to the highest affirmation of human plastic, colouristic and perspective values. From this fullness of concept and style Michelangelo went to the exaltation of sublime, tormented humanity.

All the so-called naturalism of Italian painting, or rather all humanism, was born from the frescoes in this chapel, which was and is a perpetual school of art. From Masaccio run all the pictorial experiences, and to Masaccio return all the novelties which want to make contact again with reality, after useless stylistic deviations.

In the Brancacci Chapel Masaccio is as ancient as the Greeks and as modern as the more solid Post-impressionists. He is truth, not truism; he is nature, not naturalism; he is human, not humanistic. His creatures have the characteristics of the real Adam, his landscapes are sentiments, his compositions have the pulse of life and at the same time the absoluteness of an idea. In his art, nature and spirit, intellect and sentiment, body and soul meet in a unique expression. And consequently form and colour, line and perspective, unite in a poetic representation which perhaps has no equal. Masaccio's painting is a synthesis of form, feeling, colour and psychology.

We must think of a prodigy of artistic grace, if we consider that Masaccio, son of Ser Giovanni di Mone Guidi, was born at San Giovanni Valdarno in 1401, and that he died mysteriously in 1428; so that the Brancacci chapel is the work of a young man between 25 and 27 years old.

Given the importance that this chapel has in the history of art, it will not be useless to recall its origin. The Brancacci were silk merchants, who received their coat-of-arms of nobility through good actions towards the Republic. Felice, of this family, just in the year in which Masaccio came to Florence from San Giovanni Valdarno (1422), was sent by the Signoria as ambassador to the Sultan, in Cairo. On his return from Egypt, he thought of embellishing the family chapel and called MASOLINO DA PANICALE to fresco it.

One could say that the themes proposed, even imposed, for the decoration of the chapel foresaw the spirit of Masaccio's painting. They were those of original sin, and of the life of St. Peter. Humanity, primogenital in Adam and Eve, rough and generous in the fisherman Cefa regenerated by Grace, really seems to call for the interpretation of the painter of rough and gentle nature, of severe, potent beauty.

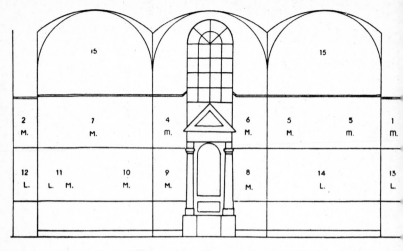

FRESCOES OF THE BRANCACCI CHAPEL.

1. MASOLINO: *Adam and Eve.* - 2. MASACCIO: *Expulsion from Paradise.* - 3. MASO-LINO: *Resurrection of Tabitha.* - 4. MASOLINO: *St. Peter preaching.* - 5. MASACCIO: *St. Peter healing the Cripple.* - 6. MASACCIO: *St. Peter baptising.* - 7. MASACCIO: *The Payment of the Tribute.* - 8. MASACCIO: *St. Peter and St. John giving alms.* - 9. MASACCIO: *St. Peter healing by his shadow.* - 10. MASACCIO: *St. Peter enthroned.* - 11. MASACCIO and FIL.NO LIPPI: *St. Peter raising the Emperor's nephew.* - 12. LIPPI: *St. Paul visiting St. Peter in prison.* - 13. LIPPI. *Liberation of St. Peter from prison.* - 14. LIPPI: *St. Peter before the Proconsul* and *Crucifixion of St. Peter.* - 15. Frescoes of the 18th cent. (V. MEUCCI and C. SACCONI).

The decoration of the chapel was first entrusted to Masolino da Pani-cale (1424-25), believed to be the master of Masaccio, perhaps because of the affinity of the names and the vicinity of the work. But between the two painters there is no artistic similarity. Masolino still belongs to the Gothic period, while Masaccio is the full expression of Humanism and of the Renaissance.

We see how mannered and conventional in the first panel on the right, top, is the scene of the *Temptation of Adam*, by MASOLINO, confronting the panel at the left, top, with the dramatic, sorrowful scene of the *Expulsion from Paradise*, in which MASACCIO reveals his very great personality. Adam, shameful, already bent under the condemnation; Eve, desperate, already weak under the weight of pain. The two figures are modelled almost with impet-uosity, summary and yet precise masses, without hesitations in details or stylistic weakness, as if the material were still the palpitating and earthly material of creation.

The work was interrupted, it seems because Masaccio took himself to Rome, and many years after his death the frescoing of the Chapel was completed by FILIPPINO LIPPI, who forced himself to be on a height with Masaccio, but his paintings are weak and shallow in comparison.

Three painters therefore alternate in the chapel: Masolino, Masaccio and Filippino. The three scenes high up are by Masolino (they always began the work at the top). The five scenes at the bottom are by Filippino. So as not to make confusion, we must point out that there are 12 painting and 16 scenes, that is, the four large side rectangles are divided into two scenes, which in some case are by two authors.

We begin to look quickly at the scenes painted by MASOLINO DA PANICALE. They are, beginning from the right, top: the scene representing the *Temptation*; the first scene on the right of the second large painting at the top, representing *St. Peter resuscitating Tabitha*; finally, the painting high up on the altar representing the *Preaching of St. Peter*. The scenes are pleasing, drawn with elegance, full of most charming details of costumes and city life. We see a Florentine square with the clothes at the windows, animals on the loggias, among which a monkey, street scenes and scenes of daily life. And we should look, in the last painting, at the costumes of the two gentlemen who listen to the Apostle. There is good observation here, but we are still in the anecdote, not in the drama of the humanity of MASACCIO. Called to Hungary, Masolino interrupted the work (1425). MASACCIO continued it (1425-1427), completing the rectangle of the right hand wall invented by Masolino, and where we feel the hand of Masaccio in *St. Peter who heals the Cripple*. After that he passed perhaps to the painting on the right above the altar, where he painted *St. Peter baptizing*, in which the scene is no longer conventional, the nudes have a great plastic power, and the « man who trembles » is drawn with anatomic truth and surprising psychology. From there the painter went to what is the most finished manifestation of his pictorial genius, that is to the great rectangle on the left wall, at the top, with the three consecutive scenes of *Jesus who orders Peter to catch a fish* (centre), of *St Peter who takes a piece of money from the mouth of the fish* (left) and of *St. Peter who pays the tribute to the publican* (right). The whole painting is known by the title of the **Payment of the Tribute.** Around the imposing and powerful figure of Jesus, a tense and expressive look upon his face, around that figure of truth incarnate, is a crowd of men. Unforgettable heads, for the fierceness of expression, and nobility of carriage. Surrounding them, a circle of hills, distant, almost disappearing, a bare, spacious landscape with light trees in the clear air. Together with this is the solidity of form, the almost cubistic relief of the masses, the impressionistic luminosity. The perspective effect is not founded on a geometrical problem, but is derived from the depth of the feeling. The composition not balanced after a linear scheme, broadens and breathes in concentric waves, which spread out from the imperious figure of Christ as far as the extreme limit of the circle of hills. In the valley, full of airiness and of men, of glances and vibrations, Christ magnetically attracts the souls which move round him as round the axis of truth. The *Payment of the Tribute* is justly considered the pictorial masterpiece of masterpieces. In a sublime synthesis Masaccio has resolved here all the problems of art, from those of form to those of colour, from those of natural truth to those of dramatic power, from those of space to those of psychology, from rational problems to problems of feeling. We are at a culminating point, from which art either was to overflow into the powerful Michelangelesque hyperbole, or rise to the sublime Raphaelesque mannerism; but Masaccio's painting remains as an example of formal fulness and stylistic

Masaccio: Payment of the Tribute.

completion, of natural truth and sincerity of sentiment: unequalled revelation of the entire, complete man, without deviations, without defects and without bewitchments.

In the lower band, the painting on the right of the altar is by Masaccio, representing *St. Peter and St. John giving alms*, another very fine work. Besides the usual solidity and fierceness of the male figure, example of humanity which after the original sin suffers and is weary, we notice the graceless truth of the woman, who makes her hard arm the seat for the half naked child. We see how the great house is almost the symbol of man's habitation, with no longer the episodical pleasantness of Masolino's houses. Everything here seems symbolic, yet tremendously realistic: the woman with the child, the man fallen on the ground, the house, the castle which shines brightly on the edge of the distant hill.

On the left of the altar is *St. Peter who heals the sick with his shadow*. Here the effects of original sin are made even more sadly evident, in the half nude old man and in the cripple in whom the intense imploration lights up an animal face. St. Peter goes on almost impassibly, but piety and prayer are written on his face, he is the statue of authority, the rock upon which Christ has founded His Church.

Passing to the lower part of the left-hand wall, Masaccio put his hand to another fresco, that formed by two scenes: *St. Peter on his Throne*, on the right, and *St. Peter resuscitating the nephew of the Emperor*, on the left. He executed the first scene with the Apostle seated on a rustic construction, and around him the circle of a strong humanity, with solid friars in their habits.

But the figures which are lined behind the shoulders of these friars, no longer have the stamp of Masaccio's universal truth, having the minuteness of patiently studied portraits, and the wordliness of the citizens' costumes. Also the architecture is made elegant and ornate, with vases and decorative plants. Masaccio had abandoned the work (1428), to die, at 27 years of age, perhaps at the gates of Rome. FILIPPINO LIPPI, the son of Fra Filippo, had taken up his inheritance with trembling hand, completing the work carefully (c. 1483), but alas without Masaccio's amazing power. Among his figures we can easily discern the heads already executed by Masaccio, such as that of the enthroned Emperor, that of the man who looks at him, from the bottom upwards, that of St. Peter and the two faces, one shortened, the other bearded, which we see over his arm.

This scene finished, Filippino passed to the scene at the end of the left wall, painting there *St. Peter in prison, visited by St. Paul*. Then, in the lower band of the right wall, he executed the painting of the *Angel who liberates St. Peter from Prison*, and the double scene of the *Condemnation of St. Peter before the Proconsul* and the *Crucifixion of St. Peter*.

Filippino was 27 years old when he finished the painting. He supplied serious handicraft to lack of vigour, producing an admirable piece of work which is only minimized by the proximity of Masaccio's work. The artistic taste of the century liked too much realism and the portraying of episodes. So Filippino's paintings are more pleasing that moving, and we are easily influenced by superficial impressions. For example, it is interesting to know that the naked figure of the Emperor's son is that of the young Filippo Granacci; that the figure of the old man near the Proconsul is that of Antonio del Pollajolo; that the figure at the end with the cap on his head is the self-portrait of the painter, and that in the Crucifixion, the first person in profile towards the left is Sandro Botticelli.

Masaccio: St. Peter healing the sick (detail).

Coming out of the church we cross the square and enter the crowded, popular *Borgo San Frediano*. Here we come upon the **Church of San Frediano in Cestello**, surmounted by a fine *cupola* by ANTONIO FERRI (1698), which is one of the most picturesque elements of the landscape on this side of the Arno. The interior is an interesting ensemble of the arts of the Baroque period, here as everywhere in Florence, rather quiet and simple. The dome of the cupola was frescoed by ANTONIO DOMENICO GABBIANI, with the *Glory of Paradise*, considered his masterpiece (1702-18).

Continuing to the left, a stone slab marks the workshop of the sculptors BARTOLINI and ROMANELLI. We come to the fourteenth century **Porta a San Frediano,** which is the best preserved of the gates of the third circle of walls, started in 1285; its design is attributed to Andrea Pisano (1324).

Following the inside line of the old walls, we come to the *Lungarno Soderini*. Going up it we have the view of the palaces on the right bank. We arrive at *Ponte alla Carraia* and enter the *Lungarno Guicciardini*, at the end of which is the **Capponi Palace**: in the hall of honour, on the first floor, BERNARDINO POCCETTI sang the glories of the great family with a series of frescoes (1585) of notable iconographic interest and exceptional pictorial vivacity. At the level of the *Ponte Santa Trinita* the embankments by the Arno are shut off by the **Palazzo delle Missioni,** of elegant Baroque architecture by BERNARDO RADI, singularly contrasting with the nearby thirteenth cent. **Frescobaldi Palace,** which gave hospitality to Charles of Valois and his court (1301).

Crossing the *Ponte Santa Trinita*, we turn into *Via Tornabuoni*, so ending the excursion in the Oltrarno quarter in which we have seen the *Church of Santa Felicita*, built on the site of the old Etrusco-Roman necropolis and Christian cemetery; the *Pitti Palace* with its annexes, museums and gardens; the most important religious centres, constituted by the old Dominican nuns' convent of *San Felice*, that of the Augustinian convent of *Santo Spirito* and that of the Carmelite convent of *Santa Maria del Carmine*. This part of the city is entirely closed in by fourteenth century walls, which start on the left bank of the Arno, from the *Porta San Niccolò*, rising towards the *Porta San Giorgio*, running round the *Fortezza del Belvedere* or Fortezza di San Giorgio, surrounding the *Boboli Gar-*

Masaccio: St. Peter and St. John giving alms.

dens, and finally going from *Porta Romana* to *Porta San Frediano.* It is a sort of triangular rectangle, with angles formed by three gates and with the hypotenuse along the Arno, which encircles enough treasures of art to make a whole city famous.

SURROUNDINGS OF FLORENCE

Left bank of the Arno: *Viale dei Colli Basilica of San Miniato al Monte - Church of San Leonardo - Poggio Imperiale - Certosa Monte Oliveto - Bellosguardo.*

Right bank of the Arno: *Fięsole - Settignano Montughi.*

Villas in the neighbourhood.

Florentine countryside.

SURROUNDINGS OF FLORENCE

Florence should be called the « flower city » rather than the « city of flowers ». She does, in fact, lie on the banks of the Arno, and spreads like a flower-bud opening between the hills in which the town itself is set. No other city in the world has an aspect like Florence, which lies in the centre of an exceptionally sweet and marvellous designed countryside The sober and serene character of Florentine art, with no sentimental unequilibriums nor fantastic monstrosities, is really derived from the valley in the centre of which the city stands. There is no street from which, on one side at least, one does not have a view of a hill. And so, having seen her monuments, we should take time to visit the outskirts and immediate surroundings.

[The colour effect of the Florentine countryside lies between two fundamental tones : the silver-grey of the olive, and the dark green, almost black, of the cypress. All the other tones, common to rustic scenes, give variety to the picture, but do not break the tonal unity of the olive, luminous like a cloud, and of the cypress, erect, elegant, solitary even in groups. No uproarious, glaring colours, or strange, extravagant outlines; but throughout modesty, discretion, a sense of secretiveness and of aristocratic reserve, making this the most intimate and most refined of countrysides.]

Hills hung with smiling villages, slopes studded with villas, little valleys full of farm houses of pleasing architecture. Paths shut in by walls, guarded by silent cypresses and crowned by the foliage of the olive. Here is a small church, with its porch in the sunshine; there a tabernacle at the junction of two roads. Up on a hill the imposing outline of an old castle; down another hill the peace of an aged convent.

One can never end discovering and enjoying the surroundings of Florence. We should pass through it at all hours, from early light of dawn, when the white villas rejoice in the sun, to the last hours of sunset, when the windows shine between the now violet-coloured olive-trees. We pass from one surprise to another, at every turn of the road, at the opening of each valley, from every hilltop and from the terraces of the many beautiful villas.

So a guide of the surroundings of Florence is always lacking, even if not prejudicial. Here we can map out the principal itineraries, but it must be remembered that a knowledge of the Florentine countryside can be better had by chance surprises and whims. Between one itinerary and another there is a world of natural and artistic scenes, most varied and unexpected as regards shapes and colour, which should be the object of the personal discovery of the interested and sensitive visitor.

View of Florence from the Bishops' Palace at San Miniato.

THE LEFT BANK OF THE ARNO

San Miniato al Monte

There are two ways of reaching San Miniato al Monte, a long and a short one. The long one, following the *Viali di Circonvallazione*, leaves *Piazza Francesco Ferrucci* and goes up the *Viale Michelangelo*, the last stretch of the celebrated **Viale dei Colli**, laid out (1868) by the architect GIUSEPPE POGGI (1821-1901) in order to give Florence a walk with a panorama of the city and surroundings.

Following its wide curves we follow the road along the side of the hill, between shady rows of cypresses and pines, through a sylvan and most varied countryside, and we come to the **Piazzale Michelangelo**, from which we suddenly have an enchanting view of the city against the background of Monte Morello to the left, Fiesole in the centre, and to the right the hills of Settignano, Incontro, and the mountain of Vallombrosa.

In the middle of the Piazzale is a *monument* composed (1875) of the bronze reproduction of David and of the four allegorical figures of the Medici tombs by Michelangelo. In the background, raised above the Piazzale, a *Loggia* in eclectic Renaissance style, built (1873) on the plan of GIUSEPPE POGGI.

The other, the short way by foot, runs from the **Ponte alle Grazie,** which was destroyed by the Germans in 1944 and rebuilt in 1955-56. The old original bridge was the third, after the Ponte Vecchio and the Ponte alla Carraia, and was built by order of the Podestà Rubaconte da Mandello; it was therefore called the *Ponte di Rubaconte*. At the right end there was built, a century later, the *Oratory of the Madonna delle Grazie,* and from this there originated the new name of Ponte alle Grazie. Originally there were little cells on each pillar, in which there lived voluntarily recluse pious women, who later gave the origin to nunneries, among which was the monastery of the Murate, now turned into a prison. To widen the bridge the cells were demolished (1874), and the Oratory transferred to the *Lungarno Diaz*, where it still is.

On the left bank is the **Piazza de' Mozzi**, the family which had three large palaces here from the beginning of the 13th cent., among the richest in the city. Here were lodged illustrious guests and not a few decisive events in the city history took place in this charming little square and on the underlying strand of the Arno. In the greatest of the Mozzi palaces stayed Pope Gregory X and on the bank of the Arno swore to the ephemeral peace between the Guelphs and Ghibellines (July 11th, 1273). The brother of the King of Naples and his Envoy in Tuscany here signed the peace with Arezzo (1314); and the Duke of Athens, who had come to Florence (1326) as a peacemaker, took up his residence here.

To the right of the square stand two *palaces* of the *Torrigiani* family: the larger, designed by BACCIO D'AGNOLO; the smaller, the work of his son Domenico. To the left, in a strange palace the windows of which are formed by the architecture of altars dismantled from a church at Pistoia, is the **Bardini Museum,** with a very varied collection of sculptures, paintings, tapestries, and other works of art, among which some of great value. The collection was assembled by a great Florentine antiquarian, Stefano Bardini, who on his death (1923) left it, together with the palace, to the Commune of Florence.

Taking *Via de' Bardi*, on the right, we come to the little **Church of Santa Lucia de' Magnoli** which contains a fine panel with the figure of *St. Lucy* by PIETRO LORENZETTI. Next to the church two fine palaces: the *Palazzo Canigiani* of the 14th century and the *Palazzo Capponi* built in the 15th century for Niccolò da Uzzano.

Coming back towards Piazza de' Mozzi, we follow *Via San Niccolò* until we reach the **Church of San Niccolò sopr'Arno,** already in existence in 1164 and several times rebuilt and restored. Here are two fine *Holy-water basins* and a *small shrine,* all of the 15th cent. In the lunette in the shrine, a *fresco* by ALESSO BALDOVINETTI (1450); to the right of the altar, a *Trinity* attributed to NERI DI BICCI. In the room at the foot of the bell-tower, the bell-ringer of the church hid, in 1530, Michelangelo, who, having directed the construction of the walls during the siege, feared he would be persecuted after the surrender of the city.

At the end of *Via San Niccolò* rises the fine *Tower* of the third circle of walls (1324), which was the only one left at its original height. Should we wish, we can also go up to San Miniato by the steps which wind symmetrically up the side

Gate of San Miniato.

Basilica of San Miniato al Monte.

of the hill beside the tower. However, the most advisable route is the road which leaves from *Porta San Miniato* along a steep path flanked by cypresses, recorded even by Dante (**Purg. XII, 104**), which climbs up the hill named by the early Florentines, « Mons Florentinus ».

Crossing the *Viale Galileo*, which is the continuation of the Viale Michelangelo, we come to the **Church of San Salvatore al Monte**, closed in by cypresses. On the site of a more ancient oratory, this church was built after the design of CRONACA (1475), of such beauty that Michelangelo himself called it « la bella villanella » (the beautiful peasant-girl). Going up still further we come to the bastions of the fortress which Michelangelo built or, reinforced during the siege of Florence, and at last we reach the **Basilica of San Miniato al Monte**, which sprang up as a chapel about the 4th cent., founded in its present form by the Bishop Hildebrand (27th. April 1018), with the help of the Emperor Henry II.

We have already spoken of the character of Florentine Romanesque architecture; here we have an opportunity of admiring a splendid example of it; it is the most beautiful Italian church of that period. It is dedicated to San Miniato, martyr in the 3rd cent. Beheaded on the bank of the Arno,

Basilica of San Miniato al Monte: interior.

according to legend, he carried his own head coming up here to die, where there was an early Christian cemetery.

Façade: the lower half is the more beautiful, with bi-coloured arches, the upper part being more trite. Mosaic (12th cent.), with *Christ between the Madonna and St. Miniato*. At the top, the *Eagle of the Guild of Calimala*, patron of the church.

Interior. - Grandiose, austere ensemble with three naves and trestled roof. Magnificent central flooring in marble intarsia with ·signs of the Zodiac and symbolic animals. On the walls, remains of 13th, 14th and 15th cent. frescoes.

Crypt, very large, closed by and artistic gate in wrought iron (1338). *Altar* with the bones of Saint Miniato. In the vaulting, remains of frescoes by TADDEO GADDI (1341).

Raised **Chancel** with marvellous transennas, and most fine carved pulpit with marble incrustations (1207). Choir with inlaid wood stalls. Apse with windows with panels of pink alabaster. In the dome, large mosaic with the *Judging Christ between the Madonna and Saint Miniato*, intercessors for the Florentines (1297).

On the right of the Chancel we enter the **Sacristy**, entirely frescoed by SPINELLO ARETINO (1387) with the *Legend of Saint Benedict*, in sixteen stories. Wood-inlaid stalls (1472). Two DELLA ROBBIA statuettes, representing *Saint Benedict* and *Saint Miniato.*

Descending from the left side of the Chancel we come to the **Chapel of S. Jacopo** also called **of the Cardinal of Portugal,** marvellous example of collaboration between 15th cent. artists. The Archbishop of Lisbon, Jacopo, had died in Florence in 1459. His uncle, King Alfonso of Portugal, ordered a splendid tomb. And ANTONIO MANETTI, pupil of Brunelleschi, made the design for it. LUCA DELLA ROBBIA, modelled the five medallions of the *Holy Spirit* and the *Cardinal Virtues.* ANTONIO ROSSELLINO carved the sarcophagus. ANTONIO DEL POLLAIOLO painted the *flying angels.* ALESSO BALDOVINETTI executed the other pictorial decorations. PIERO DEL POLLAIOLO did the altar-painting (the original is now in the Uffizi). And it all acquired a marvellous unity of style, forming one of the most beautiful and pleasing of art ensembles.

On the road which led up to the old church of San Miniato, a Florentine noble, Giovanni Gualberto dei Visdomini, met, on Good Friday 1003, his brother's murderer. Revenge was natural; but it was a holy day, and the unarmed assassin begged for piety in the name of Christ. Giovanni Gualberto pardoned him, embraced him as a mark of peace, and led him before the Crucifix in the church; he then saw the Christ bending His head towards him as in approval. Then, retiring from the world, Giovanni Gualberto founded the order of the Vallombrosan, in the forests of Acquabella, becoming one of the great Florentine Saints. In memory of this miraculous happening, Piero de' Medici, in 1447, ordered the **Tabernacle of the Crucifix,** which is in the centre of the Church. The architectural design is by MICHELOZZO, the enamelled terra-cotta roofing by LUCA DELLA ROBBIA, the paintings on the shutters which

Antonio Rossellino: Tomb of the Cardinal of Portugal.

enclosed the Crucifix, by AGNOLO GADDI. But the Crucifix is no longer here, being in the church of Santa Trinita.

The **bell-tower**, on the design of BACCIO D'AGNOLO, (1523), was still under construction at the beginning of the siege and was used by one of the people's artillery-men, Lupo, to place two culverins. Made the target of shortrange shots by the enemy artillery, Michelangelo had it faced with wool mattresses and bales; but it still has the marks which the shots left upon it.

Next to the church is the **Bishops' Palace**, summer residence of the Florentine bishops. On the ramparts of the fortress of Michelangelo, the architect Niccolò Matas laid out in 1839, the monumental cemetery, called by the Florentines, the **Cemetery of the « Porte Sante »** (Holy Doors).

Coming down the steps designed by Gius. Poggi, turning to the left, and following the Viale Galileo, we come to *Via S. Leonardo*. To the left the narrow *Via Vincenzo Viviani* goes up towards **Arcetri**, where is the *Astronomical Observatory*, and the first tower constructed in Europe (1872) to study the sun. Further on, from the summit of the hill, opposite the restored *Castle of Torre al Gallo*, we enjoy an enchanting view. By the *Pian de' Giullari*, where Galileo died in the *Villa del Gioiello* (1642), we come to **Santa Margherita a Montici**, a most attractive church, with several praiseworthy works of art and a fortified bell-tower.

To the right of the Viale Galileo, turning into the *Via San Leonardo*, we wind down towards the city. This is one of the most picturesque Florentine walks. On the right, the beautiful little **Church of San Leonardo**, where is the so-called Dante's pulpit (13th cent.), which was originally in the destroyed church of S. Pietro Scheraggio and from which Dante possibly spoke, as centainly did Saint Antonino. On the side altars, four Renaissance paintings.

Church of San Leonardo: Pulpit (detail).

Further on, on the left, there is access to the bastions of the star-shaped *Fort of Saint George*, or *of Belvedere*, with the fine palace of which we have already spoken on our excursion in the Boboli Garden. Just past the **Porta San Giorgio**, with an interesting 15th cent. fresco (*Madonna and Saints*) and a low relief of *St. George*, of the 14th cent. (a copy; we have seen the original in the Palazzo Vecchio), we go down the *Costa San Giorgio*, and, turning to the right by the *Costa Scarpuccia* and the *Via de' Bardi*, we find ourselves back in Piazza de' Mozzi, from where we started.

View of Florence from the Viale dei Colli.

The Certosa of Galluzzo.

Poggio Imperiale and the Certosa

From *Porta Romana* a straight avenue climbs up to the **Villa del Poggio Imperiale**, grandiose building which passed into various hands and is today the seat of the Institute of the SS. Annunziata, a girls' school. The original name of Villa Baroncelli was changed to that of Villa Imperiale in 1624, after the Grand duchess Maria Maddalena, of the imperial family of Austria, bought it from the Odescalchi, making it into a luxurious country residence of the grand duchesses and princesses of the house of Medici.

Its modern appearance is due to the restorations carried out under Leopold I in the last years of the 18th cent. and continued during the first years of the 19th cent. The neo-classical front façade is by the architect PASQUALE POCCIANTI; the rear one by GASPARE PAOLETTI, by whom is also the great hall on the first floor. The rest is by GIUSEPPE CACIALLI. Of great interest are the interior decorations by painters of various epochs, from those by MATTEO ROSSELLI (after 1620), very rich in authentic details, to those of architectural decorations, landscape and mythology by various artists of the 18th and 19th cent. In the chapel, among the statues and the bas-reliefs, there is a noteworthy *altar-back* by the Danish sculptor ALBERT THORWALDSEN.

Tomb of Lorenzo Acciaiuoli (Certosa).

To the right of the Villa a picturesque winding road leads down towards **S. Felice a Ema** (church of the 11th cent., with parts of a polyptych by the Gaddi, 1387), from where we can reach Galluzzo.

The easier way, however, to get there, is to go down the *Viale del Poggio Imperiale,* turning to the left into *Via del Gelsomino* as far as the fork of the *Due Strade.* Then take the *Via Senese* which quickly leads to the village of *Galluzzo* dominated by the large Certosa (Carthusian Monastery) one of the most important monuments in the neighbourhood of Florence.

The **Certosa of Galluzzo** was founded in the 14th cent. by a great and fortunate Florentine citizen: Niccolò Acciaioli (1311-65), a politician, friend of Petrarca and Boccaccio, Grand Seneschal of the King of Naples, and Viceroy of Apulia. In his great political good fortune he did not forget the fact that he was a mortal man. He gave the hill of Montacuto and the rents attached to it to the Carthusians and had built there, from 1341 onwards, entirely at his own expense, the monastery and the church, that his name might remain « fresh and lasting ». After Acciaioli, many other Florentines gave donations to the Certosa, and also the Milanese Luchino Visconti, always embellishing more and more the church and monastery.

The architecture of the Certosa and the decorations offer examples of every style, from the Gothic to the neoclassic.

In the **subterranean chapels**, of particular historical and artistic interest for their perfect state of preservation, are the *tomb of Niccolò Acciaioli* (d. 1366), which has been wrongly attributed to Orcagna, and the very fine *tomb-stones of Lorenzo,* son of Niccolò (1353), and of two other members of the family, by unkown artists of the 14th cent., examples of a very high artistic civilization. The *tomb-stone of Bishop Agnolo Acciaioli* d. 1409), of the early Renaissance, is splendid. Notable also, in the **Chapter room**, is the *tomb-stone of Bishop Leonardo Buonafede,* the work of FRANCESCO DA SANGALLO (1545).

The **great cloister** is very fine, decorated with 66 *heads* in relief by ANDREA and GIOVANNI DELLA ROBBIA. The cloister was also decorated with some very fine frescoes by PONTORMO representing *Stories of the Passion of Christ* which have been detached and restored and can be seen in a room of the convent.

Monte Oliveto

On the left bank of the Arno, down stream, a hill takes the name of Monte Oliveto from a monastery of Olivetani, built here in 1350, now unfortunately used as a military hospital. Of the old religious centre, which had very great importance also in the artistic and religious civilization of the city, and which had Torquato Tasso as its guest (1590), there still remains visible the **Church of San Bartolomeo**, in Renaissance style, with a doorway attributed to Michelozzo.

Going up still further, we find the *Church of Saint Vitus and Modestus*, and from there we reach *Piazza di Bellosguardo*, so named for the superb view to be seen from *Via Roti Michelozzi* which leads to the 15th cent. villa called **Torre di Bellosguardo**. Other villas, all in fine positions, cover the hill. Among the others, *Villa Calamai* (at the beginning of Via Roti Michelozzi, on the left) is famous, where Ugo Foscolo lived in 1813, inspired by this landscape for his poem « Le Grazie ».

THE RIGHT BANK OF THE ARNO

Fiesole

The hill city of Fiesole is reached by many roads and lanes, all beautiful, besides by the main road, which winds up in wide curves and which has a trolley-car service, starting from Piazza S. Marco.

We can climb up to Fiesole by the *Via Faentina*, crossing the Mugnone at the *Ponte alla Badia* and going up towards *San Domenico*. We can go up on the right of the Mugnone, by *Via Boccaccio*, heading directly for San Domenico, or we can climb by the picturesque *Via della Piazzola*, or by the poetic *Via delle Forbici*. It can also be reached, on the east, by the suburb called *Africo* and by the roads which lead towards *Maiano*, where the sculptor brothers, Benedetto and Giuliano da Maiano, came from.

On this side is the church of **San Martino a Mensola,** Romanesque-Gothic, restored recently, of graceful lines and containing several works of art.

The **Badia Fiesolana** stands on the side of the Mugnone. The Cathedral of Fiesole, from the time when the early Christians gathered together outside the city walls, it grew up on the burial place of St. Romulus, the evangelist of Fiesole. In 1028 it passed to the Benedictines who built a flourishing abbey there, and kept it until 1437. Later it passed to the Lateran Canons of Lucca, called the Roccettini, who altered it with the help of Cosimo the Elder. Today it is the seat of a College of the Scolopi.

From the Benedictine period there remains the fine unfinished **façade**, nearly contemporary with that of San Miniato, and in the same style.

Badia Fiesolana.

The **interior** of the church is in the style of Brunelleschi, as also the **Sacristy,** with very fine *door-way* and *basin,* is of the Renaissance period.

The **Convent** is also in the Renaissance style, restored by Cosimo, who reserved an apartment there for himself. One should visit the very beautiful *Cloister,* the *Chapter Hall* and the *Refectory* with a graceful pulpit and a noble fresco by GIOVANNI DA SAN GIOVANNI (1629).

In this convent the Abbot Ubaldo Montelatici founded (1753) the *Accademia dei Georgofili,* which was the first agrarian academy in Europe.

Going up the *Via della Badia dei Roccettini* we come to **San Domenico di Fiesole,** a Dominican convent founded by the blessed Giovanni Dominici (1406) for the reform of the order. At first it was called « il conventino » and had great religious and political importance, before the reformed Dominican friars went down to occupy the Convent of San Marco. Saint Antonino of Florence (1406) and the Beato Angelico were novices here.

The present **façade** with portico (1635) and the **elegant campanile** (1611) are by the architect MATTEO NIGETTI.

In the **interior** of the church, altered after the prototype of Giuliano da Sangallo from 1488 to early in the 17th. cent., we can admire a *Madonna between Angels and Saints* by BEATO ANGELICO (c. 1430). The architectural background of the picture was added together with the cornice, by Lorenzo di Credi (1501), and the three stories of the predella are an unfaithful modern copy of those which passed to the National Gallery in London. By Angelico who was prior of the Convent, there remains, in the Chapter Room, one of his typical frescoed *Crucifixes* (c. 1440).

From San Domenico, we go up to Fiesole, either by the wide motor road, or by the picturesque *Via Vecchia Fiesolana,* which passes in front of the *Riposo dei Vescovi,* so called because it was the resting point of the Bishops who used to journey from Florence to Fiesole.

We have alluded in our Historical Outline to the history of **Fiesole,** that Etruscan city founded seven or six centuries before Christ, and which became, in 80 B.C., a Roman colony, with the name of Faesulae. We see remains of the Etruscan period in the strong *walls* to the north and east of the city where there also is what is left of a *gate,* and in the **Museum** arranged early in the 20th cent. Remains of the Ro-

Fiesole : Roman Theatre.

man period are in the same museum, in the grandiose **Roman Theatre,** in the remains of the *Baths,* and in those of the *Etrusco-roman temple,* of particular importance.

Of Christian Fiesole there remains the imposing Romanesque **Cathedral,** (1028), dedicated to the Martyr Bishop St. Romulus and the austere **bell-tower** crowned with battlements (1213).

In the **interior,** of solemn austerity, with three naves, crypt and raised chancel, after the typical plan of the Romanesque church, with trestled roof and unequal columns coming from pagan temples, there are collected many works of art. In the **Salutati Chapel,** the *sepulchre of Bishop Leonardo Salutati,* with a most beautiful bust of him, and the altar-back with *Madonna and Saints,* works by Mino di Giovanni da Poppi, called Mino da Fiesole (1464). On the high altar is a *Triptych* by Bicci di Lorenzo (1440). In the chapel on the left of the chancel, there is an altar whith statues of *St. Romulus* and *St Matthew* by Andrea Ferrucci (1493). In the **Sacristy,** the silver *bust of St. Romulus* (1584), a fine Florentine silversmith-work.

By a steep ascent we come to where was the acropolis of the old city and where the **Convent of San Francesco** came into being. The church has a graceful *façade,* with an outthrust arch, under which is a *St. Francis,* fresco of the 15th century.

The **interior** is in the Gothic style. On the altars to the right: *Marriage of St. Catherine,* from the Florentine school of the 15th cent. and *Crucifixion* by Neri di Bicci; on the altars to the left: *Adoration of the Child* from the school of Cosimo Rosselli and *Madonna with the Child and two Saints* from the school of Perugino. On the left wall, *Immaculate Conception* by Piero di Cosimo, one of the first representations of this subject (1480). On the high altar, *Annunciation* attributed to Raffaellino del Garbo.

Inside the convent, picturesque little **cloister** and interesting **Missionary Museum.**

From up here we command, in a really superb way, the entire panorama of the Florentine valley. The descent towards the city, especially if made along the little roads which cut into the hill, is full of surprises and enchantment.

Settignano

From Fiesole, still climbing, passing *burgunto,* and then following the *Via dei Bosconi,* coming to a cross-road we turn to the right down a sylvan road. Once we pass the *Castel*

Villa Gamberaia.

di Poggio, we come to the foot of the **Castle of Vincigliata,** example of romantic reconstruction, ordered by the Englishman John Temple-Leader and executed by the architect GIUSEPPE FANCELLI in 1855. From here, always by a most charming little road we can go down to Settignano.

We can also reach Settignano from the city (trolley-bus from Piazza San Marco), by the road which goes by *Ponte a Mensola,* and near to the *Capponcina,* a modest villa made famous by the sojourn there of Gabriele D'Annunzio.

The charming village of **Settignano** is celebrated for its architects and sculptors, among many others: Desiderio da Settignano and the two Rossellino, the two Mosca, Meo del Caprina, Luca Fancelli, the three Cioli, the two Lorenzi. Michelangelo used to say jokingly that he had imbibed his love for sculpture with the milk of his wet nurse at Settignano!

Almost entirely destroyed by the Germans in 1944, Settignano still preserves in the **Church of the Assunta** a Della Robbia *Madonna,* a *Ciborium* of the 15th cent. and a *pulpit* by BERNARDO BUONTALENTI (1602).

In the **Oratory of the Trinity,** externally decorated with four large *masks* of the 14th cent., is a *choir-loft* from the workshop of Desiderio.

Half a mile along the *Via Rossellino* is the **Villa di Gamberaia,** famous for its fine scenographic seventeenth-century Italian garden, and less known as the cradle of the Gamberelli family, of which were Antonio and Bernardo, called Rossellino.

Returning from Settignano, we stop in the city's suburbs, at the **Church of San Salvi,** near which, in the *Refectory* of the Vallombrosans, alone saved from distruction during the siege, there remains a very lovely *Last Supper* by ANDREA DEL SARTO (1519). This is the fourth of the most famous of Florentine Cœnaculums, the others being: that of Andrea del Castagno in the convent of Santa Apollonia (Via XXVII Aprile), that of Domenico Ghirlandaio in the convent of Ognissanti, that of Umbrian-Tuscan School in the monastery of Sant'Onofrio (Via Faenza).

Montughi

Outside the old *Porta San Gallo,* between the city and the industrial suburb of Rifredi, along the *Via Vittorio Emanuele*, we find on the right the **Villa Fabbricotti,** or Villa degli Arcipressi, with a large park, where Queen Victoria of England was a guest in 1894.

Further on, in *Via Montughi*, the **Villa Stibbert,** once Villa Davanzati, which an English lover of art and mediaeval costumes, Frederick Stibbert (1838-1906), transformed into a *museum* very rich in works of art, arms, furniture, materials and curiosities, and which, at his death, he donated to the Commune of Florence. It is a very fine example of what a single man can do equipped with the means, and more than anything imbued with the collector's enthusiasm.

VILLAS IN THE NEIGHBOURHOOD

Ugo Foscolo, a guest at Bellosguardo, called Florence a « blessed » city, for its « valleys filled with homes and olive groves, which send towards the sky the fragrance of thousands of flowers ». He also included here the many lovely villas which stud the surrounding hills.

It would be an impossible task to visit all the villas scattered throughout the valley, lying on the sides of the hills, or crowning their outline. Another poet, Lodovico Ariosto, wrote: « To see your hills so full of homes, one would think they were sprouting from the earth like buds and branches. If all your palaces spread around the country were gathered inside a circle of walls, under one name, two Romes put together could not compare with you ».

We are giving a list of the larger and more important villas, those most famous for their history and art, adding that to exhaust this subject, a whole volume would be insufficient.

Villa Medici at Careggi

One reaches this villa by bus from Piazza del Duomo or by car across the industrial quarter of Rifredi. Rebuilt and fortified by MICHELOZZO (1433), it was the country residence of Cosimo the Elder, of Piero « the gouty », his son, and of the Magnificent Lorenzo, his nephew. Here, around them, there gathered all the men of letters, the artists, and the scientists, who in little more than half a century were to give Florence the perennial glory of a new civilization, all of his own. Here died Cosimo the Elder (August 1st, 1464), and the Magnificent Lorenzo (April 8th, 1492).

Stripped of the works of art collected there, devastated and set fire to at the time of the expulsion of the Medici, it was later restored and decorated with frescoes by Pontormo and Agnolo Bronzino. Various works of art, the little courtyard of the early building, and the very fine park are preserved by the present owners, the Administration of the Hospital of S. Maria Nuova.

Villa della Petraia

(Florence - Sesto bus). A castle of the Brunelleschi family, it became celebrated for having resisted the attacks of Giovanni Acuto (John Hawkwood) (1364). Becoming the property

Villa Medici at Careggi.

of Cardinal Ferdinando dei Medici in 1575, the structure was completely restored by BERNARDO BUONTALENTI.

The walls of the *portico* of the entrance courtyard are covered with a series of frescoes by Baldassarre Franceschini, called the VOLTERRANO, who here represented the notable events of the house and portraits of its most worthy members, with iconographical and landscape elements of particular interest. The scene of the reception, in Pisa, of the Admiral Jacopo Inghirami and the commanders of infantry of the Knights of St. Stephen, Fabrizio di Colloredo and Silvio Piccolomini, returning victorious from the battle of Bona (1607), has obvious documentary value.

In the little chapel on the first floor frescoes by BERNARDINO POCCETTI. The remains of the furnishings are very fine, also the rich variety of brocade and velvet wall-hangings, largely from the last period of court life of the villa, which was the much-loved summer sojourn of Victor Emanuel II.

The large **park** which adjoins that of the Villa of Castello, was also designed by NICCOLÒ TRIBOLO; and the design for the very attractive, celebrated *fountain* with the figure of *Florence rising from the waters*, executed by GIAMBOLOGNA, was also by Tribolo.

Villa della Petraia.

Villa of Castello

(Florence - Sesto bus). This was another country residence of the Medici. Caterina Sforza here brought up her son Giovanni, later called « dalle Bande Nere », and Cosimo, his son, was educated here by his mother Maria Salviati, before, while still very young, he assumed the heavy crown of the second duke of Florence. The house having risen to the requirements of a reigning dynasty, the Grand duke Francesco I, Cardinal Gian Carlo and the Grand duchess Cristina of Lorraine here held splendid courts.

In the very lovely **park**, designed and laid out by Niccolò Tribolo (from 1540 onwards) and decorated with the *fountain of Hercules and Chacus*, modelled by him, which has a *group* by Bartolomeo Ammannati and *cupids* by Pierino da Vinci, is also a *Grotto* with bronze *animals* modelled by Giambologna.

In this garden, jessamine imported from the East Indies, was cultivated for the first time.

Villa Salviati

(Trespiano bus). From the *Loggia* on the *Via Bolognese,* by the lane of the *Cionfo*, going down towards the Ponte della Badia, we come immediately on the right to the majestic building which GIULIANO DA SANGALLO (c. 1470) created from a former fortress of the Montegonzi. The *courtyard* with portico is marvellously graceful, the bas-reliefs being by GIOV. FRANC. RUSTICI, by whom perhaps is also an *Annunciation*, in the *Chapel*.

The villa was celebrated in the 16th and 17th centuries for the outdoor festas which were held there, in the very fine park, and in the halls, where FRANCESCO FURINI left one of his most brilliant decorations. But more than for these festive memories, common also to all the villas of the great Florentine families, there remains, according to tradition, the harsh record of the New Year gift sent by Veronica Cibo to her husband Jacopo Salviati, duke of San Giuliano: the severed head of her rival, presented to him in a basket of clean body linen (1638).

Garden of the Villa of Castello.

Villa Palmieri

(Via Boccaccio bus). Even if there are no works of art here, this is one of the most celebrated villas in the neighbourhood, for the varied and evocative beauty of the gardens, but above all because tradition indicates it as the one in which Giovanni Boccaccio imagined the scenes of his Decameron. The beauty of the surrounding country, the enchanting restfulness, the recondite grace of the place makes it more than probable that the phantasy of the great story-teller may have felt it to be the ideal refuge for the young ladies and their lovers, anxious to escape the air and pains of the pest-stricken city, in the spring of 1348.

The villa became still more popular with the Florentines, after Queen Victoria of England chose it for her winter sojourn (1888).

Villa Medici di Belcanto

(San Domenico and Fiesole bus). Built by MICHELOZZO, in 1458, for Cosimo the Elder, something of the early architecture still remains. Its name is connected with the life of the celebrated *Accademia Platonica* which gathered round the Magnificent Lorenzo, with Marsilio Ficino, Giovanni Pico della Mirandola, Agnolo Poliziano, Cristoforo Landini, the cleverest men-of-letters of the day, in the festas in which, in honour of Plato, only rhetorical gaity reigned.

From the terrace fortified with bastions, open to the south on the side of the hill, one gets a wonderful view of Florence, and of the slopes of the hill of Fiesole, in all its inexpressible beauty.

Villa Poggio a Caiano

A visit to this splendid grand ducal residence is less easy; but time spent on it is well justified. GIULIANO DA SANGALLO (1480-85) left here the prototype of a princely country residence, with full development of space, which BUONTALENTI happily continued. For the Magnificent Lorenzo he covered the hall of honour with a beautiful panelled ceiling which, at the time, it was doubted would support itself.

With its early name of *Ambra*, from the stream which runs through its park, it was exalted in the poetry of Poliziano, and of Lorenzo himself, when he collected around him the Florentine men-of-letters, in a literary country life.

The falcon-hunts, deer-stalking, fishing, country feasts, balls, and masquerades, and the May singing had the most varied and picturesque setting in this garden and in the woods of the great park, almost every Spring, for more than two centuries.

All well-known people, coming to Florence from Bologna, via Pistoia, were entertained in this villa, which introduced them to the splendours of the city. Besides Lorenzo's court, the most brilliant though not yet crowned, here held court Pope Leo X, Emperor Charles V, Archduchess Giovanna and all the Medici dukes and grand dukes.

The dramatic love of the Grand duke Francesco I and the Venetian Bianca Cappello here had its tragic end with the almost simultaneous death of the married couple; gossip and malicious literature wrongly spread news of their having been poisoned (1587). Here the Grand duke Cosimo II

Villa of Poggio a Caiano.

Pontormo: Vertumnus and Pomona (detail of the fresco in the Villa of Poggio a Caiano).

banished his wife, the fatuous and riotous Marie Louise of Orléans (1675), before sending her back to her native Paris. Here also Victor Emanuel II passed quiet times in the country.

But besides the fascination of these memories and of the interest of court gossip, the works of art that have remained deserve admiration, a few of the many collected here through the centuries: the bas-reliefs of the *terracotta frieze* from the workshop of the Della Robbia; the *architectural decorations* of the first rooms, among the best by BACCIO BANDINELLI; the series of *frescoes* in the *Great Hall,* with stories of Roman personages, which are most evident records of the exploits of the Medici. The *Return of Cicero from exile,* referring to the repatriation of Cosimo the Elder, was begun by FRANCIABIGIO (1520) and finished by ALESS. ALLORI (1580). *Egypt sending tribute to Cæsar,* recording the spontaneous homages of the Sultan to the Magnificent Lorenzo, is by ANDREA DEL

SARTO (1512), also finished by Allori (1580). By Allori too are the other stories and one of the lunettes, with the *Garden of the Hesperides*. But the authentic masterpiece, which alone justifies a visit, is the fresco in the lunette opposite, with the rustic allegories of *Vertumnus and Pomona*, painted by PONTORMO (1532) with so much boldness, with such unprejudiced freedom of composition, with such mastery of design and originality of colours, that it is one of the most beautiful paintings of the Florentine sixteenth century.

Giambologna: Florence rising from the waters (Villa della Petraia).

INDEX

Finito di stampare nel Gennaio 1973
presso la «Fotocromo Emiliana»,
Bologna

Fotolito della Zincotecnica, Firenze

Fotografie: Alinari, Bertoni, Borri, Locchi
(pagg. 44, 46, 51, 59, 107, 125, 143, 154,
165, 233, 265, 269, 287).